To Ed

with my very best wishes

Anni Tannend

APRIL 2012

ASSERTIVENESS AND DIVERSITY

Assertiveness and Diversity

Anni Townend

First published 2007 by
PALGRAVE MACMILLAN
Houndmills, Basingstoke, Hampshire RG21 6XS and
175 Fifth Avenue, New York, N.Y. 10010
Companies and representatives throughout the world

PALGRAVE MACMILLAN is the global academic imprint of the Palgrave Macmillan
division of St. Martin's Press, LLC and of Palgrave Macmillan Ltd. Macmillan® is a
registered trademark in the United States, United Kingdom and other countries.
Palgrave is a registered trademark in the European Union and other countries.

ISBN-13: 978-1-4039-9344-1
ISBN-10: 1-4039-9344-0

This book is printed on paper suitable for recycling and made from fully
managed and sustained forest sources. Logging, pulping and manufacturing
processes are expected to conform to the environmental regulations of the
country of origin.

A catalogue record for this book is available from the British Library.

A catalog record for this book is available from the Library of Congress.

10   9   8   7   6   5   4   3   2   1
16 15 14 13 12 11 10 09 08 07

Printed and bound in China

To my partner Richard Waring and our
beautiful daughters Fern and Sofia Townend
who have supported and believed in me throughout

Contents

Part I
Overview of the Book   **1**

Who the book is for; how to use the book.

Part II
What is Assertiveness?   **9**

Introduction; Assertiveness is about self-respect and respect
for others; Assertiveness is about positive recognition;
Assertiveness is about positive emotion, thinking, and
imagining; Assertiveness is about authentic connection with
self and others; Assertiveness is about meaning and purpose;
Assertiveness is about listening to and trusting intuition;
Assertiveness is about making mind, body, and brain
connections; Assertiveness is about feeling secure;
Assertiveness is about physical, intellectual, emotional, and
spiritual awareness and integration; Assertiveness is about
acceptance and mindfulness.

Introduction; Developing self-assertion through having a
clear sense of purpose; Developing positive self-assertion
through positive self-belief and self-recognition; Self-
affirmations; Self-limiting beliefs; Developing positive

Figures

Tables

Foreword

Organizations and people are experiencing unprecedented change. Increased competition and the drive for profit in the business world have led to downsizing, restructuring, an increased number of mergers and acquisitions, organizations operating globally, and workforces becoming much more diverse. Not-for-profit organizations have also experienced change, with increased demands for them to offer value for money and be more customer-focused. Alongside these changes organizations have been faced with dramatic advancement in technology.

Change is here to stay, requiring leaders in organizations to be proactive and win the hearts and minds of people to be successful. This is a particular challenge because fear and insecurity often become the dominant emotions experienced by people. Effective leaders are becoming increasingly aware that sound strategy, effective processes and systems will not succeed unless they change the mindset of people. This requires leaders to demonstrate appropriate values of openness, honesty, and respect, to recognize and support diversity within teams and gain the necessary buy-in.

All business leaders have an important role to play in ensuring that people have the necessary skills and capabilities, and receive the right support when necessary. The capacity to build and sustain positive relationships with a diverse range of people is essential for everyone. At the personal level confidence and self-esteem are vital to operate assertively. In addition people need to value and respect difference and have the strength of character to be true to themselves. Frequently when people feel threatened they react with either the "fight" or "flight" response, and become aggressive and defensive, or retreat within themselves, becoming submissive and passive. The right infrastructure needs to be in place within organizations to support people when they are experiencing difficulties.

This book will appeal to senior leaders, human resource professionals, coaches, trainers, and business consultants. All will benefit from understanding the inextricable link between assertiveness and diversity. In addition the models used throughout the book will enable readers to demonstrate the appropriate behavior needed to become role models and support others. The case studies and case analyses highlighting lessons at the individual and organizational level are invaluable.

Readers are offered a holistic approach to assertiveness and diversity. The book emphasizes the importance of connectedness between the physical, intellectual, emotional, and spiritual energies resulting in a strong sense of self—able to be vulnerable and have the capacity to build strong relationships with others. The range of models used allows readers to look at themselves and others through different lenses resulting in authenticity, respect for others and the capacity to develop and sustain positive relationships with a diverse group of people.

Jane Cranwell-Ward
Visiting Fellow,
Henley Management College

Acknowledgments

The inspiration for writing this book has been the many, many people—friends, colleagues, clients, and teachers, family, and my children—who have over the years contributed to my exploration and definition of assertiveness and diversity.

I think "having someone to believe in you" is probably the most important gift to be given during our lives, particularly during our childhood years. I have been blessed in having people who believed in me and who guided me on my way both personally and professionally; with their help and guidance I found my *métier* and passion for working with people early on in my adult life.

I am grateful to all the people with whom I have worked, both individually and in groups, who have taught me about the power of conversation and connection to transform relationships. As a leadership coach I have been given the opportunity to lead and coach others in finding their "best selves" and developing "bigger" relationships faster.

This book would not have been written if my friends and colleagues had not seen the "writer in me." I would like to thank all of the contributors and readers of this book. It has been a true honor interviewing people from a wide range of organizations, all of whom gave generously of their time in not only talking with me, but also in reading and re-reading the case studies and stories.

I would like to thank in particular Stephen Rutt, publishing director at Palgrave Macmillan, who has throughout the writing process believed in me and my writing, and has sustained me not only with excellent editing advice but also with his enthusiasm and encouragement for *Assertiveness and Diversity*. I would like to thank Alexandra Dawe, assistant editor at Palgrave Macmillan, for helping me in the final stages of the book for her support, enthusiasm and encouragement. I would like to give special thanks to those people who worked with me on the book in its final stages. They include Jackie Newman, freelance permissions editor, Susan Curran who meticulously copy edited the book, and the team at Curran Publishing Services.

The author and publishers would like to thank the following for permission to use copyright material:

Adaptation of one diagram: 'The Johari Window' from p. 60 *Group Processes: An introduction to group dynamics* by J. Luft © 1984. Reprinted with permission of McGraw-Hill Education.

One adapted figure from *The Promise of Mediation* by Robert A. Baruch Bush and Joseph P. Folger © 2005 by John Wiley & Sons Inc. All rights reserved. Reprinted with permission of John Wiley & Sons, Inc.

'The Zig-Zag Process for Problem Solving' from pp. 161–3 *People Types and Tiger Stripes* by Gordon D. Lawrence, 1993. Reprinted with permission of Center for Applications of Psychological Type, Inc.

Figure 'The nine team roles, characteristics and strengths, and allowable weaknesses' from *Team Roles at Work* p. 22 by R. Meredith Belbin, Butterworth Heinemann 1993. Reprinted with kind permission of Belbin Associates.

'The Learning Cycle' from *Learning Styles Questionnaire (80-item)* July 2006 edition by P. Honey and A. Mumford. ISBN 10: 1-902899-29-6; ISBN 13: 978-1-902899-29-9. Reprinted with permission of Peter Honey Publications.

Figure of expressed and wanted behaviors in each of the three areas of personal need, modified and reproduced by special permission of the Publisher, CPP, Inc., Mountain View, CA 94043, from *Participating in Teams: Using Your FIRO-B® Results to Improve Interpersonal Effectiveness* by Eugene R. Schnell. Copyright © 2000 by CPP, Inc. All rights reserved. Further reproduction is prohibited without the Publisher's written consent.

One adapted figure from 'Nice girls don't ask' by Linda Babcock, Sarah Laschever, Michele Gelfand and Deborah Small, *Harvard Business Review*, 2003. Reprinted with permission of the author and Harvard Business School Publishing.

Figure 'Differences and complementarities between Human Resources and Corporate Ombuds', inspired by and adapted from 'HR and Ombuds: partners in pursuit of a common vision' by Ann Bensinger, Donald and Grace Semple. Reprinted with the kind permission of the authors.

Adapted figure from 'Organisation culture and future of Planet Earth' in *The Collected Papers of Roger Harrison* p. 249, published by McGraw-Hill. © Roger Harrison.

Every effort has been made to trace all copyright holders but if any have been inadvertently overlooked, the publishers will be pleased to make the necessary arrangements at the first opportunity.

Part I

Overview of the Book

1 Introduction

This book is about people and how we can work together to develop assertiveness, assertive relationships and assertive organizations. Assertiveness and diversity are closely entwined. It is not possible for people to be assertive if they do not feel safe. Many people do not feel safe and are not safe, and live and work in fear because they are different and unable to be themselves.

I believe that people can make a difference through developing truly assertive relationships in which we respect each other and are able to be open and honest. We can create a world in which diversity is truly valued. To be assertive, to enjoy assertive relationships and to develop assertive organizations are business goals of many organizations, expressed in values and beliefs, such as respect and dignity, openness and honesty, diversity and inclusivity. This book explores the relationship between assertiveness and diversity. The case studies and personal stories illustrate how individuals, teams, and organizations can make a difference and make it possible for everyone to be valued for who they are and respected for what they do.

Assertiveness is a way of life, a way of doing business based on mutual respect and regard. It is very much about developing relationships with each other that are based on trust, respect, openness, and honesty.

Assertive relationships are those in which people seek to understand each other, to acknowledge their differences, to challenge and support each other, to be open and honest with each other. Developing assertiveness and assertive relationships takes courage and a willingness to question personal values. It means being open to change and to new possibilities of "being"—thinking and feeling—and "doing"—behaving. Assertiveness is a personal journey of self-awareness and curiosity, of developing a strong and integrated sense of self. It is an interpersonal journey in which people engage and connect with others, with their differences and similarities, and together create organizations that are truly inclusive and assertive.

Who the book is for

The book is written for people who want to create assertive relationships and truly inclusive and assertive organizations. It will be of particular interest to business psychologists, human resource professionals, senior leaders, trainers, coaches, and leadership development consultants.

How to use the book

The book has been written to provide readers with an understanding of the relationship between assertiveness and diversity, and the importance of both to the way in which people do business with each other and to organizational success. It is imagined that some readers will read the book from cover to cover and that others will read particular chapters of interest. The book is clearly structured to help readers engage with the content and to learn from the experiences of others working with assertiveness and diversity in organizations. The book is divided into parts, each of which addresses a particular aspect of assertiveness and diversity. Each of the chapters offers readers:

- Insights into and information about working with assertiveness and diversity.
- Case studies from people working in organizations and those with individuals in organizations that show how assertiveness and diversity have been developed and achieved. In those case studies based on coaching and counseling, the confidentiality and anonymity of the clients has been respected.
- Case analyses that highlight aspects of assertiveness and diversity.

Part II: What is Assertiveness?

Part II describes what assertiveness is, and provides insights into assertiveness and the skills of developing assertiveness. Assertiveness is often confused with aggressiveness, and Chapter 2 offers the reader a number of different approaches to understanding what assertiveness really is. These approaches are referred to in the rest of the book. Chapter 3 highlights the importance of positive self-assertion, and how this can be developed through a process of personal inquiry into values and beliefs about self and others, leading to the development of positive and affirming beliefs that underpin assertive behavior. Chapter 4 explores and clarifies key assertive communication behaviors and skills, and these skills are added to in Chapter 5 in relation to developing assertive relationships. Chapter 6 offers the reader ways of managing conflict assertively, and of seeing conflict as an opportunity for developing assertive relationships. The final chapter of the part, Chapter 7, explores bullying and the negative impact that this can have on individuals and organizations, and gives the reader a range of assertive communication skills that are helpful in dealing with bullying behavior.

Part III: Working with Personality Differences

Part III is about understanding personality differences. It shows how through understanding these differences people are able to appreciate their individual differences and similarities, and through a recognition of each other's differences and similarities work together more effectively. In Chapter 8 four models of understanding personality differences are described. Chapter 9 shows how the use of the Myers-Briggs Type Indicator (MBTI), a strength-based model, can help people develop confidence in themselves as leaders, how the MBTI offers people a language with which to talk about their strengths and differences, and finally how the MBTI can help people appreciate their unique selves. Chapter 10 shows how using Fundamental Interpersonal Orientations Relations—Behavior (FIRO-B) can greatly help in an understanding of the three areas of interpersonal need and their associated behaviors. Chapter 11 illustrates how using Belbin team roles can help team members appreciate their differences and use them for greater team effectiveness. Chapter 12 shows how the learning cycle and the theory of different learning styles can be hugely helpful in understanding the different ways in which people learn, in developing greater self-awareness, and awareness and appreciation of others.

Part IV: Multicultural Differences, Differences of Sexual Orientation, and Gender Difference

Chapter 13 offers the reader a model for working with multicultural differences, with particular reference to race and ethnicity. Chapter 14 highlights how the denial of difference in sexual orientation is under-mining of self-confidence, and ultimately of people giving of their best in the working environment. Chapter 15 explores gender differences and how they are influenced by values, beliefs, and role models about what is expected of women and men. Chapter 16 illustrates, in particular through the case study, how working with multicultural differences is the way of doing business.

Part V: Assertiveness and Diversity in Organizations

Part V shows how assertiveness and diversity go hand in hand in devel-oping organizations that are truly inclusive and valuing of people. Chapter 17 builds on the previous parts of the book and strongly makes the case for diversity. It shows how recognizing and valuing diversity in the way people are and do things increases business success. Chapter 18 shows how respecting people and their different work–life balance needs increases their personal effectiveness and overall organizational success. Chapter 19 illustrates how Corporate Ombuds gives people a sounding board where they can explore their options when dealing with a difficult work related issue in absolute confidence. Chapter 20 shows how workplace counseling and employee assistance programs acknowledge that people may have personal issues, at different times in their working lives, and can benefit from counseling. Chapter 21 illustrates the importance of having values that are understood by everyone in their relationships and in how they do business. Chapter 22 shows how 360 review feed-back develops assertiveness and diversity through encouraging open-ness and honesty in relationships. Chapter 23 shows how assertive leadership underpins the development of truly assertive organizations in which diversity is lived. Chapter 24 illustrates the power of coach-ing to support people in their learning and development, and how it is encouraging of inclusivity and assertiveness. Chapter 25 shows how promoting happiness at work helps build strong working relationships as well as outstanding organizational success.

Conclusions and Resources

Chapter 26 offers the reader some conclusions about the importance of assertiveness and diversity in organizations. Appendix 1 lists the names and contact details of people who have directly contributed to the book either by giving a case study or story, or by reading the book and giving feedback. Appendix 2 gives a brief description and website details of contributing organizations. Appendix 3 is a resource section giving readers information about training and consultancy related to the themes covered in each part of the book. Finally there is an extensive bibliography of books relating to each chapter.

Part II

What is Assertiveness?

2 Philosophy of Assertiveness

Introduction

The purpose of this chapter is to give a brief description of the concepts that have informed the approach to assertiveness and diversity that is developed in this book and illustrated through the case studies and case analyses. Each of the approaches relates either to developing self-confidence and positive self-esteem, or to the development of working relationships that are assertive, inclusive, and transformational between people.

The key concepts of assertiveness are listed on the left of Table 2.1, and the theories from which they are drawn listed on the right.

Assertiveness is about self-respect and respect for others

Self-respect involves being self-aware, of being aware of who one is. Respect for others involves being aware of who they are, in both their differences and their similarities. This enables people to respect each other for who they are, for their differences, at the same time as being able to explore and work with them knowing that there is an underlying basis of respect and regard for each other as people, for each others' humanness.

The theory of transactional analysis (TA) (Berne, 1975) and in particular the concept of "life positions," is a useful one in differentiating between assertiveness and non-assertiveness. The underlying philosophy of TA is that people are all born "OK" and that in childhood people make decisions based about themselves and others based on

Table 2.1 The key concepts of assertiveness and the theories from which they are drawn

Assertiveness is about:	Theory of:
Self-respect and respect for others	Transactional analysis
Positive recognition	Transactional analysis and positive psychology
Positive emotion, thinking and imagining	Positive psychology, appreciative inquiry, solution-focused brief therapy
Authentic connection	Positive psychology and existential time-limited therapy
Meaning and purpose	Existential time-limited therapy
Listening to intuition	Intuitive intelligence, energy medicine
Mind, body, and brain connections	Affective neuroscience
Feeling secure	Attachment theory
Physical, intellectual, emotional and spiritual awareness	The four intelligences or energies
Acceptance and mindfulness	Cognitive behavioral psychology

the kind of recognition and acknowledgement that they receive from significant others. The decision that many people make is that they are "not OK," and this becomes their "life position." Eric Berne, the originator of TA, believed that people can change this decision, and that through self-awareness and positive recognition from others, they can choose to be OK.

The theory of "life positions" proposes that the only healthy position is that of I'm OK: You're OK (Harris, 1995), in which people feel secure and self-confident in themselves and respect others for who they are. The three other life positions are all non-assertive, and are underpinned by feelings of insecurity and a lack of self-confidence.

The writer Pamela Butler (1981) uses the theory of life positions to highlight the difference between assertive—I'm OK: You're OK—and the non-assertive behaviors of passivity—I'm not OK: You're OK—and aggression—I'm OK: You're not OK. Table 2.2 shows the four life positions and the thoughts, feelings and behaviors associated with passivity, aggression, and with manipulation and divisiveness—I'm not OK: You're not OK.

Table 2.2 I'm OK: You're OK: The four life positions showing the difference between assertive and non-assertive feelings, thoughts, and behaviors

4. I'm OK: You're not OK Aggressive/defensive I win: You lose	**1. I'm OK: You're OK** Assertive/creative I win: You win
Thoughts/beliefs: Lack of self-respect and respect for others Negative thoughts and beliefs about self and others Believes others are to blame Conflict is seen as something to win and other person to lose	Thoughts/beliefs: Self-respect, and respect of others Positive thoughts and beliefs about self and others Believes that she/he is responsible for thoughts, feelings and behaviours Conflict is seen as an opportunity for transformation and change
Feelings: Lacks self-confidence Negative self-esteem Feels insecure in self Lack of awareness Distrusting of self and others Disconnected from self and others	Feelings: Self-confident Positive self-esteem Comfortable and secure within self Aware of feelings Trusting of self and others Connected to self and others
Behaviors: Uses language to blame others: "You did this." Avoids eye contact Interrupts, talks over and sometimes shouts at others Makes statements rather than asking questions Closed body posture Gives negative feedback to others Is overly critical and judging of others	Behaviors: Uses "I" statements Makes eye contact Listens to others Addresses people directly Engages with others, asks open questions, and is curious Open body posture, and uses gestures that reflect content Asks for feedback from others Gives positive and constructive feedback to others

Table 2.2 continued	
3. I'm not OK: You're not OK Manipulative/divisive I lose: You lose	**2. I'm not OK: You're OK** Passive/submissive I lose: You win
Thoughts/beliefs: Lacks self-confidence Lack of self-respect and respect of others Negative thoughts and beliefs about self and others Thinks others are "out to get her/him" Suspicious and wary of others Sees conflict as something destructive	Thoughts/beliefs: Lacks self-confidence Lacks self-respect Compares self with others, and finds self lacking Believes other people are better than her/him Expects to be put down Sees conflict as something that others win over her/him in
Feelings: Feels insecure in self Feels undeserving of praise Feels resentful towards others Feels hopeless, and depressed	Feelings: Feels insecure in self Feels miserable Feels not worthy Feels insignificant
Behaviors: Avoids eye contact Uses negative language to talk about self and others Does not hear positive feedback or give it	Behaviors: Hides from others Avoids eye contact Close body posture Does not hear positive feedback or give it

A life position is made up of beliefs about the self and others; these beliefs about the self and others are then used to justify decisions and behaviors. A life position is decided early in childhood; Berne suggests that the decision is made by the age of 7. Claude Steiner (1990) suggests that we are all born with a healthy life position, with positive beliefs about self and others, but that this position is very quickly lost and the young child adopts a negative belief about the self, and in some cases about others. Whatever the decision, people can choose to make new decisions about their self-beliefs and beliefs about others. We can choose to develop a healthy assertive life position, one in which we have positive self-belief and positive beliefs about others.

Inside and outside of work people whose life positions are aggressive/defensive and passive/submissive can be drawn to each other. They develop what is known as a symbiotic relationship in which people with the aggressive/defensive life position put others down in order to feel better about themselves, and those people with the passive/submissive life position have their beliefs about self and others confirmed as they are once again put down and found to be lacking in some way.

People whose life position is manipulative/divisive believe that they are not worthy, and nor are other people. In the working environment few people have chosen this life position. However when times are very hard some people may find themselves sinking into this life position, and during this time may benefit from the support of a counselor.

The challenge for everyone is to develop and maintain the healthy life position, I'm OK: You're OK, which is assertive/creative. In choosing this life position people are choosing to respect themselves and to develop relationships in which there is an underlying respect of other people and their differences.

Assertiveness is about positive recognition

The fastest and most effective way of developing and maintaining an I'm OK: You're OK life position is through giving, receiving, and asking for positive recognition. People who feel positive about themselves appreciate and value others; they are able to give and receive positive recognition. Positive recognition inspires and motivates people.

In TA recognition is known as "strokes." A "stroke" is a "unit of recognition," and can be non-verbal or verbal. We are giving each other strokes all the time. "Strokes" can be positive or negative, unconditional or conditional. A positive unconditional "stroke" is a unit of recognition that communicates to others that they are appreciated and valued for who they are, irrespective of what they do, or have done. By contrast a negative unconditional "stroke" is a unit of recognition that communicates to others that they are not liked for who they are.

People generally would prefer to get a negative recognition than to be totally ignored. For most people, to be ignored is worse than receiving a negative piece of feedback. To not be seen, noticed, or heard is to be discounted for who one is, to be disregarded and dismissed.

In the working environment people typically give, receive, and ask for conditional "strokes" that are either positive or negative. Those that are positive conditional are acknowledgements for what we have achieved, while negative conditional "strokes" are messages that are negative and typically undermining of self-confidence.

Recognition can make the difference between joyless achievement and joyful mastery. Once you know that what you have done matters to people who matter to you, then what you have done becomes more uplifting to you. You feel more closely connected to the people who have recognized you.

(Hallowell, 2002: 147)

Recognition for achievement takes many different forms, and people value different forms of recognition depending on their personal values and beliefs, and their cultural background. In the working environment recognition by way of merit is increasingly valued. People expect to be given recognition for what they achieve, and for this recognition to be fair and based on merit.

Recognition for achievement can include:

- promotion
- compensation increase
- change in benefits (such as a company car)
- increased responsibility
- further development and training
- job rotation (transfer to another area of the business that enhances the person's portfolio of skills and job experiences)
- mentoring from a more experienced person in the business
- coaching from a line manager or external coach
- co-coaching, or buddy coaching with a peer from another area of the business
- a special mention in the company newsletter
- formal company "recognition schemes."

Recognition communicates to people that they are valued for their achievements, while encouraging excellence in their performance. At the same time they will feel that they matter to others, are valued for who they are, and feel connected to their organizations.

Assertiveness is about positive emotion, thinking, and imagining

A number of theories are helpful in deepening an understanding of what it means to be one's "best self," to be assertive, positive, and authentic. In particular the theories of positive psychology, appreciative inquiry and solution-focused brief therapy, all of which focus on people's strengths by way of their values, qualities, and skills, are useful.

The theory of positive psychology, developed by Martin Seligman (2004), focuses on positive emotions of optimism about the future, confidence, hope and trust, and builds on people's strengths. People who have developed the positive emotion of optimism are able to interpret adverse situations and setbacks very differently. They are able to hold on to hope and a sense of purpose, and to find meaning in the most challenging and difficult situations. They look for the positive, for the "gift" in the situation, and for the opportunity for personal and relationship transformation.

The focus of appreciative inquiry, developed by David L. Cooperrider (Cooperrider and Whitney, 1999), involves drawing out what are people's best experiences, their best achievements, and to draw on these "positively exceptional moments" to effect profound change. The process of transformation encourages a shift in thinking and feeling about how people shape their futures, and in doing so develops positive self-esteem.

The language of appreciative inquiry is positive and assertive. The questioning encourages everyone involved in the process of inquiry to focus on the positive in their experience, to focus on their "best selves," and the best in others and in the organization. The process is collaborative, and encourages people to be open and honest with each other, to be creative, and to recognize that they are all responsible for what they have created, are creating, and can create together.

The theory of solution-focused brief therapy is that people have the resources within themselves to find solutions to their problems and difficulties (George, Iveson, and Ratner, 2002). The approach is based on respect for people, and the belief that everyone knows what is best for them, and with the appropriate intervention they will be able to resource the solution. People are perceived as much more than their problem and/or difficulty. They are encouraged to recognize and appreciate their inner resources and to draw upon them, and to imagine themselves in challenging situations in which they are their "best selves."

Assertiveness is about authentic connection with self and others

The theory of positive psychology emphasizes the importance of connection with one's self and with others. Connectedness is about relationship, and the power of relationship to transform people's lives.

Key elements of connectedness, as described by Edward Hallowell (2002), include:

- unconditional love from someone; being loved and recognized for who you are
- friendship; having close friends with whom feelings and thoughts can be shared
- community; belonging to friendship groups, groups and teams
- organization; working with others within the same organization
- environment; having a connection with the environment within which one works and lives, as well as nature and animals, and the wider world.

Developing assertive relationships with others promotes the feeling of connectedness, of colleagueship in the workplace, of being able to work things out together.

The theory of existential therapy provides useful insights into the relationships between self-esteem and connection (Strasser and Strasser, 1999). Relationships matter, and being able to be real in relationships is part of feeling secure and of having assertive patterns of behavior. Only through having a true connection with one's self is it possible to truly connect and engage with other people. Every interaction and encounter that people have impacts on how they think and feel about themselves.

> Every stimulus that we receive has some kind of impact on our self-construct and in turn that affects our concept of self. Other people's opinions are usually at the forefront of how we view ourselves, how we feel about ourselves and how we change our convictions. Generally our self-esteem and self-concept are on a continual "roller-coaster," dependent on the opinions of others.
>
> (Strasser and Strasser, 1999: 106)

Assertiveness is about meaning and purpose

People's values give meaning to and help make sense of their world. Without values, without meaning, people feel insecure and worthless. Many value and behavior patterns are bound up with the culture and place in which people live, and are affirming of positive self-esteem and assertive relationships. Others however can be non-assertive and negative, devaluing of self-regard and regard of others. Whether positive or negative, the values and behavior patterns can become sedimented and stuck in such a way that they are never explored or clarified. They are lived in a rigid and unquestioning way, and in some cases misunderstood and misinterpreted not only by those upholding the values but also by others who uphold different values.

Existential therapy offers useful insights into how people can become rigid in their thinking and the importance of flexibility in thinking for developing assertiveness and inclusivity. Strasser and Strasser (1999) liken rigidity in values to sedimentation. It is made up of values and behavior patterns that are deposited (like sediments) deep within people; they become part of people's sedimented self-construct.

Rigidity in values can lead to negative and self-limiting beliefs about oneself and others, and to patterns of behavior that are non-assertive. People are helped in this therapy to look at their rigid sedimentations and to recognize that they have a choice about how they interpret and look at experiences.

> We can be dogmatic or stuck to such an extent that it is often hard to realize that there might be other ways of viewing the world or other ways of conducting our lives.
>
> (Strasser and Strasser, 1999: 94)

Typically people become rigid in their thinking when they are feeling insecure, threatened, lacking in confidence, and feeling disapproved of by themselves or others. There is a basic assumption in this therapy that within all of us there is the possibility to change, and that with help we can make the shift in thinking, feeling, and behaving. The shift is from feeling unsafe and insecure, and lacking in self-confidence, towards feeling safe and secure, and feeling confident in oneself and in one's abilities.

The shift extends outwards from the individual into relationships with others. For example when people experience conflict with each other they often feel insecure and unsafe, leading them to feel, think, and behave more rigidly. The tendency is to become defensive and to behave non-assertively, resorting to either aggressive or passive behavior, through a lack of security and lack of self-confidence.

Developing positive self-esteem and assertive relationships involves exploring what really matters and a willingness to view things differently and to make different choices of interpretation. Through the exploring of personal values people can choose to make changes in their patterns of behavior, to make different connections within themselves and with others that are more assertive. In doing this people are choosing to stir up previously rigid value and behavior patterns, to stir the sedimentation that has become rock-like and reinforced over the years and to shift their self-constructs through questioning and through becoming less rigid and more flexible and open to change.

Assertiveness is about listening to and trusting intuition

Positive self-esteem gives people the courage to act on their intuitions. Without positive self-esteem people will not act on their intuitions because they fear being criticized or judged by others. These fears are often based on past experiences that they have perceived as negative. As a result people hold back from being creative, from taking risks, or from offering help. When people hold themselves in positive self-regard, they think less and worry less about what other people will think of them.

Caroline Myss (2005), a well-known and recognized author and speaker on how people use their personal power, has most recently focused on the need for people to develop positive self-esteem in order to have the courage not only to listen to their intuitions but also to act on them in service of others. Myss suggests that an act of service to another person or group of people is about being honest and direct with them. It may mean disagreeing with or challenging them, for example, by giving them difficult feedback on their performance. She comments, "Our fear of others' opinions can be a very real controlling force. Many people repress their intuitive guidance for fear of how others will judge them" (Myss, 2005: 135).

Most global organizations uphold the value of integrity. While this will mean different things to different people depending on their background and experiences, generally people know when they are behaving with integrity because they are behaving in line with their values and beliefs about themselves and others. People behave with a lack of integrity when their fears and anxieties get the better of them and take over. Behaving with integrity involves listening to one's intuition, doing what feels right and is required in a situation. It means overcoming fears and anxieties about what others might think or say. This takes the courage to "speak one's truth."

Assertiveness is about making mind, body, and brain connections

Affective neuroscience refers to that part of the brain concerned with the development of neuronal connections related to emotional development, and the ability to connect with oneself and others. Recent research into affective neuroscience (Wilkinson, 2006) has much to offer to those looking to understand assertiveness, and in particular understand the internal connections that are made between the mind, body, and brain and how they relate to the external connections that people make with each other. People are able to make new neuronal connections throughout life; however, early infancy and adolescence are the times of most growth and development.

In infancy, between birth and the age of 18 months, the child's brain is undergoing huge neuronal development, with connections being made through the process of the child being mirrored by her or his primary care-giver. The right hemisphere of the brain is concerned with the processing of emotions; connections are made and are also unmade during this time. Positive experiences create positive connections in the brain, and are nourished by further positive reinforcing experiences of the self and others. In the absence of positive experiences of mirroring, the neuronal connections are not made.

The left hemisphere of the brain is concerned with cognition and language recognition. The neuronal connections between the right and left brain enable people to put "feelings into words," to be able to express themselves. We need good connection between the right and left hemispheres in order to get good interpersonal connection; equally, good interpersonal connection facilitates right and left hemisphere brain connection.

Affective neuroscience very much supports the transactional analysis theory that early decisions can be remade through positive experiences with others. People can learn how to relate to self and others positively and assertively, and to enjoy a healthy I'm OK: You're OK life position; new neuronal connections can be made through engaging with new and positive experiences of the self within relationships.

Assertiveness is about feeling secure

People who feel secure have an inner self-confidence and feelings of positive self-esteem. The theory of insecure and secure attachments developed by the psychologist Dr John Bowlby during the 1940s and known as "attachment theory" helps in an understanding of what assertiveness is, and how early childhood experiences impact on feelings of self-esteem and patterns of behavior (Bowlby, 2006a). For people who experience secure and positive early attachments in their relationships with primary care-givers, the mind, body, and brain connections are positive. They are able to express how they feel towards others without fear, and to respond to others' feelings without fear; they know what is right for them, and are able to self-manage and to be assertive.

By contrast people who experienced negative, uncertain, and insecure attachments in their primary relationships in early infancy can fear their own and others' feelings, and may respond by avoiding and cutting off from feelings, or by cutting off from them and then having an angry outburst.

Table 2.3 summarizes the difference between a secure early attachment and insecure early attachments, and shows the relationship between assertive and non-assertive behaviors and the kinds of relationships that people are likely to experience based on their experience of having their attachment needs met in infancy. Only the assertive/

Table 2.3 The four life positions related to early attachment patterns and the impact of these on relationships

4 Aggressive/defensive	**1 Assertive/creative**
I'm OK: You're not OK	I'm OK: You're OK
Insecure in self, lacking in self-confidence	Secure in self, self-confident
"Avoidant" pattern of attachment, early attachment needs not met	Early attachment needs met through positive, responsive engagement of primary care-giver
Affective neuronal connections not made	Positive affective neuronal connections made in brain
Mistrusts others, keeps self at distance, is controlling	Confident in self, and comfortable with others, is trusting and open
Fears rejection and rejects others first	Connected with self and others

3 Manipulative/divisive	**2 Passive/submissive**
I'm not OK: You're not OK	I'm not OK: You're OK
Insecure in self, lacking in self-confidence	Insecure in self, lacking in self-confidence
"Disorganized" pattern of attachment, early attachment needs not met	"'Ambivalent" pattern of attachment, early attachment needs not met
Affective neuronal connections not made	Affective neuronal connections not made
Moves between being "Ambivalent" and "Avoidant" in relationships; appears to others as unpredictable, and not safe to be around	Fears abandonment
	Fearful towards others and of others, is anxious
	Withdraws from others through lack of confidence and uncertainty; appears vulnerable to others and needy
	Mistrusts and is unsure in relation to other people

creative life position is a reflection of a secure attachment; the other three insecure attachments are all based on an underlying belief that "I am not OK."

Assertiveness is about physical, intellectual, emotional, and spiritual awareness and integration

The four intelligences or energies are physical, intellectual, emotional, and spiritual, and developing an awareness of these parts of ourselves, and integrating them, is central to developing assertiveness.

The theory and model of the four intelligences or energies is described by international organizational consultant Steven Covey (2004) and by Tim Laurence (2003), founder of the Hoffman Institute in the UK. The model is used increasingly in organizations to help people develop greater self-awareness, and to know who they are when they are fully present in themselves, and are leading from within, with energy and vitality. This means paying attention to, and noticing, how one is feeling physically, intellectually, emotionally, and spiritually, and at the same time being aware that everyone else is also made up of physical, intellectual, emotional, and spiritual energy. Not paying attention to one or more of these overlapping energies or intelligences may result in imbalance and ill-health. Assertiveness is about the integration of all four intelligences. Figure 2.1 summarizes the different characteristics associated with each of the four intelligences or energies.

Assertiveness is about acceptance and mindfulness

Recent developments in cognitive behavioral psychology (Orsillo et al., 2004) shed useful light on how people can develop greater self-awareness and self-confidence. The acceptance approach is based on acceptance of thoughts, feelings, and behaviors that people have linked to what really matters to them in terms of their values and aspirations.

> Mindfulness is a process that involves moving toward a state in which one is fully observant of external and internal stimuli in the present moment, and open to accepting (rather than attempting to change or judge) the current situation.
>
> (Orsillo et al., 2004: 77)

Mindfulness is about noticing and bringing into awareness how we are feeling, physically, intellectually, emotionally, and spiritually in the

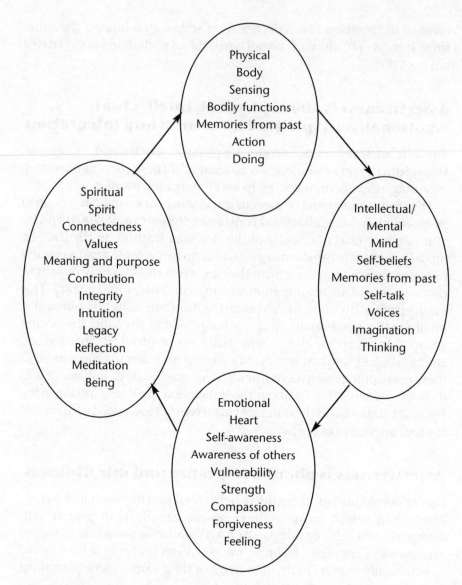

Figure 2.1 The four intelligences or energies

present moment, the here-and-now; it is about being fully connected internally and externally. It involves being able to differentiate between thoughts and feelings, acknowledging them as being transitory.

The acceptance and mindfulness approach draws upon those spiritual practices that encourage observation of the self, and recognition that we have a choice in how we perceive situations and respond to them. In this way possibilities are opened up, and people are encouraged to take responsibility for their feelings and thoughts, to acknowledge and to accept them, and to let go of those that may not serve them well in terms of their values and aspirations.

Through increasing self-awareness and awareness of possibilities people can be helped to be both more accepting of themselves and others, and to enjoy more engagement and connection in their lives.

3 Positive Self-Assertion

Introduction

Developing assertiveness and diversity in organizations is about developing people, in particular developing self-awareness and awareness of others, as well as the impact people have on each other. Positive self-assertion is about people having the confidence to be themselves, to know and be true to their values and beliefs, and to have the courage to speak their truth. Key to this is developing a strong connection with oneself—physically, intellectually, emotionally, and spiritually, through which there is awareness of one's qualities, abilities, and limitations. People who have a strong sense of self are able to be vulnerable, and know when to ask for help. The stronger and more connected people are to themselves, the stronger is their connection and relationship with others.

Assertive relationships are those in which people speak their truth, are able to live their values and beliefs, be honest and open, while respecting, supporting, challenging each other, and especially giving feedback to each other. Assertive relationships are "bigger relationships":

> The bigger the relationship the larger the opportunities for envisioning possibilities, for imagining and connecting with the spiritual; for thinking and planning, leading to taking action and getting results.
> (Ian Lock, leadership development consultant, conversation, 2006)

In this chapter the skills of developing positive self-assertion are explained, and the case study which follows shows how, through the process of developing positive self-assertion, people can and do make a positive difference through increased self-awareness in particular through overcoming self-limiting beliefs, and through developing a stronger connection with the self.

Developing self-assertion through having a clear sense of purpose

People who have a sense of purpose and know what matters to them are able to be more assertive. They are aware of, and take responsibility for, their decisions and choices based on their values and beliefs. Thus exploring and clarifying the values and beliefs people hold is central to everything else that they do and the way in which they interpret experiences. This is true at an individual and organizational level. In order for people and organizations to live their values and to act with integrity, they need to know what their values are, and how to communicate these values assertively.

Developing positive self-assertion through positive self-belief and self-recognition

Self-recognition refers to the kinds of beliefs and thoughts that people have about themselves (intellectual), and the kinds of feelings (emotional) and body sensations (physical) that they experience associated with these beliefs and thoughts. How people feel spiritually is very much connected to their intellectual, emotional and physical energies.

In any situation thoughts run through the mind: this is sometimes referred to as "inner self-talk." Thoughts may be accompanied by memories of the self in earlier and similar situations. Some people visualize themselves in previous situations; others hear what was said to, or by them, in that situation. The "inner self-talk" is also related to how people feel in their bodies. Particular body sensations are associated with particular thoughts and situations. For example when people feel anxious their breathing tends to be shallow, and when they are feeling relaxed their breathing is deeper. How people think and feel about themselves influences their behavior, which in turn influences the behavior of others.

Self-affirmations

When people feel self-confident their self-beliefs and beliefs about others are positive, they feel relaxed and positive, and their behavior is assertive, I'm OK: You're OK. People are more likely to give to and receive positive recognition from others, and this in turn increases thoughts and feelings of self-worth and positive self-esteem.

Positive self-affirmations are statements about self that are affirming of self. They are always specific and positive, and usually begin with the personal pronoun "I," to emphasize that the person is taking responsibility for the affirmation. People may not always think or feel as positive as the self-affirmations suggest, nevertheless when preparing for a situation it can be extremely useful to think of positive self-affirmations as well as visualizing oneself in the situation behaving assertively and creatively. Other ways of practicing positive self-affirmations include writing, singing, and saying them to oneself in a mirror.

Examples of positive self-affirmations:

- I am good at making presentations.
- People will be interested in my views.
- I communicate my ideas clearly to others.
- I am confident in my abilities as a leader.
- I enjoy positive working relationships.

When people enter into a situation holding self-affirming beliefs and positive thoughts about others, they are more likely to enjoy positive, creative relationships with people in which there is openness and honesty. See Figure 3.1.

Self-limiting beliefs

When people lack self-confidence, their thoughts about themselves are negative and limiting. They may feel physically uncomfortable and tense, and are more likely to give negative recognition to others and receive it from them. This in turn increases their negative thoughts and feelings about themselves and others, leading to low self-esteem.

Self-limiting beliefs are usually general and are all encompassing of people, leading to a loss of meaning and purpose in their lives. Very often these beliefs were decided upon early in life as a response to the messages people received from their primary care-givers and the underlying life position is "Not OK."

Examples of self-limiting beliefs and negative self-recognition:

- I'll never be any good as ....
- I know I'm useless at managing others.
- They'll never agree to what I'm suggesting.

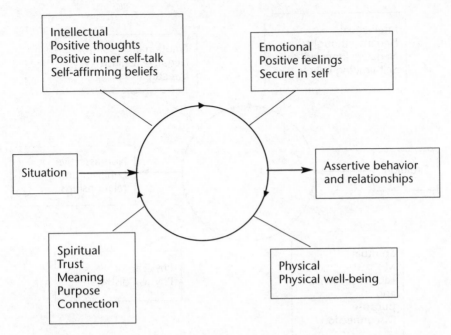

Figure 3.1 Positive inner self-talk and self-affirming beliefs linked to emotional and physical well-being, spiritual connection, and assertive behavior

- I know I'm stupid.
- I might as well give up now.

Negative thoughts such as these often result in people feeling uptight, with headaches and low physical energy. People communicate what they are thinking and feeling about themselves non-verbally and verbally to others. Once people focus on the negative it is easy to spiral down, finding more and more not only in oneself, but also in others, that is negative. See Figure 3.2.

Developing positive self-assertion through intuitive intelligence

Intuition is, first of all, an expression of power.

(Myss, 2005: 17–18)

Paying attention to intuition is what assertive people do. They listen to and trust their intuition; they pay attention to and have the courage to

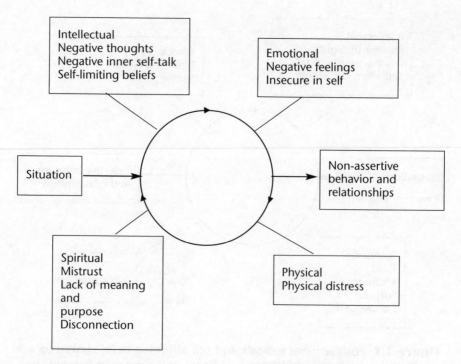

Figure 3.2 Negative inner self-talk and self-limiting beliefs linked to emotional and physical distress, lack of spiritual connection, and non-assertive behavior

act on it—to speak their truth. Sometimes people refer to their intuition as a "gut feeling," others to it being a "hunch about something" or their "sixth sense." They are not afraid of their intuition, the feelings that connect them with their environment and the people in it. Most importantly they are open to connecting at this level within themselves and with others. This is frequently described as a kind of spiritual connection since it is not physical, nor is it intellectual or emotional.

Developing self-assertion involves developing intuition and trusting what the intuition is sensing, both within oneself and between others. Very often people do sense something at an intuitive level, knowing what to do in that moment, but do not have the courage to act on their intuition. People who have positive self-esteem and who trust themselves are more able to act on their intuition and behave with integrity.

Developing positive self-assertion through taking personal and interpersonal risks

A personal risk may take the form of allowing oneself to become aware of, and then to challenge, a previously held negative self-belief, to think the unthinkable and to do what seemed to be undoable.

An interpersonal risk may take the form of choosing to share some personal information with another person or give them some feedback about their behavior and its impact. Either way there is often a risk involved, a stepping into the unknown and sometimes a fear of what the other person will think or do in response. Table 3.1 lists what having the courage to be assertive involves.

Table 3.1 Having the courage to be assertive

- Listen to one's intuition.
- Speak one's truth.
- Know what gives one meaning and purpose.
- Act with integrity.
- Trust.
- Be brave physically, intellectually, emotionally, and spiritually.
- Be vulnerable physically, intellectually, emotionally, and spiritually.
- Not know always how to do something.
- Make mistakes.
- Take risks.
- Have fun.
- Live with passion.
- Do something differently.
- Shift and change thinking and feeling.
- Question self and others.
- Challenge negative thinking about self and others.

Case study: The essence of assertiveness, positive self-assertion, and assertive relationships in organizations

It was feedback about his behavior at the final stage of an interview process that was the beginning of a journey of personal and interpersonal transformation for Atif Sheikh. Others perceived him as "hanging back" and "self-deprecating" in group situations. This came as a surprise to him as he perceived himself as being "big, brown and very public school" and that making fun of himself was a way of managing situations with charm and humor.

Atif got the job and struggled during the first few months until he went on a leadership course where he was given the opportunity to explore and clarify his values and self-beliefs. In the business simulation on the course he found himself hanging further and further back, having not been voted by the group to be the leader. Challenged by one of the tutors he realized that he only stepped into a leadership role when given permission by others to do so, as had been the case both at school and at university where he had been the chosen leader. This realization was a huge learning and "un-learning." Through feedback from the tutor he identified the following self-limiting belief:

I am not good enough and I never will be for my father.

Linked to this self-limiting belief Atif realized that he spent much of his time being the kind of person he thought other people wanted him to be. Thus if he was chosen as a leader, he would be the kind of leader that others wanted him to be rather than being himself. He worked on being himself and not someone else's idea of who he was.

Two years later, on a team retreat, Atif realized that he had a deeper self-limiting belief that was underneath his hanging back, not saying what he really thought, backing down and staying quiet in group and team situations. This self-limiting belief was based on a fear of being himself, and was expressed as:

I fear that I am a coward.

Assertiveness is about having courage, having the courage to be oneself and to speak one's truth. Atif realized that what was holding him back from being himself was his fear that he did not have the courage to truly be himself, and that he had some shame around his ambition. Deep down he thought ambition was a dirty word, that it was somewhat ugly and competitive. It was not until the tutor on the team retreat said to him, "Your ambition is a beautiful thing," that Atif was able to see that his ambition was, and is, something that helped and could be used for the benefit of other people. Far from it being something to be ashamed of, it is something to be proud of.

The process for Atif was one of reclaiming and accepting himself and his values—honesty, ambition, and pride—and valuing them as positive. He now has an honest set of values and in his words "simple ways of looking at the world." He describes these simple ways as transformational:

> Now I know who I want to be and can stop taking responsibility for others whilst being aware of the impact I have on others. I try to be proud of everything that I do, in every moment, and in everything that I say. These simple ways are helping transform my relationships especially with my father. I am now able to be more assertive with him, to be honest and open.
>
> (Atif Sheikh, interview, 2005)

Atif has a positive and affirmative self-belief, he is proud of who he is and what he stands for. He wakes up feeling good about the previous day. He believes that once people get to this place of positive and affirmative self-belief they have the courage to be assertive in their relationships, and that their conversations are transformational, no matter how difficult the relationship. He lists his values as:

- flair
- passion
- ambition
- intellect
- strength
- laughter
- generosity.

Atif's self-limiting beliefs have been replaced by positive and life-changing beliefs:

> I have the courage to be who I am and to act in a way that I am proud of.
> I am everything that I can be.
> I step up into being a leader. I do so with the right intent. I make a real difference.
> I am the kind of son that I want to be.
> I say what I think and feel in relationships.

In 2005 Atif was in a new job and brought his learning to what was a relatively new department following a restructuring. Together the department identified five key values, each with an accompanying behavior and action. The values, behaviors, and actions are listed in Table 3.2.

Table 3.2 Values, behaviors, and actions

Values	Behaviors	Actions
1. Focus	Work together as a team, take "collective action," manage cross functionally-"together management."	Work hard at enrolling others, need their help to be successful. No meetings before 10.00.
2. Integrity	Be transparent and honest-when things are bad say so, when we make a mistake say so. Air our views with positive intent.	Take responsibility for how we feel, what we think, and say so clearly.
3. Challenge with respect	We will have tough conversations with each other and be assertive. Understand where others are "coming from."	Have a crib sheet to help us do this with five simple "tips." Training. Atif as "buddy" for department.
4. Plan for success	Go cross-functional and pick up the phone always. Share knowledge.	We will involve others in planning, be totally inclusive.
5. Passion	Celebrate success; tell success stories at meetings, celebrate jobs. Praise.	We will lead with passion, say who we are and how we operate. We will let people know of our successes.

CASE ANALYSIS: OVERCOMING SELF-LIMITING BELIEFS AND TRANSFORMING RELATIONSHIPS THROUGH CONVERSATION

Atif's journey has been one of not knowing and questioning, through to finding, knowing, and accepting his own values. For him values are deeply personal and discovering those values has been a profound journey. He has reclaimed his humor and now sees the intent behind it as coming from a very different, much more positive place than previously. He enjoys using it to challenge others and to remove status from around the table.

The process of becoming himself, of having the courage to be himself and to be open and honest in relationships, started with feedback from others about his behavior. Atif used the feedback to explore and clarify his true values and the beliefs about himself and others; and to further and better his understanding of himself and his relationship with others. The feedback provided Atif with an opportunity to "stir" those values and beliefs about himself that had become "sedimented" (see pages 18–19).

Once a self-limiting belief is identified, it is possible for people to look at how this gets in the way of them living the life that they want to and creating the future that they want to create. Atif was able to do this, and in so doing opened up the way to peel a further layer of the onion and to identify a deeper self-limiting belief based, as many self-limiting beliefs are, on fear. For Atif it was the fear "of being a coward," of not having the courage to be himself, in particular to lead with his values of ambition, honesty, and pride.

Fear is often accompanied by shame, shame of the fear, and fear of the shame. Atif was given a huge gift when the tutor honored him for his ambition, describing it as a "beautiful thing." This enabled Atif to see himself differently, to celebrate who he was, and the things that mattered to him, and to see them as positive rather than negative. Atif describes himself now as being at peace with himself, of living an honest and open life of which he is proud. Out of the uncertainty of "unknowing" and not knowing his values he now knows what matters to him, and feels secure and confident in himself to be able to have any conversation no matter how challenging the subject or relationship. A key ingredient of feeling secure and confident is trust. Atif trusts that providing he lives his truth that great things will happen, and do! He enjoys an inner peace and enjoys relationships that are assertive, based on honesty, openness, and respect.

4 Assertive Communication

Introduction

Assertiveness is about self-respect and respect for others, of communicating from an I'm OK: You're OK life position with other people. The language of assertive communication reflects the values and beliefs that underpin assertiveness, of self-awareness and awareness of other people, in particular of being aware of choices that we are making in terms of how we interpret situations, and how we behave towards others.

Assertive communication is a language of connection in which each person is self-aware and aware of others, physically, emotionally, intellectually, and spiritually. When people are communicating with each other assertively they are listening to each other, asking questions and talking about what they notice and observe, think, and imagine, and how they feel openly and honestly; they are connected to themselves and to others.

In the first part of this chapter the key assertive communication skills and behaviors that express a truly I'm OK: You're OK life position are outlined. They are:

- listening
- observing
- using "I" statements
- questioning
- giving, receiving, and asking for feedback.

The case study shows how assertive communication can be learnt and how through doing so people can develop assertive relationships and more assertive organizations.

Listening

Listening is key to all communication and underpins assertive communication and all assertive behaviors. People listen and respond differently depending on the situation, and how they feel about themselves and other people. Listening from the life position I'm OK: You're OK, with respect for self and others, with a positive attitude and intent, makes all the difference as to whether the behavior is assertive or non-assertive, and to the kind of connection that people make with each other.

People show that they are listening usually by looking at the person who is talking, by paying attention to him or her non-verbally. By looking at the person they are giving her or him positive recognition, whether or not they agree with what the person is saying. Other ways of communicating that we are listening to each other include nodding, and sometimes making a sound—either of agreement or disagreement. People listen with their bodies, and communicate to each other that they are listening by the way in which they are sitting, standing, or moving as they are listening. In situations in which people are not able to see each other, they communicate that they are listening and/or have heard by making a sound.

Letting people know that we have heard them is important, and equally so through electronic and written communication. A quick response "Thanks for the email" is for most people better than no response at all.

How people listen in different situations

How people listen impacts on what they pay attention to. Ian Lock, leadership development consultant, gives the example of listening to the safety instructions being read out at the start of a flight, and asks people to think about how they listen in that situation. He then asks people to think about how they listen to the same instructions during a flight when it has been announced that there are problems and undue turbulence ahead, which could necessitate an emergency landing at some point.

Listening with positive self-respect and self-awareness

When people feel positive about themselves they are more likely and willing to see the positive in themselves, other people, and in the situation. Bringing self-awareness to how we communicate with others is vital to assertive communication.

How people listen when they are feeling happy, sad, angry, or fearful will make a difference to what they hear and to how they respond to the other person. People who are feeling happy are likely to have more energy to listen to the other person. By contrast when they are feeling sad, angry or fearful they are less likely to be able to hear what the person is saying. When people feel happy they are more able to be in the present than when they are feeling sad, angry, or fearful. These feelings of sadness, anger, and fear tend to get in the way of people being able to listen and hear what is going on around them or what is being said to them.

Listening with positive regard and respect for others

How people regard other people impacts on how they listen to them. Being aware of what determines that regard is an important part of developing assertive communication and listening to people who are different, who bring a different way of communicating, of looking at things and doing things. Recognizing one's own bias and prejudices is a necessary part of assertive communication. It is often only through reflecting on possible biases, or through receiving feedback, that people become aware of subtle prejudices which impact on how they listen to others.

Observing

Noticing and paying attention is a skill of assertiveness, associated with mindfulness and acceptance, self-awareness, and authentic connection. Noticing how we are feeling and what we are thinking in a situation and being able to express these feelings and thoughts to others is an important part of assertive communication, as is observing others, truly paying attention to them without making value judgments about their behavior, or assumptions about them. The skill of observing, of noticing self and others, helps people to be fully present in their communication and to be more aware.

Noticing how we are feeling physically, intellectually, emotionally, and spiritually is an important part of self-responsibility and of self-management. The more aware we become of how we are feeling as whole people, the more we can make an authentic connection with ourselves, and with others through being truly present to ourselves and to others.

Using "I" statements

The use of "I" statements is a central part of communicating assertively, and follows on from listening to self and others, and observing self and others. It is a very simple and yet powerful way of communicating self-responsibility, and makes assertive communication much more possible and real.

When people use the personal pronoun "I" rather than "You," "We," "One," or "It," they communicate much more powerfully a sense of self, and of taking responsibility for their feelings, thoughts, and behavior. It can sometimes be difficult for people who are used to saying "You," "We," or "One," to use "I." When they do, they notice a qualitative difference in both how they communicate and what they are communicating, and the impact that they have on others. In particular they have a much stronger sense of self, of being their own person.

There is more risk involved when people use the personal pronoun "I." They are risking more of themselves by expressing their thoughts and feelings. By not using the personal pronoun people can distance themselves from how they are feeling, and what they are thinking.

The benefits of using "I" statements, of taking self-responsibility, are huge in that others are more able to hear what is being said, and to listen with acceptance. They can hear more clearly people's passion, their commitment to what they are talking about, and are more likely to understand and engage with the person. In a situation where someone is making a criticism or is in conflict with someone else, the combination of listening, observing specific behaviors, and being able to express thoughts and feelings using "I" statements makes the criticism or the difference easier to hear. Consider the difference between the following two statements:

I feel uncomfortable with what happened when ....

You made me feel uncomfortable when ....

The first statement gives both speaker and listener an opportunity to explore their feelings and thoughts about what happened without judgment, or any implied blame of each other. The communication is assertive and there is the possibility of arriving at a deeper understanding of each other. The second statement is accusatory. The person is putting the responsibility for how she or he feels onto the listener who is likely to feel defensive in response to the perceived accusation. The communication is non-assertive, and the possibility of arriving at a deeper understanding of each other is potentially closed down.

Clearly there are times when saying "We" is more appropriate than saying "I," for example when what has been done or agreed is by a group and/or team of people. Indeed saying "I" on such occasions can suggest that the person is claiming sole responsibility and disregarding the contribution of others, and is definitely not assertive communication.

Questioning

Building on the assertive communication skills of listening, observing, and making "I" statements is the skill of asking questions, especially open questions. When people ask questions they are making a connection with the other person, or people. They are demonstrating that they are interested in them, and perhaps curious about them. In a discussion or conversation, asking questions related to what people have been saying lets them know that they have been listened to, and heard. Questions can be used in a number of ways, including gathering more information, showing interest, and checking something out—for example checking out an assumption. Being clear of the intention behind the question, and asking with positive intent, are important to assertive communication and to building open, honest, and trusting assertive relationships.

Open questioning

Typically, open questions are those that, as the word "open" implies, allow people to respond in any way that they choose, and are non-directive. Open questions can be more or less open; they can provide and point the person in a direction depending on the words used and when the question is asked during an exchange.

Some examples of open questions are:

What do you think happened?
How do you think we could have done this differently?
What else do you think we could have done?
How do you feel about things now?

Open questions require that the person asking them really listens to the other people. It is important to be aware of the extent to which an open question is truly open in the sense of being non-directive and the extent to which it could be directive, directing someone towards a particular response.

Closed questioning

By contrast, closed questions are those that elicit either a "Yes" or "No" response, and are directive of the conversation. They are necessary and appropriate in certain situations.

Noticing and listening to the kind of language that a person uses to describe his/her experience of something helps the listener determine how to respond and what kinds of questions to ask. Using "I" statements and a mix of reflecting back what the person has said and a question is a useful assertive communication skill. For example:

I thought we had decided X. You said that you thought that we had decided X. How do you feel about our having made that decision now?

Giving, receiving, and asking for feedback

We are giving feedback to each other all the time, be it verbally or non-verbally, informally or formally. Feedback is about giving each other recognition. Through the process of giving, receiving, and asking for feedback, people make stronger connections with each other and become more self-aware. The Johari Window (Luft, 1984) is a useful model for illustrating the dynamics of giving information about self (self-disclosure), and receiving information and/or feedback from others. See Figure 4.1. It shows how people can develop more assertive relationships with each other—that are open, honest and trusting, through the giving, receiving of, and asking for, feedback. The more people give information about themselves, including their feelings and thoughts, the more open and honest and giving of information other people will be towards them. In asking for feedback from people, people are able to develop relationships in which assertive communication becomes the "way of doing things" and reflects both self-respect and respect for others.

The dynamics of giving, receiving, and asking for feedback mean that "window pane" 1 (in Figure 4.1) gets larger, as the relationship gets "bigger" and energy is released. The goal of assertive communication is to facilitate assertive and inclusive relationships through creating a large open "window pane" in which everyone is able to be their true and "best selves."

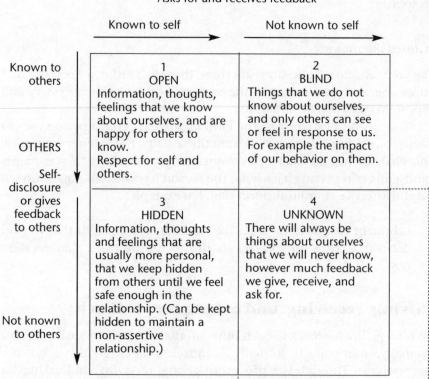

SELF
Asks for and receives feedback

	Known to self	Not known to self
Known to others	1 OPEN Information, thoughts, feelings that we know about ourselves, and are happy for others to know. Respect for self and others.	2 BLIND Things that we do not know about ourselves, and only others can see or feel in response to us. For example the impact of our behavior on them.
Not known to others	3 HIDDEN Information, thoughts and feelings that are usually more personal, that we keep hidden from others until we feel safe enough in the relationship. (Can be kept hidden to maintain a non-assertive relationship.)	4 UNKNOWN There will always be things about ourselves that we will never know, however much feedback we give, receive, and ask for. Unconscious

OTHERS — Self-disclosure or gives feedback to others

Figure 4.1 Developing self-awareness and assertive relationships through giving, receiving, and asking for feedback

Source: Adapted from Luft (1984: 60).

Feedback can be positive and it can be constructive. Either way it is important that giving, receiving, and asking for feedback is done well and with positive intent, self-respect, and respect for the other person. When given with positive intent, feedback is usually well received and experienced as a gift. It is useful to remember when giving feedback that it can say as much about the person giving the feedback as the person receiving it. Feedback that helps develop self-awareness and assertive relationships:

■ is specific rather than general
■ is based on observable behaviors

■ is timely and close to the event
■ is given from an I'm OK: You're OK life position
■ takes into account the other person's readiness to hear the feedback
■ takes into account the person's cultural differences
■ gives people a choice about whether to respond immediately
■ gives people an opportunity to ask questions
■ is developing of positive self-esteem
■ is developing of an interpersonal connection
■ is motivating of creativity and ongoing learning and development
■ is received with interest, curiosity, and positive intent.

Table 4.1 summarizes key assertive behaviors and what they communicate to others.

Table 4.1 Summary of assertive behaviors and what they communicate

Assertive behavior:	Communicates:
Using "I" statements: I feel, I think	Self-responsibility, self-awareness
Listening	Respect for other/s
Making appropriate eye contact	Connection and listening
Nodding	Connection and listening
Asking open, and closed, questions	Interest and curiosity
Giving specific feedback	Connection and engagement
Seeking feedback	Learning and development
Saying "No" with respect	Self-responsibility, and boundaries
Saying "Sorry"	Self-responsibility
Congruency between verbal, non-verbal	Integrity
Positive feedback	Appreciation of person
Critical feedback well given	Learning and development

Case study: Assertiveness training

Paul Turnbull, former head of learning and development at Guardian News and Media (GNM), describes how an interpersonal effectiveness course helped a team of 25 administrators within the advertising function to "add value" through developing greater assertiveness.

The project manager for the advertising function responsible for the development of people was keen to find a way of adding value. Together with Paul Turnbull, the idea of assertiveness training was agreed upon for the administration team. Paul asked team members a number of questions and identified a series of focused workshops covering different areas of assertiveness. All the workshops were between one and a half hours and two and a half hours and took place monthly. The second and third workshops were led by The Mind Gym (www.themindgym.com), and the first and last workshops led by Paul.

The first workshop focused on "Understanding myself and others," and a psychometric questionnaire, the Myers-Briggs Type Indicator (MBTI), was used to help people appreciate their strengths and differences, and to better understand the impact of their style of communication on others. (See Chapters 8 and 9 for more on MBTI.) Participants were able to better understand their own strengths and to think about what strengths their line managers might have, and how best to work with their differences.

The second workshop focused on "Saying "No," and helping people to say what they want, as well as being able to say "No," and to understand what gets in their way of saying "No." Participants practiced saying "No," and worked on a recent situation from the working environment in which they would have liked to say "No" and didn't.

The third workshop focused on "Managing upwards," and people were encouraged to find assertive ways of asking for what they wanted from their line managers. This involved them looking at situations from their line managers' perspective, and trying to identify changes that that they would like to see in their line managers, and to decide what they can do to facilitate the changes.

The fourth and last workshop focused on "Influencing others," and helped participants to explore a range of different strategies that can be used to influence people, including making the moral case for doing something.

Six months after the last workshop, all the participants and their line managers were sent a follow-up questionnaire asking them "Where are you at now?" The five assertiveness workshop issues were:

- is able to say "No" in an assertive way
- demonstrates behavior to show that they value the opinion of others
- is able to say what they are thinking in an assertive way
- is able to say how they are feeling in an assertive way
- is able to ask for what they want in an assertive way.

In each of the five factors evaluated, the participants rated themselves higher than their line managers, suggesting that the behaviors were not happening as much as the participants thought they were, or that managers were not noticing the behaviors. Either way the feedback was useful to the participants and indicated that they needed to be really clear in their assertive behaviors.

CASE ANALYSIS: SELF-AWARENESS AND AWARENESS OF OTHERS

Developing assertive communication was at the heart of the interpersonal effectiveness training, in particular developing self-awareness and awareness of others, and respect of one's own differences and others. Knowing that people have different styles of communicating helps people to appreciate their differences, and also to communicate with each other more effectively through an understanding of these differences.

Through increased self-awareness people are able to identify their personal and professional boundaries, and how to take responsibility for managing these boundaries. Saying "No," from an I'm OK: You're OK life position, is an important part of being clear, open, and honest in relationships. A combination of assertive communication skills—listening, open questioning, and making clear "I" statements that communicate both thoughts and feelings—helps people to say "No" in a way that is developing of an assertive relationship in which there is mutual respect and regard.

Giving people an opportunity to reflect on their relationships with their line managers and how they can make these relationships really work so that they and their line managers can work together effectively is an important part of people taking responsibility for their relationships, and recognizing that they have a choice about how they "live the relationship." Assertive communication underpins influencing others. Influencing from an I'm OK: You're OK life position is about being taking responsibility, being clear in the communication about what is wanted, using clear "I" statements, and being willing to work towards a win: win outcome.

The use of The Mind Gym workouts by organizations is increasingly popular as they can be easily integrated into the working day as well as complementing other initiatives of organizations. The workouts are high-energy and give people a boost and a set of tools, techniques, and tips that can be readily applied in the working environment.

The follow-up questionnaire was a useful feedback tool, and gave people an opportunity to reflect on their assertive communication and the extent to which they had communicated more assertively with their managers following the training. In particular it helped to further participants' awareness of the difference between the impact that they intended and the impact actually felt by their line managers. It highlighted the need for them to continue to ask for feedback from their line managers on how their communication was received.

5 Assertive Relationships

Introduction

Key to developing assertive communication skills is the underlying attitude of self-respect and respect of others, the I'm OK: You're OK life position. This chapter adds to those skills described in Chapter 4 with an exploration of some of the key communication skills offered by neuro-linguistic programming (NLP) (McDermott and Jago, 2001). NLP draws on a number of theories and practices, and is about making it possible for everyone to be more effective and assertive in their relationships. The skills outlined in this chapter are:

- mirroring and rapport
- representation systems
- reframing
- anchoring
- compelling futures
- association and dissociation.

The first three case studies focus on using NLP in one-to-one coaching, and helping people to develop positive self-esteem and assertive relationships. The fourth case study illustrates how the rapport-building skills of NLP can be learnt as part of assertiveness training.

Mirroring and rapport

Mirroring is about making a connection with another person. Very often people mirror each other without realizing that they are doing so, particularly non-verbally—for example in the way that they are sitting or standing. Equally people mirror each other verbally by using the same words. By doing this people feel heard and understood by each other. Mirroring helps build rapport between people.

Representation systems

Listening and noticing are skills that underpin assertive communication to. Listening and noticing how people use language to make sense of their experiences and then mirroring this back to them is a powerful way of building rapport and giving recognition to people. By using the same language people communicate that they have heard what the other person is saying, and that they speak some of the same language. Representation systems refer to the way in which people make sense of the world, the way in which people process information and communicate it to others. The five representation systems are:

- visual (sight and imagination)
- auditory (sound)
- kinaesthetic (touch and feel)
- gustatory (taste)
- olfactory (smell).

The three senses—sight, hearing, and feeling—are described in further detail below. The senses of taste and smell that are used by people to make sense of particular situations are not described.

Visual

People who use a visual representation system to make sense of the world picture things in their mind, literally either visualizing past, remembered experiences or imagining possible future experiences. When communicating with others they use specific language that reflects this representation system, such as "see, look, imagine"; for example, "I see what you mean." When people use their visual representation system they look up either to the left or right depending on whether they are accessing past memories or imagining a future situation.

Auditory

People who use an auditory representation system use their hearing to make sense of the world, and communicate using language such as "hear, sound, listen"; for example, "I hear what you are saying." People's eyes move from side to side when they use their auditory representation system.

Kinaesthetic

People who use a kinaesthetic representation system make sense of the world through how things feel to them physically and emotionally. They talk about how things feel to them, and look down when they are using their kinaesthetic representation system. For example, "I sense that what you are saying is ...."

Reframing

Reframing is about seeing things differently, and is an excellent way of opening up possibilities for experiencing things differently. It is about recognizing that people have a choice about the meaning and purpose they attribute to experiences, and that they can choose which "frame" to look through. The skill of reframing experiences is one that links closely with choosing positive emotion, thinking, and imagining. Reframing is often used to help people explore a different and more positive way of looking at experiences. Reframing can be as simple and as profound as changing one or two words in a sentence, for example, "I can't find the time to exercise" to "'I choose not to make time to exercise." This shift from "helplessness" to an awareness of choice and responsibility opens up the possibility for the person to choose to do something differently—to create the time.

Anchoring

Anchoring is a fantastic skill for literally "anchoring" a thought, feeling, and behavior in the mind and body. It is frequently used as a skill alongside imagining or visualization, whereby people imagine a situation in which they are feeling, thinking, and doing what they would really like to be doing—for example, behaving assertively. People are then asked to choose an image, a sound, a feeling in the body, smell, or taste that they associate with behaving assertively, and to really see, hear, and feel this association so that they can draw upon it when they are next in a situation in which they want to behave assertively.

Anchoring supports people in affirming themselves—in self-recognition, positive emotion, thinking, and imagining—by way of acknowledging that they have the resources within themselves and can draw upon them as and when they need and want to. It acknowledges the mind, body, and brain connection, and helps people to strengthen positive affective neuronal connections. In giving people a choice about how they anchor, it also acknowledges that people have different representation systems and will find their own "best" way to anchor.

Compelling futures

The skill of creating a compelling future involves people using their preferred representation system to create a future for themselves that is compelling, so much so that it is "as if" it is already happening. People feel self-empowered and motivated from within when they can create their desired future right now. This helps them know what it is that they need to do to bring that future into the present.

Association and dissociation

The skills of association and dissociation can be helpful in terms of people developing positive self-esteem and assertiveness.

Association is helpful when people wish to connect with their emotions. They may wish to connect with distressing feelings in order to express them, and in so doing to let go of them. People often hold on to feelings in their bodies, and being helped to associate with, and to express them, can facilitate them in letting go and moving on. For people who have low self-esteem it is empowering to connect with positive experiences, feelings, and thoughts that they may have filtered out.

Dissociation can be usefully used by people to create distance between themselves and their feelings, for example when those feelings are negative and overwhelming, and they feel out of control. Dissociation is unhelpful when people create distance between themselves and their feelings, when they "cut off" from themselves for long periods of time. They can feel withdrawn and isolated from others, and can be experienced by others as distant and difficult to connect with. They are disconnected from themselves and disconnected from others.

Case study 1: Reframing and anchoring

Paul Turnbull, former head of learning and development at Guardian News and Media (GNM), describes how he uses the tools of NLP in his career

coaching practice to help people create possibilities and to clarify a positive way
forward in their working lives. The focus is on helping people to become more
curious and aware of possibilities and to learn how to behave more positively,
creatively and assertively. Paul encourages people to see experiences as learning
projects.

> I encourage people to get curious. To ask themselves questions like—
> What's going on? Why is it like this? What can I learn?
>
> (Paul Turnbull, interview, 2005)

Reframing

Paul uses reframing to help people view situations differently and more
positively. He gives coaching clients an opportunity to explore difficult
situations from a number of different positions and points of view, to help
them to better understand what is going on. He invites the client to view
situations differently by physically moving from one position to another,
and to sit in different chairs representing the different positions.

Jane came to Paul for coaching to help her deal with her line manager,
whom she found difficult. In particular she experienced her line manager
as behaving inconsistently and becoming defensive when Jane
approached her. Jane wanted to "do something about it." With this in
mind Paul arranged two chairs in relation to where Jane was already
sitting; and explained that these chairs were Second and Third Positions.

He asked her to talk about how she was feeling and thinking from First
Position—the chair that she was already sitting in. Paul encouraged her
to take responsibility for herself, using "I" statements, beginning "I am
feeling ...," "I think that ...."

He then asked her to sit opposite in Second Position, to be in the
mindset of her line manager, to become her, and to describe the situation from her point of view. Again he encouraged Jane to use "I"
statements, and he asked a number of questions to help Jane in this position to think and feel herself into the "shoes" of her boss.

Finally he asked her to move to Third Position, in between First and
Second Position, and to look to her left and right, and consider what she
had learnt from the First and Second Position. He then asked her to
move from the Third Position over to First Position, taking with her the
learning she had gained; and asked her, "How are you feeling now?"

Jane felt physically more relaxed, and was visibly so. Her shoulders
had dropped and she was breathing more calmly. Her speech was slower,
calmer, and more expressive than it had been when she started out in

First Position. She described herself as feeling calmer and more in control of her feelings, and able to do something about the situation.

Anchoring

When asked by Paul whether there was a color, sound, sensation, smell, or taste of which she was aware when feeling physically relaxed, calmer, happier, with which she could anchor this experience and use when in the situation to remind herself of this experience, the color yellow came to mind, and "the warm sun on her skin." Paul suggested to her that she could draw on this color and sensation not only in the situation with her line manager, but also in other situations in which she felt unsure and anxious, and that this would help her to feel more confident in herself and reconnect her with her feelings of positive self-esteem and self-acceptance.

CASE ANALYSIS: SEEING THINGS DIFFERENTLY

Through the coaching, Jane was helped to express her feelings and thoughts about the situation that she was in. Through the language that she used she was encouraged to take responsibility for her feelings and thoughts. She had been stuck with negative feelings and thoughts, critical of herself for feeling this way. Moving from the First Position to the Second Position shifted her physically—she saw things from the perspective of her line manager.

Moving to the Third Position enabled her to see both perspectives and to incorporate what she had felt and thought in the Second Position as well as how she had been feeling and thinking in the First Position, and to see, hear, and feel differently about the situation. She took this new awareness back into First Position, and was able to reframe the situation.

Case study 2: Dissociation

Paul uses dissociation in coaching when people are stuck in negative feeling and thinking about themselves, others, and a situation. It is used when they have become totally identified with negative feelings and thoughts, and are no longer able to talk about their experience of the situation in any other than a negative way.

Sue came to Paul for coaching as she was finding it really difficult to handle customers who were complaining on the telephone. She referred to these people as "the old gits." She was feeling upset and angry and unable to think differently about them, and was feeling upset to be thinking in this way when otherwise she enjoyed positive and assertive relationships with people. However this dread of answering the telephone and feeling so negative was affecting her in other areas of her work, and she was talking about this negative experience a lot of the time.

Paul asked Sue to close her eyes and to select one of these negative situations, and to put the experience on a movie screen and to watch, listen, and notice the feelings of the people on the screen. He asked Sue to be really curious in her observations. After a few minutes he asked Sue to open her eyes to tell her what she had learnt. Sue was amazed at the difference in herself and her feelings, about both herself and the other people on the screen. She had learnt, she said, that she needed to prepare differently for answering the telephone; and to think positively about it so that she could listen to the people without judging, and to be more curious about what was going on. He asked her if there was any way that she could describe the people other than "the old gits" and she came up with "the old codgers"—this made her smile rather than grimace.

CASE ANALYSIS: THE POWER OF POSITIVE THINKING

Dissociation through observing from a distance was really helpful for Sue, who had got caught up in negative feeling and thinking. Through dissociation Sue was helped to view things differently. She was able to create some distance between herself and the experience, and to be curious in what was going on for her and the people in the situation. Once the distance was created she was able to "stand back" and learn from her observations by paying attention to what was going on. She realized that she had choices about how she viewed the situation, and that she could change the way she thought and felt about the experience. She was given an opportunity to talk about the experience differently, to move away from the negative, rigid thinking towards positive, flexible thinking about the situation, allowing her to learn from it; bringing some humor and lightness of touch to her experience by thinking of the people as "old codgers."

Case study 3: Compelling futures and representation systems

Max sought coaching following an appraisal in which he and his manager had agreed that there was nothing else available to him by way of development in his current role. He had been with the company for 12 years. His purpose in seeking coaching was to answer the question, "What do I do next?" Related questions were, "Are there any other things in GNM for me—in different parts of the group?" "What other roles might there be for me?" "How can I expand my horizons?"

In response to these questions Max identified that he would like a role, possibly in people management, that was fast paced and responsive. Paul asked him whether there was anything else that he would like to do. Max replied, "I'd like to have a shop in which I sell stuff that I have made."

Paul then asked Max if there was anything else that he might like to do. Max replied, "I'd like to teach, primary school children." Max was then invited by Paul to close his eyes and to do the following:

> See yourself as a teacher in a primary school. What do you see? What are you doing? What do you look like?
> How do you feel in this role?
> What can you hear?

He then asked him to repeat the above exercise:

> See yourself in another role within the GNM group. What do you see? What are you doing? What do you look like?
> How do you feel in this role?
> What can you hear?

And then once more to do the exercise for having a shop:

> See yourself in the shop selling stuff that you have made. What do you see? What are you doing? What do you look like?
> How do you feel in this role?
> What can you hear?

At the end of this exercise Max was asked to open his eyes and to talk about what he saw, felt and heard in each of the three situations. He described seeing himself engaged in the teaching, bending down, helping the children in their school work. He felt energized and around him he heard chatter. Working in another area of the GNM group was more difficult for him to be able to see, feel, or hear. He saw himself working with people, heard talking, and felt flat in terms of energy. His experience of seeing himself in the shop was similar to that of teaching, in that he saw himself helping people, serving them in the shop; he felt energized and around him he heard chatter.

When he reflected on what he had just described, he said, "I know what I have to do next. I have to leave."

CASE ANALYSIS: "DOING IT!"

NLP is very much about helping people to "do it." Using the skill of compelling futures helps people to create a picture of their experience, and tricks the brain into feeling the feelings that the person would feel if he/she was actually in the situation. In this case study Max was helped to achieve his objective of finding out what do next by being in the future and experiencing himself in that future through what he saw, felt, and heard: the three representation systems—visual, kinaesthetic, auditory.

The process of asking Max, "Is there anything else (that you might like to do)?" allowed him to go deeper and wider in terms of expanding his horizons and really tap into what he wanted to do next. Through engaging in this process he also discovered that what really mattered to him was working with people, and that he really wanted to do something which was about helping people and making a difference.

Case study 4: Rapport-building skills

Julian C. Mount is one of the directors of Big Top Business Training, and uses NLP skills in working with people to develop more assertive communication behavior.

As part of the assertiveness training people practice assertive communication skills. Initially participants can feel uncomfortable with the behaviors: for example, making eye contact with everyone else in the group. Although this sounds simple it can be hugely difficult for people to make eye contact with each other without feeling embarrassed and awkward. Practicing making eye contact with each other helps people to feel more comfortable and enabled them to do so after the course.

Noticing the language that people use and matching use of words helps build rapport with people. Participants practice picking out the different representation system words and also using words from the same representation system to communicate that they have heard and understood what the person is saying. For example if someone uses language that is very visual, participants will reflect back visual words such as see, picture, imagine, vision.

Julian describes assertive behavior as follows:

> Assertiveness is about rapport, it is like the oil in a combustion engine that helps things to run smoothly between people. It helps people build a better quality of relationship with each other.
> (Julian Mount, assertive inquiry dialogue with author, January 2005)

Participants pay attention to the non-verbal aspects of what is being communicated: the gestures, voice tone, and where the person is looking during what they are saying. All the time people are learning how to connect more deeply and openly with others through communicating more clearly and assertively in both their listening and their talking. They are connecting with themselves more strongly, being more aware of how they themselves are communicating, and ensuring that there is a congruity between what they are saying and how they are saying it.

CASE ANALYSIS: THE POWER OF LANGUAGE

Assertiveness training courses using NLP offer participants an opportunity to develop greater inner self-confidence and to practice the skills of assertive communication. People become aware of the power of language, and how small changes in language can make a huge difference to how a message is received by others. The value of being on a course that focuses on assertive communication is that people can reflect on their own behavior and ask for feedback from others in a safe environment. They are able to practice different communication skills with each other, and experiment with different ways of behaving. People become more self-aware and also more aware of others, and can really hear, see, and feel the difference when someone communicates, taking full responsibility for what they are saying.

Julian refers to there being a high level of respect and honesty in assertive relationships: people are able to be themselves with each other and feel respected for who they are. The quality of the assertive relationship differentiates it from other non-assertive relationships, and is a characteristic of relationships that are based on the I'm OK: You're OK life position, in which people take full responsibility for who they are, and the choices that they make—including choices about how they communicate with others.

6 Managing Conflict

Introduction

Assertiveness is about connection between people. Conflict can provide people with an opportunity to develop assertive relationships and to connect with each other more honestly. A fundamental attitude of self-respect and respect of others underpins managing conflict assertively. The conflict may not necessarily be resolved; however, people who have managed conflict assertively are able to develop "bigger" relationships in which there is a deeper and greater understanding of each other.

In this chapter the transformative approach to conflict is explained in relation to developing I'm OK: You're OK assertive relationships. The assertive communication skills that facilitate the development of a transformative approach to managing conflict and developing assertive relationships are described, and a summary of the different approaches to understanding conflict and managing conflict is given. The first case study illustrates how through understanding conflict people can change their perspective and behavior, and deal differently with conflict. The second case study shows how an understanding of and working with conflict can help board team members lead their organizations more effectively.

The transformative approach to conflict

The transformative approach to conflict, developed by Robert A Baruch Bush and Joseph P Folger (2005), is a relational approach that acknowledges people, their goals, and needs. The approach is one in which people are encouraged to become more aware of the choices that they are making in their perceptions and interpretations, and to recognize that the other people in the conflict situation are making their own choices too. With this awareness people are enabled to listen and to talk with each other about their differences, and arrive at an understanding, although not necessarily a resolution.

> When people can talk through difficult issues—making clear choices with greater understanding of those with whom they differ or disagree—they learn how to live in a world where difference is inevitable. They move outside themselves in attempting to understand and connect with others whilst remaining true to their own decisions and choices.
>
> (Bush and Folger, 2005: 35)

The experience of conflict

Conflict is an inevitable dynamic in human relationships; people move between reconciliation and conflict all the time. For many people the experience of conflict is alienating and disempowering. They feel themselves to be "not OK," and experience a downward spiral into negative thinking and feeling. They feel physically, intellectually, emotionally, and spiritually disconnected from themselves, and from others. Physically people become ill, suffering from a range of stress-related illnesses. Intellectually people become less creative and imaginative, thinking only about the conflict situation. Emotionally people feel anxious, fearful, and angry; they feel a loss of self-esteem and self-confidence. Spiritually they feel disconnected from themselves and others, often lacking in purpose and meaning.

People involved in conflict experience a break in their interpersonal connection, and often feel alienated from each other and self-focused. They may avoid or attack each other in a number of different ways. For example, they may withdraw from each other and withhold information, exclude each other, and choose not to include themselves in an activity. They may attack each other, for example by interrupting, not listening, or finding unnecessary fault with each other. This is detrimental not only to the working relationship, but also to those with whom they work, as energy is used in fueling the conflict rather than in furthering the performance of the individuals or of the team.

The conflict also fuels further conflict as the people involved interpret each other's actions negatively in relation to the conflict. As a consequence people experience a loss in self-confidence, especially in relation to their ability to manage difficult working relationships and difficult interpersonal situations. This leads to feelings of worthlessness, negative self-talk, and non-assertive behavior. The key principles of assertiveness—respect and trust—can be lost when people are in conflict, in particular respect of oneself and for the other. Trust is broken between the people concerned, and this is often accompanied by a loss of trust in the organization. People who feel alienated and powerless to manage conflict perceive themselves as ineffective, unable to effect any change, and are often suspicious of those who are.

In some conflict situations it may be that only one of the people is experiencing the conflict, with the other unaware that there is a conflict at all. Conflict situations like this can arise when people are in conflict with their line manager, often over a perceived injustice. The employee fears raising the conflict with the line manager, believing that by doing so she or he will make matters worse. The relationship connection with the line manager is already weakened, and the employee fears further alienation.

The transformative approach to managing conflict

The transformative approach encourages people to make a dynamic shift from negative to positive thinking and feeling, about self and others; and to do so through empowerment and recognition. When people make an "empowerment shift" they move from feeling weak to feeling strong in themselves and the relationship, when they make a "recognition shift" they move from being self-absorbed to having a greater understanding of the other person and being more open in the relationship. Figure 6.1 shows the dynamic shifts of empowerment and recognition that transform negative beliefs about self and others into positive beliefs about self and others.

The shift from non-assertive to assertive

When people are in the I'm OK: You're OK life position, their experience of conflict is one of self-confidence and positive self-esteem at the same time as engaging fully with the other person. They show self-respect and respect for others. They enjoy positive emotion, thinking, and

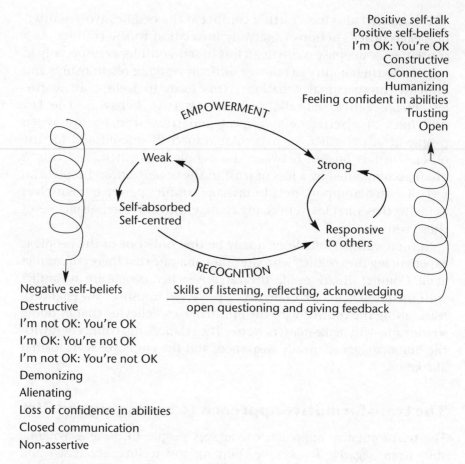

Positive self-talk
Positive self-beliefs
I'm OK: You're OK
Constructive
Connection
Humanizing
Feeling confident in abilities
Trusting
Open

EMPOWERMENT

Weak

Strong

Self-absorbed
Self-centred

Responsive
to others

RECOGNITION

Negative self-beliefs   Skills of listening, reflecting, acknowledging
Destructive   open questioning and giving feedback
I'm OK: You're OK
I'm OK: You're not OK
I'm not OK: You're not OK
Demonizing
Alienating
Loss of confidence in abilities
Closed communication
Non-assertive

Figure 6.1 The transformative approach to managing conflict

Source: Adapted from Bush and Folger (2005: 55), 'Changing conflict interaction'.

imagining. Table 6.1 shows how people manage conflict from the four different life positions.

The shifts from non-assertive to assertive management of conflict are similar to those described in the transformative approach. The transformation takes place at the relationship level, and in doing so is enabling of the people in the conflict situation to change their way of managing conflict.

The shift is from the negative conflict spiral to a positive spiral that is empowering, enabling, and connecting, through the relationship skills

4. I'm OK: You're not OK Aggressive/defensive/competitive I win: You lose	**1. I'm OK: You're OK** Assertive/creative/collaborative I win: You win
Assert needs and goals with no concern for relationship.	Relational, transformational. Focus on needs, goals, and relationship. See each other as equal problem solvers. Conflict seen as opportunity for creativity and different choices.
3. I'm not OK: You're not OK Manipulative/divisive I lose: You lose	**2. I'm not OK: You're OK** Passive/submissive/withdraw I lose: You win
Each forgoes own needs and goals. Lack of asserting goals so ultimately relationship suffers through lack of openness, trust, and honesty.	Avoid conflict, comply with others' needs and goals. "Anything for a quiet life." Go along with others but do not commit.

Table 6.1 How people manage conflict from the four different life positions

of listening, reflecting, acknowledging, open questioning, and giving feedback. Without the shift at the relationship level, the conflict issues can be dealt with but the people involved are likely to fear similar situations arising in the future, and as a result avoid the possibility of future conflict.

Different styles of managing conflict, influencing, and negotiating

Table 6.2 compares and contrasts the different styles of managing conflict that have been described by a number of different authors writing about conflict, influencing, and negotiating. The transformative and I'm OK: You're OK approaches are aligned with the win: win, collaborating, and principled negotiating styles, all of which focus on the relationship as well as the goals, needs, and wants of the people involved.

Table 6.2 The different styles of managing conflict compared and contrasted

Benfari	Thomas and Kilmann	Bush and Folger	Fisher and Ury	Assertive/non-assertive
Win/lose style. Personal goals asserted. Focus is on winning. Belief is that there has to be a winner and a loser.	*Competing style.* Personal needs are the focus; no concern for others' needs.		"Hard" positional bargaining/ negotiating position and power matter.	I win: You lose. I'm OK: You're not OK. Aggressive/ defensive.
Lose/yield style. Belief that conflict is detrimental to relationship.	*Accommodating style.* Meeting needs of others' at expense of own needs.		"Soft" positional bargaining/ negotiating position, focus on relationship.	I lose: You win. Passive/ submissive/ withdrawn.
Lose/leave style. Belief that conflict is a waste of time.	*Avoiding style.* Neither personal needs are stated nor is there interest in others' needs.			I lose: You lose. Manipulative/ divisive.
Win/win style. Belief that conflict can be managed and solution found. Style and skills can be learnt.	*Collaborating style.* Desire to meet own needs and all needs of others.	*Transformative approach.* Empowerment and recognition are key. Relational and engaging. Skills can be learnt of listening, reflecting, open questioning.	*Principled negotiating,* "negotiating on merits." Relationship and issue matter. Perceptions are made explicit. Skills of negotiating can be learnt. People are seen as separate from the problem.	I win: You win. Assertive/ creative, collaborative. Develops "bigger" relationships. Belief that conflict is an opportunity for engaging, learning, and making different choices.

Table 6.2 continued

Benfari	Thomas and Kilmann	Bush and Folger	Fisher and Ury	Assertive/ non-assertive
			The focus is on interests, and not on positions. A range of options for mutual gain are generated prior to any decision making. Objective criteria are agreed upon by which a decision is made.	Develops self-esteem and confidence in ability to manage conflict. Skills can be learnt.
Compromise style. Belief that conflict is about giving a bit and losing a bit.	*Compromising style.* Desire to partially meet everyone's needs a bit; outcome will be partially satisfying to everyone.		*Soft and hard "positional" bargaining,* relationship matters more but only so much.	*Compromise* between I win: You lose and I lose: You win. Relationship is compromised.
Contextual style. Use of all of the above five styles depending on situations. Can be confusing for people.				*Movement between all four life positions,* attitudes and beliefs. Not consistent and not helpful in developing culture of trust, openness, and honesty.

Assertive communication skills used in managing conflict

The communication skills that are used by people to make the "dynamic shift" from non-assertive to assertive, and to develop assertive relationships, include:

■ listening
■ reflecting
■ acknowledging
■ open questioning
■ giving feedback.

Table 6.3 illustrates the dynamic shift from managing conflict non-assertively to managing conflict assertively that takes place through using assertive communication skills.

Table 6.3 The dynamic shift that takes place through using assertive communication skills

From:	To:
Alienation	Connection
Lack of recognition towards others	Recognition of others
Distrust	Trust
Blame of others	Self-responsibility
Self-doubt	Self-confidence
Negative self-limiting beliefs	Positive self-affirming beliefs
Insecurity	Security
De-powering of self	Empowering of self
Weakness	Strength
Closed communication	Open communication
Feeling stuck	Feeling open to possibilities

Case study 1: From weakness to strength

Frances Middleton is an executive coach. Her approach to working with conflict is that it is an inevitable part of everyday life, and as such is very akin to the existential approach in which conflict is understood as one of life's "givens." Frances facilitates clients in their understanding of conflict: in particular, their awareness of choices with regard to their interpretation of the conflict

situations and their behavior in them. People are encouraged to take responsi-
bility for their part in the conflict and to explore their options for how they
might deal with it differently. She gives the example of a client, Jane, who
through her understanding of the conflict that she was experiencing with her
line manager was empowered to manage the conflict very differently.

At the time Jane sought coaching from Frances she was feeling weakened
by the conflict she was experiencing with her line manager. She explained
to Frances that whenever she met her line manager to discuss ideas and
issues he always challenged and questioned her. She experienced him as
opposing her through his questioning and challenging, and felt overwhelmed by him and his opinions. Within minutes of talking with him
about an exciting idea about the future of the department, she would feel
frightened and want to run out of the door. The experience was impacting
on her self-esteem. She felt vulnerable not only in relationship to her line
manager but also that her job was threatened. She feared that if she made a
mistake when she responded to his challenges, he would fire her. On one
occasion she described feeling frightened but that she had decided to
"fight" as a way of managing her desire for "flight" from the conflict situation. When he raised his voice she had shouted back at him, and they had
had a head on shouting match. Initially Jane had felt her approach had
been successful in piercing his overpowering image; however it had also left
her feeling weakened, having compromised her own values.

Jane was enabled through the coaching to talk about her feelings of
vulnerability, in particular how small and vulnerable she felt whenever
she talked about her ideas with her line manager. At other times,
however, she described the relationship with him as being positive. She
was curious why she felt so threatened when it came to putting her ideas
forward, and realized that she went in with a strong emotional attachment to her ideas. This strong emotional attachment meant that she
immediately felt personally criticized by any questioning or challenging
of her ideas, and that her choices were either to "flee" or to "fight."

She became aware that she perceived any questioning or challenging
of her opinions as being a direct criticism of herself as a person, in which
she felt belittled. She recognized this as a pattern from her childhood.
Her parents had both been people who enjoyed debating and arguing
their ideas with each other, seemingly competing with each other. Jane
had found it difficult to put forward her ideas, and often felt put down
and criticized when she did offer an idea. She had felt squeezed out of
arguments, weakened, and insecure in herself.

Frances encouraged her to describe situations in which she had
experienced presenting an idea and putting a point of view across in which

she had felt confident and empowered, and to explore what was different between these situations and those in which she had lost confidence and felt weakened. Through this exploration she realized that she felt overwhelmed and challenged when she perceived her line manager as questioning her value system, and specifically her sense of fairness and equality. This realization encouraged her to present ideas from a business rather than personal perspective—focusing on business impact and outcome.

Through this shift in perspective Jane was enabled to engage with her line manager in a discussion about ideas keeping the focus on the business context, and through seeing herself and her line manager as being engaged in a discussion together about what would be best for business success. She reported back to Frances that she had been able to enjoy a conversation with her line manager in which she had put her ideas forward. They had listened to and asked questions of each other, and given feedback to each other. She felt confident in herself, and that rather than working against her line manager she was working with him. The working relationship was transformed into a more authentic relationship in which there was greater engagement, awareness of each other, and mutual respect, although not necessarily agreement.

CASE ANALYSIS: FROM WEAKNESS TO STRENGTH

Through the coaching Jane was enabled to make a shift from weakness to strength, from disconnection from herself and her line manager, to connection with her own values and beliefs, and connection with her line manager. She became aware of the possibility of partnership with her line manager and of having an I'm OK: You're OK relationship with him. The case study highlights how through an understanding of the experience of conflict Jane was able to make a shift in her perspective which empowered her to stay in the I'm OK: You're OK life position. Previously she had quickly moved into the I'm not OK: You're OK position, perceiving her line manager to be in the I'm OK: You're not OK position, and thus creating what often happens in conflict situations: a symbiotic relationship between these two life positions. On the occasion when she had decided to choose the "fight" rather than "flight" option, she felt she had compromised her own values and beliefs. She was able to be strong in her values and to offer her ideas within the business context. She maintained an I'm OK: You're OK position in which she felt confident and from where she experienced herself as being in partnership with her line manager, engaged in an exploration of what would be best for business success.

Case study 2: The spirit of inquiry

Ian Lock is a leadership development consultant, and his experience of working with boards of directors is that they often work in an environment of unhealthy conflict. The way in which they manage this conflict is, in turn, reflected in the way the organization works.

Ian's first question to a board is, "What is it like to work here?" or "What is the current reality?" People initially respond very positively to each other. However as this conversation continues the team dynamic starts to play out—with people displaying non-assertive behaviors such as aggressive and passive behaviors. Ian encourages people to notice what is going on in the conversation, who is engaged and who is disengaged, and how they are feeling right now. This enables board members to draw parallels between how they are communicating with each other in the conversation, and how this plays out in their meetings in the working environment.

Ian's next question is designed to help people understand what is blocking them from working together as a leadership team. He asks, "What gets in the way?" or "What is getting in the way right now?" He invites board members to notice how they are feeling as opposed to what they are thinking. This allows people to connect with themselves and each other.

Ian's next question helps people deepen their inquiry into the context of their personal leadership: "What is really important to you, what are your values and beliefs?" This helps people to be truly congruent in their leadership behaviors, and allows them to transform their approach to conflict through being their authentic selves. Sharing their values with each other creates a willingness to understand and work with difference. Ian believes that this helps people build "bigger" relationships with each other, in which there is a deeper recognition of each other as people and as leaders. Through listening and understanding, board members create a safe environment in which they feel secure enough to disclose their fears, uncertainties, and doubts that get in the way of them being their "best selves."

Ian then asks, "What are your personal blockers—fear, uncertainties, and doubts?" Board members have an opportunity to be listened to nonjudgmentally as they share where they feel vulnerable, and what it is about themselves that they are protecting or hiding from others. Through these conversations people feel acknowledged for who they are: in particular for what is often the small child within them who fears, for example, not being liked, being judged by others, not being good enough. This experience of being seen and heard helps people to see beyond their differences, to connect, really trust and respect each other.

With this deeper and broader understanding of each other the board are ready to address the question, "What is your purpose as a leadership team?" Their confidence in themselves and each other is stronger. They recognize conflict as a natural occurrence, and are able to engage with each other from a very different and more empowering perspective. The possibilities have just got much bigger.

CASE ANALYSIS: FROM NON-ASSERTIVE TO ASSERTIVE CONFLICT MANAGEMENT

Conflict is more effectively managed within "bigger," assertive relationships that are based on mutual respect and trust. Ian uses the spirit of inquiry to help people explore what is fuelling their interpersonal conflicts, and to make the shift from an unhealthy to a healthy experience of conflict. His approach is similar to that of the transformative approach in that people are both empowered and recognized through personal reflection, and through engaging with each other. The questions Ian asks facilitate people in developing greater self-awareness and awareness of each other. People are helped to make the shift from a non-assertive life position and aggressive, passive, and manipulative behaviors to the I'm OK: You're OK assertive life position. In making this shift people understand conflict as something to be managed within the context of creating relationships and organizations in which differences are acknowledged and respected. Through engaging with each other in a spirit of inquiry people draw on the communication skills of listening, reflecting, acknowledging, open questioning, and giving feedback to each other, leading to personal and organizational transformation.

7 Dealing with Bullying

Introduction

The business case for developing assertiveness and an assertive business culture is huge, and the cost for not doing so great. A business culture that is non-assertive is one in which non-assertive behaviors are manifest, and at worst one in which bullying is the norm rather than the exception. Developing assertiveness is key to addressing bullying behavior in organizations. Translating organizational values of integrity, honesty, openness, and trust into assertive behaviors is critical in the development of a truly assertive business culture that seeks to understand and work with difference in order to ensure outstanding business performance.

Bullying is a major cause of absenteeism and stress-related illness in the workplace. It is costly for individuals in terms of their physical, intellectual, emotional, and spiritual well-being, and can cause long-term damage; for organizations it is costly financially and is damaging to their reputation, especially in high-profile court cases. The need to develop individual assertiveness and to deal with bullying as and when it happens is critical in developing assertive business cultures that are inclusive and diverse.

This chapter builds on the previous chapters and explores the attitudes that underlie bullying behavior and its impact on people. The benefits of developing an assertive business culture in which everyone is responsible for behaving assertively, and in particular of developing assertive leadership, are described. The skills of assertiveness used to deal with bullying are highlighted, and build on the assertive communication skills outlined in the previous four chapters. The two case studies illustrate the damaging impact of bullying behavior on people, and how through an understanding of what bullying behavior is, both the bully and the bullied can be helped to develop assertiveness.

Understanding bullying behavior

Bullying behavior is the opposite of assertive behavior; it is always negative and destructive. Underlying bullying behavior there is a lack of self-confidence, low self-esteem, and low self-respect as well as low respect and mistrust of others. The life position is "not OK." The bullying is a mix of two non-assertive behavior patterns—aggressive/defensive and passive/submissive; I'm OK: You're not OK and I'm not OK: You're OK respectively, and in its extreme form is manipulative and divisive, I'm not OK: You're not OK. The bullying behaviors are usually evidence of the people having been bullied themselves, and having learnt the behaviors from others, often in childhood.

Bullying behavior can be motivated by envy and jealousy of the bullied person, who is perceived as being "better than" in any number of ways, for example, "more clever," "more popular," "more attractive." People are sometimes unaware of the impact that their behavior has on other people, and can be surprised that their behavior is perceived as bullying. This is well illustrated in the first of the two case studies. At other times people are aware of their bullying behavior but unaware of the underlying negative self-beliefs and beliefs about others that give rise to the behavior.

People can learn to behave assertively, and to appreciate that there are different ways of communicating with people that are more positive, creative, and effective. This in turn can lead to new, positive beliefs about self and others, as well as to more assertive relationships in which people give and receive positive feedback that is affirming of their self-esteem, self-confidence, and competence.

The impact of bullying on people

The impact of ongoing bullying can be long-lasting and devastating for the bullied person. Many people are frightened to speak out about bullying, fearing that they will not be heard or that the bullying will get worse. This is despite most organizations having clear anti-bullying policies, procedures, and channels of communication including Corporate Ombuds and employee assistance programs (see Chapters 19 and 20). Some of the impacts of bullying behavior on people include:

- high levels of anxiety, including panic attacks
- feeling out of control
- fear—that they will not be believed, or are being overly sensitive
- erosion of self-confidence and self-esteem
- feeling insecure and anxious
- feeling shame at being bullied
- feeling isolated and alienated
- self-blame
- sleeplessness
- loss of appetite
- over-eating
- over-drinking, smoking, drug taking
- withdrawing from others (at home and work)
- lashing out at others (at home and work).

People who are bullied can experience a number of symptoms commonly associated with panic attacks. These include:

- palpitations
- sweating
- trembling and shaking
- shortness of breath
- feeling of choking
- chest pains
- nausea
- feeling dizzy or light-headed
- numbness and tingling sensations.

An assertive business culture versus a bullying culture

Developing an assertive business culture in which bullying is unacceptable is the responsibility of everyone in an organization; people need to be given the opportunity to reflect on their own behavior and to be able to reflect on the values that underlie their behavior. Developing and maintaining assertiveness involves supporting and challenging each other to behave in a way that is inclusive and respectful of difference. This can take the form of regular team meetings in which time is taken to check in with how people feel they are working together as well as focusing on the task. Whilst policies and procedures for dealing with bullying are necessary, the real development of assertive relationships is how people are with each other in the day-to-day.

Table 7.1 contrasts the behaviors of the two different business cultures.

Table 7.1 The differences between assertive and bullying business cultures

In an assertive business culture people:	In a bullying business culture people:
Take responsibility for their behavior, they self-manage	Blame others
Appreciate each other's qualities and competencies	Criticize others and focus on mistakes
Recognize that they have a choice about their behavior	Do not take responsibility for their behavior
Respect difference, and treat people with respect	Disrespect others who are different, and disregard them
Give, receive, and ask for feedback that is open and honest	Do not give feedback, unless it is criticism and do not ask for feedback
Are inclusive of others, seeking to involve people when appropriate	Are excluding of others, often leaving people out "on purpose" or without thinking
Are aware of and look after their own and others' well-being	Are not concerned with well-being
Talk directly to people when there are issues to be resolved	Go behind people's backs rather than talking directly to people when there are issues
Are consistent in their assertive behavior in relationships—with colleagues, peers, line managers, customers, suppliers	Are inconsistent and unpredictable in their behavior, appearing sometimes to be assertive and other times to be non-assertive
Are open	Are fearful and closed

Assertive leadership versus bullying leadership

Leaders within organizations have a particular role to play by way of modeling assertive behavior that is inclusive and respectful of diversity. This means living the values of the organization through their own behavior towards others, and creating a business culture that is assertive, inclusive, and respecting of difference. Whilst everyone is responsible for their own behavior, and for "living the values," business leaders and those who manage others have a particular responsibility for engaging with people in an assertive, I'm OK: You're OK way.

For those leaders whose behavior is typically aggressive/defensive, learning that there are alternative ways of "getting people to do things" and "of getting results" can be hugely challenging, especially as they have been rewarded for "what they do" rather than "how they do it." Equally it can be challenging to give feedback to leaders whose behavior is aggressive/defensive, as they are likely to reject the feedback. Leaders whose behavior is bullying can be helped through coaching and feedback to reflect on their behavior and the values and beliefs that give rise to the behavior; through becoming more self-aware people are given opportunities to change their behavior, and to understand the impact of assertive behavior on creating a working environment which is positive, inclusive, and diverse.

Communication skills that are helpful in dealing with bullying

Protective techniques are assertive communication skills that can be used in addition to the skills already described in the earlier chapters of Part II. Protective techniques include:

■ broken record
■ negative assertion
■ negative inquiry
■ selective ignoring
■ disarming anger in others.

Broken record

This technique is, as it suggests, about repetition, and involves making the same assertive statement over and over until people on the receiving end have heard and acknowledged that they have heard what has been said. Tone of voice and body language are important in how the message is delivered and repeated.

Negative assertion

Negative assertion is a technique that acknowledges valid criticism as well as communicating self-awareness and taking responsibility for feelings and thoughts. For example:

> I do find it difficult to work under pressure and can be very irritable when I am feeling stressed.

Negative inquiry

Negative inquiry is a powerful protective technique that involves the bullied person asking questions of the bully in order to gather more information about alleged criticisms of behavior. The bullied person's intention is to hear all the criticisms until there are no more left unsaid, without responding, other than asking, "Is there anything else?" from an assertive life position. This is a particularly useful protective technique when someone is being bullied and open communication has failed.

Negative assertion and negative inquiry

The two techniques can be powerfully used together in facilitating open and honest communication between people. It is a combination of self-disclosure and questioning as to whether there is a negative impact on the other person. For example:

> I do find it difficult to work under pressure and can be very irritable when I am feeling stressed. Do you think that I have been irritable with you recently?

Selective ignoring

This technique is about choice, and choosing what to respond to and what not to respond to when someone is behaving in a way that is unacceptable.

Disarming anger in others

This is a useful protective technique to use when one person is very angry and the other is frightened of the person's anger. It involves the person on the receiving end of the anger finding a way of drawing the other's attention into the present and then acknowledging the anger. The steps are:

- Draw angry person's attention into the present, by saying her or his name.
- Make and maintain eye contact.
- Acknowledge the person's anger: "I know you are angry."
- Acknowledge that the desire is there to hear what the person is saying and that the shouting is getting in the way of her or him being heard. "Please stop shouting so that I can hear what you are saying. If you do not stop shouting then I will walk away from this conversation." If the person does stop shouting this may lead on to the next step. If the person does not stop shouting then it is important to walk away from the conversation as indicated.
- Acknowledge the fear: "When you are angry like this I feel frightened."

Case study 1: Alleged bullying

Karen Davison is an organizational consultant and counselor who specializes in the areas of trauma, workplace bullying, assertiveness and de-escalation of aggression, and behavioral risk management. In this first case study she describes working with someone who was allegedly bullying, and in the second working with someone who had been bullied over a period of months.

David worked in the engineering department of a large organization. He was referred to Karen following two complaints from staff members and an employee who left the department because of his unacceptable bullying behavior. In the first session David seemed very perplexed about why his behavior was unacceptable. He was genuinely surprised by the complaints about his behavior. He felt hurt by the criticism and misunderstood. He and Karen explored the situations that had led to the criticism and complaints from staff.

In doing so David was able to better understand his own behavior in relation to his upbringing. The way in which he behaved towards others was the way he always behaved. He came from a male-dominated family and social background, in which making fun of each other, telling others what to do and defending one's own territory was the way people got on with each other. The technical department in which he worked was similarly male-dominated and David related to people in the same way that he had always done. When under pressure or feeling threat-ened, he defended himself by putting other people down and using humor. David recognized that he had learnt these behaviors as he grew up from his father and brothers. His strategy had been to do the same back to them.

In the second session Karen helped David explore the particular behaviors for which he had been criticized, and which caused people to feel bullied. David had already mentioned that he used humor when he felt pressured, and his use of humor had been cited as inappropriate behavior. David talked about his use of humor, and with Karen's help began to appreciate the impact of his humor on others. He realized that he had as a child frequently felt hurt, and consequently made an early decision to protect himself by using humor to hurt others first. He was previously unaware of having made this decision and the motivation for making the decision.

David had also been criticized for his use of sarcasm towards other members of the department. Again he was genuinely taken aback by the criticism and that he was perceived as aggressive and undermining of them. Examples of sarcasm had been given, and while David remem-bered the occasions, he was truly perplexed as to why people felt belittled by his comments. Karen helped him to explore the kinds of things that he said and how he said them to his colleagues and when. Through this process he realized that he used generalized statements that were pinpointed on one person in front of everyone else in the department. He used a particular sneering tone of voice when making these statements. Again he was totally unaware of how the tone of his voice or his body language could impact on other people.

In the third and fourth sessions David explored new and different ways of behaving, in particular of motivating others through effective communication. Karen asked him to practice his new skills and to keep a journal inbetween sessions, recording his use of different communica-tion behaviors. She also gave him reading material to support the sessions. In these two sessions David practiced developing the assertive communication skills of:

- asking open questions to gather more information before responding
- asking for more time to think about his response to request
- saying "no" to people in a way that was clear and that acknowledged the other's right to make the request
- giving positive feedback to others, in particular appreciation for a job well done

- giving criticism to others that would help them to further develop and improve in their performance.

In the fifth and final session David reviewed his progress, and reported feeling very different from how he had felt at the start of the counseling process. Some months later he was promoted into a more senior managerial role.

CASE ANALYSIS: SELF-AWARENESS THROUGH REFLECTION

Workplace counseling provided David with the opportunity to develop greater self-awareness and awareness of others. Until the counseling he had not considered his behaviors, nor had he realized that he could behave differently when he was feeling pressured, overwhelmed, or anxious. He realized that his learnt behavior was inappropriate in the work environment and that he had a choice as to how he behaved.

Aggressive and defensive behavior in the form of inappropriate humor and sarcasm is very typical of people who are feeling unsure and insecure. Underneath aggressive behavior is often a person who feels insecure and lacking in confidence and competence, "not OK," and the only way in which she or he can then feel more secure is by belittling or humiliating others. David learnt that there were other ways of behaving that were more appropriate and assertive.

Case study 2: Being bullied

Susan was referred for counseling, having been bullied over a period of time by her manager. This first session, which was face-to-face, gave Susan an opportunity to talk about why she was seeking help, and included a detailed assessment of the impact of her experiences on her mental and physical health. She was feeling extremely anxious, full of dread at going into work, not sleeping at night and feeling very tired during the day, being physically sick and bursting into tears.

Susan was an attractive and popular young woman in her thirties. She was successful in her work and had had good feedback on her performance. However her line manager appeared to take pleasure in undermining Susan's standing within the department. She demanded more and more of her, setting impossible targets and unreasonable workloads. The pressure on Susan increased over a period of six months. The line manager favored two of Susan's colleagues. They were given less work, and both of them colluded with the line manager in alienating Susan.

During this time Susan felt increasingly inadequate, and blamed herself for what was happening to her. She thought that "if only" she could meet certain targets and do the things asked of her, the bullying would stop. She thought that if she "was nicer," things would get better. They did not. At the end of this six-month period her manager went on prolonged sick leave. Susan expected that she would feel better now that the main bully was away from the workplace, but lived in fear of her return. The sight however of the manager's two friends immediately triggered anxiety and panic in Susan. She turned to the senior manager for help, who referred her for counseling.

The subsequent eight sessions were by telephone, and this proved to work extremely well for Susan. Karen was able to offer a degree of flexibility according to Susan's needs while maintaining very clear boundaries with regard to timings of sessions. There were three main strands to the telephone counseling, all of which were supported by targeted reading material about:

- the physiology of the anxiety response and addressing the anxiety
- the psychology of bullying
- understanding and developing assertiveness.

The first telephone session focused on Susan's anxiety. Karen explained the physiology of the anxiety response, enabling Susan to understand why she responded as she did when she felt threatened. Karen taught Susan breathing and relaxation exercises, providing her with a tape that she was encouraged to use on a daily basis to lower her anxiety. These exercises became the basis for anxiety management strategies that Susan was later able to employ to control her anxiety in stressful situations.

During the second session Karen talked to Susan about the psychology of bullying. Karen explained that bullies typically target those who are popular and successful. Understanding this helped Susan to see that what she had experienced was not unique, and was something other people understood. In particular she was helped to recognize that she was not to blame for the bullying. She had, up until this point, decided that she was to blame and that it was her fault. She was helped to let go of this belief about herself and to see that it was the manager's behavior that was the problem—not she. No matter what she did by way of her own behavior she would not be able to appease the bully.

Sessions three and four focused on understanding and developing assertiveness skills that Susan could use to develop positive self-belief, self-confidence, and confidence in her abilities. A key confidence builder for Susan was her inner strength, and Karen reflected this back to her. She had continued to perform well and to work well despite the hugely stressful working environment and the constant bullying from the manager and the two colleagues. She was able to build on this and to learn assertiveness skills. This was an important starting point for Susan and a reconnecting with her strengths. She was asked by Karen to do homework between sessions by way of practicing assertive skills and challenging self-limiting beliefs.

The final session on the telephone was a summary of all that Susan had learnt and incorporated into her life. She reported feeling much more in control of her feelings rather than at the mercy of debilitating anxiety and panic attacks. She had learnt some helpful ways of relaxing and alleviating tension and anxiety, and continued to add to her list of positive self-affirmations. She was putting into practice the assertiveness skills that she had learnt, and was feeling much more positive about herself and about others.

CASE ANALYSIS: THE HEALING OF PSYCHOLOGICAL DAMAGE

The anxiety and physical symptoms that Susan experienced as a result of ongoing bullying from her line manager are very typical of people who are being bullied. Learning about the psychology of bullying greatly helped Susan to think differently about herself and not to see herself as a "victim" of bullying. A combination of self-affirmations, developing positive emotion, and using positive imagining in the form of visualization and relaxation tapes helped Susan to re-find her positive self-esteem. Through practicing assertive communication skills Susan further affirmed her ability to assert herself.

The message from this case study is very clear: assertive communication skills can be learnt and in so doing psychological damage can be healed.

Part III

Working with Personality Differences

8 Models for Working with Personality Differences

Introduction

The purpose of this chapter is to outline a number of models that are useful in furthering an understanding of assertiveness and personality differences. The chapters that follow in this part of the book show how using and working with these models and theories can help develop assertiveness and difference in organizations.

The four models that are outlined in this chapter related to assertiveness and personality differences are:

- Psychological type: Myers-Briggs Type Indicator (MBTI)*
- Interpersonal needs: Fundamental Interpersonal Relations Orientation –Behavior (FIRO-B)*
- Team roles: Belbin team roles
- The learning cycle and learning styles: Honey and Mumford

Each of the four models encourages people to become aware of their strengths and differences while acknowledging areas for development. As strength-based models they support people in becoming their "best selves," and help people to appreciate and work with their differences. In particular they help people to recognize that through working with difference they can become more effective as individuals, teams, and organizations.

---

* Myers-Briggs Type Indicator and MBTI, Fundamental Interpersonal Relations Orientation-Behavior (FIRO-B) are registered UK and US trade marks of Consulting Psychologist Press, Inc.

Psychological type: Myers-Briggs Type Indicator (MBTI)

The MBTI is one of the most widely used self-report psychometric instruments in organizations to help people understand themselves and appreciate their differences. Katherine Briggs and Isabel Myers-Briggs (Briggs-Myers with Myers, 1980) developed the theory to make Jung's theory of psychological type accessible to people in order that they could better understand each other, appreciate differences, and work together more effectively. The results from the questionnaire indicate people's preferences for how they are energized, acquire information, and make decisions about that information, and how they like to organize their lives. It is concerned with people's strength of preference rather than whether they have a skill in a particular area. As such it is very much a strength-based theory of personality, and is therefore very affirming of people. There are four dimensions of preference, and people have a preference for one or the other in each of the dimensions.

Extroversion–Introversion (E–I)

How people are energized, whether by the outer world of people, things, and activities, or drawing energy from their inner world of thoughts and ideas.

Sensing–iNtuition (S–N)

How people gather information, whether by taking in information through the five senses, preferring to focus on details, or through using a "sixth sense"—their iNtuition, and focusing on the bigger picture.

Thinking–Feeling (T–F)

How people make decisions, whether by structuring decisions through taking an objective, logical approach or through taking a more subjective approach based on personal values and impact on others.

Judging–Perceiving (J–P)

How people like to live their lives, whether being planned and liking to arrive at conclusions or preferring to go with the flow, adapting to situations as they go along.

Preference is rather like left and right-handedness: although they have a preference, people can use their less-preferred hand if it is necessary or they are required to do so. Indeed for some tasks they may use this writing hand quite comfortably. However if required to draw upon this lesser preference over a period of time people usually report feeling tired, awkward, and sometimes lacking in self-confidence.

Knowing one's preferences and having an awareness of the four dimensions of preference is for many people like a "homecoming" in which they know themselves for who they are, and can help in identifying when they are their "best selves," feeling self-confident and behaving assertively, and when they are "not themselves." Once people have knowledge of their preferences they are able to look to develop greater self-confidence and assertiveness in each of the four dimensions, and to become "more of themselves."

Type dynamics and self-confidence

The four functions are Sensing and Intuition, Thinking and Feeling. The results from the questionnaire indicate people's preference in each of the four dimensions. The middle two letters of people's MBTI type refer to the two functions that they prefer to use to gather information or make decisions. Type dynamics refers to the order in which people use these two functions and their "hidden" opposites. Thus people who prefer using their iNtuition and Thinking have as their "hidden" opposites Sensing and Feeling. When they are not being their "best selves" and are using one of these lesser preferred functions—perhaps when they are tired or stressed, and are not using it well—they can be described as being "beside themselves." Naomi Quenk writes about this experience in her book *Beside Ourselves* (1993) for each of the 16 MBTI types.

A knowledge of the model and the four functions, Sensing–iNtuition, Thinking–Feeling, is helpful to people—whether or not they have completed the questionnaire—when they are communicating with others who may gather information and make decisions differently from them. Figure 8.1 shows the relationship between all four functions, and is commonly referred to as either the zig-zag process or the "Z" diagram (Lawrence, 1993). Using the zig-zag process as a method of preparing material that appeals to and can be readily understood by all four functions is very effective. Knowing that in any gathering of people there will be a mix of the functions can help in the delivery, such as at a meeting or presentation. For example:

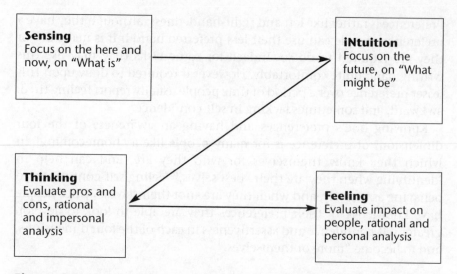

Figure 8.1 The "Z" diagram showing the relationships between the four functions

Source: adapted from Lawrence (1993).

- ■ Have I gathered all the necessary information? (Sensing).
- ■ How have I related it to the bigger picture? (iNtuition).
- ■ What principles and logic have I used to make the decision/s? (Thinking).
- ■ How does the decision I have made impact on people's values, beliefs, on what matters to them and those affected by the decision? (Feeling).

Interpersonal needs—Fundamental Interpersonal Relations Orientation-Behavior (FIRO-B)

Will Schutz (1966) identified three basic interpersonal needs that people express through behaviors towards others, and the desire for the behaviors associated with each of these three needs to be demonstrated towards them. The three interpersonal needs are Inclusion, Control, and Affection (also known as Openness). Table 8.1 shows the three interpersonal needs, the feeling need underlying each of the needs, the main preoccupation related to the behavior, and the key issue for people.

People differ in terms of the extent to which they satisfy each of the three interpersonal needs. Completion of the questionnaire gives people a score between 0 and 9, which indicates how much they express

Table 8.1 Interpersonal behaviors, feeling needs, preoccupations, and issues

Interpersonal behavior	Inclusion	Control	Affection
Underlying feeling need	Significance	Competence	Likeability
Preoccupation	Prominence, being noticed	Dominance	Emotional closeness
Issue	"In" or "out"	"Top" or "bottom"	"Close" or "far"

a behavior towards others, and the extent to which they want that behavior from others.

A low score, 0–3, means that people are selective about satisfying particular needs; a high score, 7–9, means that people seek to satisfy these needs in most situations, and a medium score (4–6) that in many situations they are likely to satisfy these needs but not all. There are no "right" or "wrong" profiles—some people have low scores in all three areas of interpersonal need, and others high scores. Those people with low scores are highly selective about how and where they seek to get their needs met. Those people with high scores in all three areas seek to get their needs met in most situations. Many people have a mix of higher and lower scores, and understanding the dynamic relationship between the three areas of interpersonal need is helpful in developing greater self-awareness and assertiveness. Table 8.2 shows the scoring of expressed and wanted behaviors in each of the three areas of interpersonal need.

For most people an understanding of their FIRO-B is affirming of who they are and helps them to understand interactions between people. Learning about the different behaviors associated with each of the interpersonal needs encourages people to think about their underlying feeling needs and how they can get these needs met assertively. Equally, an understanding of the model is helpful irrespective of whether people have completed the questionnaire and received individual feedback. The descriptions that follow give an overview of behaviors associated with each of the interpersonal needs.

Table 8.2 Inclusion, control, and affection, expressed and wanted scoring			
	Inclusion	**Control**	**Affection**
Expressed towards others	The extent to which people include themselves and others in activities 0–9	The extent to which people take control and give direction to others 0–9	The extent to which people seek closeness and intimacy with others 0–9
Wanted from others	The extent to which people want others to notice them and include them in activities 0–9	The extent to which people want others to lead them and to provide direction 0–9	The extent to which people want others to be close and intimate towards them 0–9

Source: adapted from Schnell (2000: 9).
Modified and reproduced by special permission of the Publisher, CPP, Inc., Mountain View, CA 94043 from *Participating in Teams: Using your FIRO-B® results to improve interpersonal effectiveness* by Eugene R. Schnell. Copyright 2000 by CPP, Inc. All rights reserved. Further reproduction is prohibited without the Publisher's written consent.

Inclusion and assertive behavior

The behaviors associated with inclusion include:

- participating in discussions
- involving others in discussions
- associating with and making contact with others
- seeking recognition
- seeking acceptance
- acknowledging others.

People's self-confidence is closely linked to being recognized, and being seen by others for who they are, whether or not they have a high need for inclusion. When people's need for "significance" is not met they can experience a loss of self-confidence which may over time lead to feelings of isolation and exclusion. Learning about the behaviors associated with inclusion can help people in getting their needs met more effectively and assertively. When expressed from an I'm OK: You're OK life position there is a congruency between what people are saying and how they are feeling.

Control and assertive behavior

The behaviors associated with control include:

- taking on positions of authority
- focusing on the task, driving for results
- influencing others' opinions
- establishing clear rules and procedures
- gauging others' competence
- seizing control of a situation
- being directive
- being decisive.

Many people's self-confidence is linked with feeling "competent," and this is the area in which they assert themselves. Again learning the kinds of behaviors that are associated with the interpersonal need for control can help people assert their needs in this area. All too often people express their need for control through non-assertive behavior that is aggressive. Learning how to express control from an assertive, I'm OK: You're OK life position makes a huge difference to their leadership.

Affection and assertive behavior

The behaviors associated with affection are:

- showing appreciation of others
- sharing personal opinions or feelings about issues
- being flexible and accommodating
- being warm and friendly
- building trust and openness in a group or team
- differentiating between people in a group or team
- forming close relationships with a few people
- coaching and developing others.

Everyone has a need to be liked and loved, to like and love others. Learning the behaviors associated with affection can help people to develop self-confidence in this area, and to develop more assertive relationships with people in which there is a deeper level of trust and openness.

FIRO-B and self-confidence

The underlying feeling needs for "significance," "competence," and "likeability" are closely linked to people's feelings of positive self-esteem and self-confidence. Table 8.3 shows how each of the underlying feeling needs is linked to people's feelings of positive self-esteem and self-confidence.

People are usually able to recognize which of the three areas of interpersonal need are linked to their feelings of self-confidence and positive self-esteem. One way of recognizing whether an area holds a lot of energy for people related to their self-esteem is to ask, "What happens when this need is not met?" For example, some people for whom inclusion is very important are very affected by not being invited to an event, and can experience a downward spiral in their self-confidence. For others for whom inclusion is not so important, not being invited to events is generally unlikely to impact on them. However not being invited to a particular event, perhaps by people who really matter to them, may be difficult, although that may not necessarily have a huge impact on their positive self-esteem.

FIRO-B and assertive relationships

A knowledge and experience of working with the FIRO-B model helps people to appreciate differences in relationships, and to understand and work with these differences in order to develop more assertive relationships. For example people with low scores on inclusion and high scores on expressed control are able to understand why their leadership is on occasions resisted by others within the team—they may have over-

Table 8.3 Underlying feeling needs linked to feelings
of positive self-esteem and self-confidence

Underlying feeling need	Significance	Competence	Likeability
Feelings of positive self-esteem and self-confidence related to:	Being noticed Being seen for "Who I am" Associating with people	Being respected and acknowledged for my abilities and skills	Being liked for who I am; being close and intimate with some people

looked the inclusion needs of team members and moved straight into getting their control needs met. Taking time to acknowledge people, albeit briefly, can make all the difference to how people's leadership is then received and responded to by others.

Belbin team roles

The theory of team roles and of people playing to their strengths within teams fits comfortably with people feeling confident in who they are and competent in what they can do to make a contribution to team work. Meredith Belbin (1993) identified nine team roles, each of which is complementary, and which relate to how people work in teams, rather than to their operational or technical contributions. Belbin refers to people as having real strengths which make up particular team roles, and explains that these strengths are facilitated by what he describes as "allowable weaknesses." When people are being their "best selves" they draw on the strengths of the role and make a positive contribution to team working. Equally when people are, for whatever reason, not drawing on their strengths they may lapse into the negative side of what is otherwise a strength. In this way Belbin sees "allowable weaknesses" as areas to be aware of, and to self-manage. Table 8.4 shows the nine team roles, their characteristics and strengths, and "allowable weaknesses."

The theory of team roles suggests that people in an effective team make complementary contributions, while teams that succeed less well may have people making competing contributions. Teams made up of people with a mix of strengths, abilities, and characteristics, who communicate positively and assertively with each other and with other teams, are likely to be successful. Less effective teams may also have people drawing upon weaker roles and therefore be under-performing. The theory further suggests that drawing on less-preferred roles may work in the short term, but in the longer term the team will suffer. A person is rarely strong in all team roles, and for most jobs a range of team roles is an asset. A certain flexibility and willingness to develop less-preferred roles is also necessary as and when a person's functional role changes. People can and do learn the behaviors associated with different team roles when a job requires them to do so.

Effective team working depends on members having an awareness of their strengths and then being able to transcend these and make contributions from other roles as and when necessary or appropriate.

Table 8.4 The nine team roles, characteristics and strengths, and "allowable weaknesses"

Team role	Characteristics and strengths	"Allowable weaknesses"
Plant	Creative, imaginative, unorthodox. Solves difficult problems.	Ignores details. Too preoccupied to communicate effectively.
Resource Investigator	Extrovert, enthusiastic, communicative. Explores opportunities. Develops contacts.	Over-optimistic. Loses interest once initial enthusiasm has passed.
Coordinator	Mature, confident, a good chairperson. Clarifies goals, promotes decision making, delegates well.	Can be seen as manipulative. Delegates personal work.
Shaper	Challenging, dynamic, thrives on pressure. Has the drive and courage to overcome obstacles.	Can provoke others. Hurts people's feelings.
Monitor evaluator	Sober, strategic and discerning. Sees all options. Judges accurately.	Lacks drive and ability to inspire others. Overly critical.
Teamworker	Co-operative, mild, perceptive, and diplomatic. Listens, builds, averts friction, calms the waters.	Indecisive in crunch situations. Can be easily influenced.
Implementer	Disciplined, reliable, conservative, and efficient. Turns ideas into practical actions.	Somewhat inflexible. Slow to respond to new possibilities.
Completer finisher	Painstaking, conscientious, anxious. Searches out errors and omissions. Delivers on time.	Inclined to worry unduly. Reluctant to delegate. Can be a nit-picker.
Specialist	Single-minded, self-starting, dedicated. Provides knowledge and skills in rare supply.	Contributes on only a narrow front. Dwells on technicalities. Overlooks the "big picture."

Source: Belbin (1993).

The learning cycle and learning styles

Peter Honey and Alan Mumford (Mumford, 1993) have developed a model of learning styles and of the learning cycle, encouraging people to think differently about learning and to think of everyday experience as an opportunity for learning. The model offers insights into how people learn, and how to provide learning opportunities for people in which they can fully engage, and through doing so feel confident and competent about themselves. For many people an understanding of their preferred learning styles and the learning cycle is transformational. The theory explains why people find it difficult to learn in some situations and easy in others, in line with their preferred learning style. Providing opportunities for people to learn effectively helps develop their self-confidence and positive self-belief. People can be helped to move round the learning cycle in order to get the most learning from their experiences—using their preferred way of learning and experimenting with their lesser preferred ways of learning. The four stages of the learning cycle are shown in Figure 8.2.

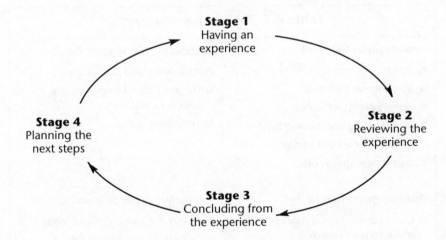

Figure 8.2 The learning cycle

Source: Honey and Mumford (2006).

The four learning styles associated with each of the four stages of the learning cycle are:

- Activists, Stage 1: Having an experience.
- Reflectors, Stage 2: Reviewing the experience.
- Theorists, Stage 3: Concluding from the experience.
- Pragmatists, Stage 4: Planning the next steps.

In the business environment the emphasis tends to be on "having the experience," on getting on with what has to be done, with insufficient time built in to review and reflect on the experience before doing it again. Building in opportunities for people to reflect on their experience and to ask questions encourages them to be more self-aware and to develop more assertive relationships in which difference is valued and appreciated. Some people, for example those with a preference for Introversion (MBTI), may need more time to think through an experience prior to discussing it with others. Allowing time and space for people to "gather their thoughts" can help the review process. Others, for example those with a preference for Extroversion (MBTI) need very little time for individual reflection,

---

Table 8.5 The four learning styles

Activists prefer to learn by:	Reflectors prefer to learn by:
- doing - thinking on their feet - having plenty of variety - participating and having fun - having an element of risk - trying new things out.	- observing and listening - thinking about things before making a decision - preparing well.
Theorists prefer to learn by:	Pragmatists prefer to learn by:
- using concepts and models that make sense to them - exploring and making links between facts and ideas - being intellectually stimulated - structuring and setting clear objectives.	- trying out strategies and ideas - applying ideas to real life situations - having credible role-models - having proven techniques - putting theory into practice.

preferring to review the experience through talking with others. As part of the review people are able to give each other feedback and to learn from each others'—often different—experiences of the same situation.

Once people have reviewed their experience individually and collectively, they can draw conclusions and make new decisions with regard to going forward. Together they can explore what they need to do differently, at the individual, team, and task level, in order to ensure business success. This encourages individual and shared responsibility for success, and an awareness of the choices that people are making about what they are doing and how they are working.

The final stage in the cycle is planning; deciding what to do next and how to do it. At this stage it is useful to take into account the different ways in which people gather, and make decisions, about information using the MBTI, and in particular the "Z" diagram, Figure 8.1.

9

Using the MBTI

Introduction

As a strength-based theory the Myers-Briggs Type Indicator (MBTI) lends itself to developing assertiveness, in particular self-confidence and positive self-belief. The MBTI highlights people's "gifts differing" and the importance of appreciating differences in how people are energized, gather information, make decisions and prefer to organize our lives. Indeed the theorists and practitioners Paul D. Tieger and Barbara Barron-Tieger (2000) suggest that according to their research psychological differences are more significant and pertinent than gender differences.

Certainly understanding and appreciating psychological differences is important in developing assertiveness and relationships in which people can be their "best selves." For many people learning about their MBTI type is a journey of self-discovery and an appreciation of difference. They are able to understand why they feel very similar to some people and very different from others. Through an understanding of psychological type people are helped to appreciate how they are different, and to understand and work with their differences for greater effectiveness.

The MBTI is used in many different ways in organizations. Frequently organizations use the MBTI and 360 review feedback as core elements of their personal and professional development programs. A key benefit of the MBTI is that it gives people a model with which to understand each other and a language for talking about their differences that enables them to be more open and honest with each other.

In this chapter the case studies offer different ways of using the MBTI to help develop people's positive self-esteem and self-confidence and an appreciation of differences. The first case study focuses on the use of the MBTI in developing the "leader within," and the second describes how coaching, using the MBTI, can help people to develop their own strengths and to appreciate difference.

Case study 1: The leader within

Maria Fay is an executive development consultant. She uses a range of instruments to help people develop greater self-awareness and interpersonal effectiveness including the MBTI, FIRO-B, and 360 review feedback. Maria works with senior people in organizations helping them to find their "leader within," to find what she describes as "their unique leadership voice."

As people develop more personal awareness and interpersonal effectiveness they are enabled to work with difference more. They are able to appreciate their own uniqueness and that of others. Maria defines leadership "as getting things done through the support of others." To do this, leaders need to be able to develop positive and assertive relationships with the people that they lead, and influence the people they may not necessarily line manage. The three key elements to assertiveness involve the leader paying attention to both the task and relationship, and are described by Maria Fay (in unpublished material, 2005) as:

- being clear about the desired outcome or goal in a situation and expressing this in a positive and assertive way, stating what is wanted rather than what is not wanted
- anticipating people's situation and how they might perceive it, and responding by "walking in the other person's shoes" without making assumptions about their perceptions or responses
- communicating in a direct, honest, and confident way that inspires trust and enhances the individual's professional reputation and credibility.

When Maria introduces the MBTI to people she usually issues a "health warning" explaining that "Type is our 'hardware,' our 'default setting.' Learned skills and behaviors are the 'software' that sit on top and give us versatility and range allowing us to flex and adapt to different situations and people" (Maria Fay, correspondence with author, 2006).

Leaders can be more effective and assertive when they have an awareness of the different ways in which people process information and make decisions, as well as an understanding of how people direct their energy and are energized, and organize themselves. When a relationship is difficult it can be useful for leaders to think about what they could have done differently, and how perhaps using their preferred natural strengths may not have served the situation well. For example a very enthusiastic, outgoing, and interactive person with a preference for Extroversion may not always appreciate the impact of his or her behavior on those with a preference for Introversion, who may feel unable to "get a word in edgeways."

People can in their enthusiasm for psychological type use it as a way of "typecasting" themselves and getting out of doing something that they are less comfortable with or find challenging. Maria emphasizes to leaders the importance of seeing that "Psychological Type helps to explain what we enjoy and why some things feel harder and require more effort from us but it doesn't excuse us from doing something—for example: I'm an iNtuitive, I don't do detail! (Sensing)" (Maria Fay, correspondence with author, 2006).

CASE ANALYSIS: TRUSTING SELF AND FEELING CONFIDENT

Learning how to use their own strengths and the skills associated with their different preferences helps leaders to be more assertive and effective in their leadership. They are helped to feel confident about their own way of leading and to trust themselves. At the same they are able to consider their relationships with others, and to use the MBTI as a tool for talking about differences and how best to lead people to be their "best selves."

Case study 2: Using the MBTI for personal development and professional fulfilment

Jenny Rogers is an experienced coach, trainer, and author. John, a senior manager in a large retail company, sought career coaching from Jenny. He was feeling unhappy in his current role and was finding it difficult to be motivated, which was impacting on his performance and he felt on his team's performance. He was obviously concerned not only for himself but also for his team, and expressed his deep regret at what he felt to be an inadequacy on his part.

He had received feedback from others that he was an excellent retailer and good at his job but—and it was the "but" that caused him to feel concerned—that he lacked the ability to think strategically, necessary for the top-level positions within the company.

In the first of three coaching sessions Jenny explored with John his MBTI profile—ENFP—on which he had had feedback at a team building session. From this session John knew that he was the only person in the senior management team with a preference for the Feeling function. The dominant team type preferences were Thinking and Judging (one other team member shared a preference for Perceiving but all other members shared a preference for Thinking). He had known that he was different from other team members and indeed felt that his strengths as a retailer were reflected in his MBTI profile. He was outgoing, warm and friendly towards people, enjoyed developing relationships with people and finding out what their needs were, and seeking to meet these needs. Meetings could be challenging for him as he felt he was constantly at risk of seeming "touchy feely." On occasions he felt that he was being made fun of when people looked to him to "save the staff."

His challenge as he saw it was to find a career in which his people skills and his desire to help people could be met, and to work in an environment in which these talents would be acknowledged and appreciated. In the second and third coaching sessions John explored further his strengths and how best he could use them in the service of others. He identified that serving others was hugely important to him, and that this was an underlying and informing value for him. He felt sad that he hadn't been able to be himself and to work with others who were different from him. Nevertheless he recognized that his strengths were such that he wanted to use them in a more rewarding and fulfilling work environment. He recognized that it would take courage to leave his highly paid position in the retail company, but that this was what he had to do in order to be true to his values and beliefs. Coaching led him to place much greater value on his spiritual gifts and interests. Within a year he had left his highly paid job and was retraining to be a Christian minister, a role in which he is now thriving.

CASE ANALYSIS: FEELING DIFFERENT AND BELONGING

Being different from others is for many people a huge challenge. People can feel that they do not belong; and that others do not really value or appreciate who they are. In this case study John felt that sometimes he was made fun of for being different. This can happen when people feel ambivalent towards the person who is different from them; they can feel challenged by the person and as a way of handling this challenge make fun of, or mock the person. At worst people can turn to bullying the person.

The MBTI is non-judgemental and encourages people to value their preferences to appreciate their and other people's strengths and to work with them. At best people realize their own strengths and the value of difference in making their lives a richer mix.

10 Using FIRO-B

Introduction

Developing assertive relationships and assertive communication is greatly facilitated by an understanding of the three basic interpersonal needs described in the theory and model of Fundamental Interpersonal Relations Orientation—Behavior (FIRO-B). FIRO-B offers people an insight into their own interpersonal needs and those of others, and helps people to better understand their differences and to work together more effectively. Applying FIRO-B to team working is especially helpful in understanding and working with team dynamics and stages of team development.

This chapter describes and explores using FIRO-B to understand the interpersonal needs of people related to the different developmental stages of teams. In the case study a business consultant describes how he uses FIRO-B in organizations to help people better understand their own and others' interpersonal needs in order to be more assertive as individuals and to develop more assertive relationships.

Interpersonal needs and stages of team development

Research into small groups and teams working together has shown that they go through predictable developmental stages. Tuckman (1965) identified five stages of team development—forming, storming, norming, performing, and adjourning, sometimes known as mourning. At each developmental stage people express their interpersonal needs through their behaviors towards each other. Working together assertively and effectively is greatly facilitated by an awareness of the interpersonal needs experienced at each of the developmental stages, and the questions that people are asking of themselves and about others. Table 10.1 shows the relationships between the developmental stages, interpersonal needs, and the questions being asked by team or group members.

Teams are more effective in their performance when they recognize the interpersonal needs of team members, and people are acknowledged. Understanding the interpersonal needs and behaviors associated with each of the stages of team development and learning to express the behaviors from an I'm OK: You're OK life position can

Table 10.1 Interpersonal needs experienced at the different stages of team development

Stage of team development	Interpersonal need	The question being asked of self	The question being asked of others
Forming	Inclusion	How much do I want to be "in" or "out"?	Who is "in" or "out"?
Storming and Norming	Control	How much power and influence do I want to express towards others? How much power and influence do I want from others?	Who is "top" or "bottom"?
Performing	Affection	How close do I want to be to others? How close do I want others to be to me?	How "close" or "far"?
Mourning	Affection –control –"exclusion"	How do I feel about ending?	

make all the difference to whether a team succeeds in achieving outstanding performance. Teams can and do get stuck in Inclusion and Control behaviors and can find it difficult to move through them into Affection. Usually the getting stuck is the result of people's interpersonal needs not being addressed. An awareness of the kinds of behaviors associated with each of the stages greatly facilitates the moving towards the Affection stage.

Inclusion

Inclusion is key to assertiveness and diversity. Inclusivity and diversity go hand in hand. When people first meet and work together as members of a group or team they are "checking each other out"; underlying their Inclusion behaviors there is an interpersonal need for "Significance." At this initial "Forming" stage of team development people want to be noticed and recognized. The interpersonal challenge is one of being recognized as an individual and differentiated from others while at the same time fitting in and being accepted by and accepting of others. Depending on people's individual interpersonal needs they will engage in more or less Inclusive behaviors.

Table 10.2 shows the kind of Inclusion behaviors which a team leader and team members can express towards each other from an assertive, I'm OK: You're OK life position in which there is self-respect and respect of others, in order to facilitate people being their "best selves" and to meet their Inclusion needs.

Control

Once people have addressed the Inclusion needs they move into meeting their need for Control. At this stage of team development people begin to reveal much more of themselves to each other, including their values and beliefs; differences begin to be felt between people. This is a critical stage of team development when conflict between people is most likely. Underneath what appears often to be a relatively small issue over which there is conflict, people are working out with each other how much influence and control they want to have over each other, and who has the most power and influence in the team.

It as this stage that the skills of assertive communication, and maintaining an I'm OK: You're OK life position are vital to the success of the

Table 10.2 Inclusion behaviors used by the team leader and team members to facilitate meeting the interpersonal need for Inclusion

Inclusion is expressed assertively by team leader and team members through:	And helps everyone in the team feel:
Saying "Hello" to everyone	Acknowledged for being present
Using everyone's name	That they have been recognized individually—and are "significant"
Looking at the person who is talking, (if face to face)	Listened to
Talking briefly about something which everyone can relate to	That they can contribute to a general discussion
Asking everyone if they have the relevant papers, and if not ensuring they can see them	That their participation in the team activity is valued
Going "round the table," or "round the room"—even if it is a virtual room as in a conference call	That they have an opportunity to more formally say "Hello" and to be heard—and to feel "in"
Being clear about the time, and timings, and checking that everyone is clear	That their time is valued, and that have been recognized and are "important"
Asking questions of people	That what they have to say is of interest, and they are interesting to others

team. Seeing potential conflict, and actual conflict, as opportunities for the team to develop more assertive relationships with each other in which they can work towards win: win solutions and discover even more creative outcomes is part of moving through Storming into Norming.

Table 10.3 shows the kinds of Control behaviors which expressed from an I'm OK: You're OK life position help the team leader and team members meet the interpersonal need for Control.

Table 10.3 Control behaviors used by the team leader and team members to facilitate meeting the interpersonal need for Control

Control is expressed assertively by team leader and team members through:	And helps everyone in the team feel:
Asking for people's opinion on a subject	Valued for their "competence"
Encouraging people to use the personal pronoun "I"	That they are responsible for their own views and interpretations
Different people providing direction and guidance	That they can follow the lead of others, and that they will be followed
Allowing differences of opinion and listening without interrupting	That difference is appreciated
Asking for different views and opinions	That their views and opinions do really matter
Acknowledging that people will have different opinions, values, and beliefs	More comfortable with expressing difference
Paying attention throughout to relationships between people as well as their goals and needs	Issues and differences can be discussed and not "personalized"

Affection

At the Performing stage of the team development people feel more trusting of each other, and there is more affection and openness between them. Respect for their differences at the same time as an appreciation of their similarities is a characteristic of teams at this stage. The skills of assertive communication become the way in which people communicate with each other and part of the team culture. The relationships between people are based on the I'm OK: You're OK life position. People feel confident about who they are, and competent in their abilities.

Table 10.4 shows the kinds of Affection behaviors which expressed from

Table 10.4 Affection behaviors used by the team leader and team members to facilitate meeting the interpersonal need for Affection

Affection is expressed assertively by team leader and team members through:	And helps everyone in the team feel:
Giving to, receiving from, and asking for feedback from each other	That they can be open, trusting, and learn from each other—increasing self-awareness and awareness of each other
Giving positive appreciation to each other	That they are likeable and appreciated for who they are and what they do
Asking for help as and when needed from each other	That it is OK to ask for help

an I'm OK: You're OK life position help the team leader and team members work together effectively and achieve outstanding performance.

Teams may stay together for varying lengths of time, and during this time new members may join and members leave. Any change in membership impacts on the dynamics of the team and the relationships within the team. An understanding of the three key interpersonal needs can help the team address the interpersonal needs of everyone when someone joins or leaves the team.

At each stage of team development the team leader will use different assertive communication skills ranging from the directive through to the non-directive. Typically teams, and individuals, need more direction when they initially meet and less direction when they have worked together for a period. These skills are summarized in Figure 10.1.

Within one team meeting the team leader is likely to use the full range of assertive communication behaviors, starting with more directive at the beginning in order to provide direction and to ensure inclusivity, moving through to more non-directive behaviors during the meeting. Towards the end of the meeting the team leader may once again provide direction in confirming actions and agreeing the way forward. Table 10.5 shows the different stages of team development, team members' interpersonal needs and team leader behavior.

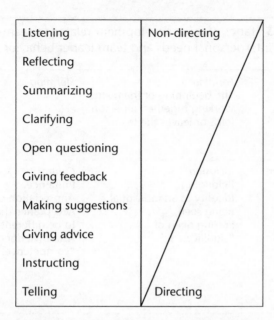

Figure 10.1 The range of assertive communication skills from non-directive though to directive used by the team leader

Case study: Using FIRO-B

In this case study Phil Lowe, a coach, facilitator, and writer, describes using FIRO-B in a team-building workshop to help people better understand their own and others' interpersonal needs and behaviors. All participants were members of a senior management team that was struggling with difficult interactions between individuals, the team, and the rest of the organization. Everyone brought to the workshop a difficult interaction that they had recently experienced, and their FIRO-B profile.

One team member, Jill, shared how difficult she found interacting with people when she first met them; her worst scenario was being introduced to someone at a conference and being expected to talk with this person.

Phil used an actor to play the part of a person at a conference with the rest of the team as observers, making notes of their observations. The team gave feedback that, in the work situation, they perceived her as being friendly and informal with people but that they had experienced her as being awkward in situations in which she was expected to network with people that she did not know. Phil related this to her FIRO-B scores that revealed she had very low Inclusion and low Affection scores.

Table 10.5 Stages of team development related to team members' interpersonal needs and team leader behavior

Stage of team development	*Forming* The beginning of the team working together; a person joins or leaves the team.	*Storming*
Team members' interpersonal need.	*Inclusion* Belonging. Identity as an individual. Being seen. Feeling need of "significance."	*Control* Influence. Appreciation of difference. Acceptance that it is OK to be different. Acknowledgement of "competence."
Team leader behavior	Providing direction, giving team clear instructions; making clear expectations. Offering guidelines. Ensuring everyone is included.	Providing direction, and offering support through ensuring that everyone is heard. Acknowledging that there are differences. Encouraging of differences being explored. Offering a model for giving, receiving, and asking for feedback.

A team member with high Inclusion and high Affection scores offered to be in the role play with the actor and for Jill to be the observer. Jill observed the ease with which her colleague engaged with the person, asking him about his job, how he was getting on, and what had brought him to the conference. She made it look easy and effortless. Jill decided that she would talk more with people who find it easy to talk with people on first meeting, and find out what they do, starting with her colleague. Knowing that she could learn some of the behaviors of Inclusion, and that with practice they would become easier for her, was hugely empowering. She did not need to become someone else rather she was able to learn behaviors that would enable her to be herself and to feel more comfortable with herself.

Table 10.5 continued		
Norming	*Performing*	*Mourning* The ending of team; a person leaves or joins the team.
Affection Developing own ways of working, on getting on with each other, and with the task. Finding own ways of working. Evolving own team culture.	*Affection* Getting on with the task and taking care of each other, enjoying each other. Liking being with each other and feeling "likeable".	*Affection, Control, and Inclusion* Dealing with loss, managing change. Feeling happy with changes, feeling angry with changes. Feeling insecure and unsure about identity.
Stepping back from the team, while being present. Allowing the team to find their own way, and checking in through regular meetings. Encouraging review of performance and relationships with each other.	Being available to offer support and direction if needed. Listening and appreciating people for their contributions. Giving positive and timely feedback. Being open and honest.	Providing support and some direction by way of acknowledging experience of loss and impact on people; working with uncertainty and feelings of insecurity.

CASE ANALYSIS: UNDERSTANDING AND LEARNING NEW BEHAVIORS

FIRO-B is a wonderful tool not only for helping people to understand their interpersonal needs and interpersonal dynamics but also for recognizing the different behaviors associated with each of the interpersonal needs. The use of FIRO-B facilitated team members in understanding their own particular interpersonal needs and the way in which they expressed these needs through behavior. With this awareness team members were enabled to see each other more clearly and to appreciate their differences.

For Jill understanding that her low scores did not mean an absence of interpersonal need for Significance or Likeability, rather that she was very selective about the people to whom she expressed this behavior and from whom she wanted it, was very reassuring. Equally realizing that she could learn some of the behaviors associated with Inclusion and Affection helped her to feel more confident in herself.

Using the actor provided a tangible illustration of how the interpersonal dynamics behind the FIRO-B express themselves in observable behavior, making it much easier for team members to see the impact of their behavior, and for conscious behavior change to take place. The role of the actor in feeding back how she felt on the receiving end of particular behaviors facilitated the feedback process and helped all the team members to engage with each other in giving, receiving, and asking for feedback. They were enabled to have "bigger" conversations with each other in which were able to be open and honest, and to find more effective ways of working together.

11

Belbin Team Roles

Introduction

An understanding of the different strengths that people bring to teams helps both individuals and team members to be their "best selves." People can feel confident in the team roles that they bring to team working, and appreciate that other people bring different strengths. The theory of Belbin team roles gives people a language with which to talk about their differences as well as to appreciate their "allowable weaknesses."

In this chapter, using Belbin team roles is explored in relation to developing assertive relationships between people working together in teams. In particular the verbal communication behaviors associated with each of the team roles are described, and it is explained how, when used from an I'm OK: You're OK life position, they encourage people to appreciate their strengths and differences and leverage them for team effectiveness and business success. The case study shows how Belbin team roles can be used as a tool for developing self-awareness and awareness of others, and for developing greater self-respect and respect of others.

Belbin team role strengths and assertiveness

People usually have very clear strengths in at least three of the nine team roles, and draw upon a number of the other team roles as and when they need to do so. Typically people have one or two team roles that they rarely use, because they either are reluctant to do so, or know that they are not very skilled in this particular role. They are able to think about situations in which they felt self-confident and used their strengths well, as well as those situations in which they could have used their strengths to greater effectiveness. Equally knowing that strengths can sometimes be "allowable weaknesses," if overused or used inappropriately, is an important part of assertiveness.

Completing the Belbin Team Role Self-Perception Questionnaire and the 360 Belbin Team Role Questionnaire in a team can greatly help the team to become more assertive and effective. Team members gather feedback from other team members, and from people outside of the team. The feedback is then used as part of a team exercise in which people have an opportunity to reflect on their self-perception and on how other people perceive them. Team members are encouraged to share their feedback with each other, and to ask each other for examples of what they could do differently in order to be more assertive and effective.

Verbal communication behaviors

Table 11.1 shows the range of verbal communication behaviors that can be observed in team interaction and team working. The behaviors are divided into two broad categories "Seeking" and "Giving," with an example of the behavior and the team role that most uses these behaviors.

Team roles and assertive team working

All the behaviors are used by some or all of the team roles, and are examples of assertive communication when expressed towards others from an I'm OK: You're OK position. It is useful to remember that in any team there are likely to be several people who share similar team role preferences, and are therefore contributing using similar communication behaviors. When a team is working well together there is a rich mix of all the team roles, with people drawing on their strengths and building on each other's, at the same time as being tolerant of each other's "allowable weaknesses." Some of the team roles are more likely to use some of the behaviors more than others: for example, Coordinators are likely to use more seeking behaviors in order to coordinate the efforts of the team.

When a team is working assertively and well, everyone is involved whether they are listening or talking. People engage with each other through asking questions, seeking more information, and building on each other's ideas. There is healthy interrupting as people spark off each other's enthusiasm. Conflict is experienced as an opportunity for further creativity, and for working together. Everyone feels able to

Table 11.1 Seeking and giving behaviors associated with the different team roles

Seeking behaviors

Category	Description of behavior	Example	Team role most likely to use behaviors
Seeking suggestions	Behavior intended to gain ideas from other	"How shall we handle it?" "What shall we do next?"	Coordinator
Seeking clarification	Behavior intended to gain further explanation of a point	"How exactly would that work in practice?"	Coordinator Monitor evaluator Completer finisher
Seeking reactions	Behavior intended to check out with others their understanding	"What do other people think about the idea?" "What is your understanding of the point?"	Coordinator Shaper Resource investigator Teamworker
Seeking information	Behavior that seeks facts and opinions	"What does the report say by way of the figures?"	Specialist Monitor evaluator Plant
Proposing	Behavior that puts forward an idea or proposal and at the same time invites others to respond	"How do you feel about our going forward with it?"	Plant Shaper Monitor evaluator Completer finisher Specialist

Giving behaviors

Telling	Behavior that puts forward an idea or proposal in a way that tells people this is what we are going to do	"OK, we are going to take this forward as follows."	Coordinator Shaper

Table 11.1 continued

Category	Description of behavior	Example	Team role most likely to use behaviors
Building	Behavior that extends or develops an idea that has already been put forward	"I like the idea of going forward in the way you have proposed and would suggest that we add this."	Teamworker Coordinator
Agreeing	Behavior that expresses agreement	"I agree with the idea to move forward as suggested."	Teamworker Coordinator
Supporting	Behavior that expresses support to another person	"I really appreciate your courage to share your opinion, thanks."	Teamworker
Disagreeing	Behavior that expresses a difference of opinion or disagreement	"I disagree with the idea put forward and would like to explore an alternative."	All team roles
Disagreeing and blocking	Behavior that expresses a difference of opinion and blocks movement forward	"We have tried this before and it didn't work. It won't work this time."	All team roles
Giving information	Behavior that offers facts, opinions, or clarification	"I feel uncomfortable about the idea because of my experience of ...."	Specialist Plant Monitor evaluator Shaper
Interrupting and/or talking over others	Behavior that cuts others off and/or silences people	"I think that we ..." over someone else	All team roles

Source: adapted from unpublished handout (Henley Management College, 1986).

contribute, and takes responsibility for themselves at the same time as noticing the contributions of others—and bringing each other in to discussions.

> The essence of a team is of players who have a reciprocal part to play and are dynamically engaged with one another.
>
> (Belbin, 1993: 87)

Increasingly teams are made up of people from different cultural backgrounds, and team working may take place regularly via conference calls and video conferencing. Knowledge and awareness of the different team roles and the different kinds of verbal contributions that people make can be hugely helpful when working in geographically dispersed teams. Combining this knowledge with that of FIRO-B can assist team members, for example, in a conference call to use "seeking behaviors" to facilitate meeting people's interpersonal need for Inclusion at the beginning of the call. Those people for whom talking over and interrupting each other is more of a cultural norm are helped through a knowledge of team roles to appreciate that others may participate differently, and need to be "brought in." Equally people who may find it difficult to interrupt can be encouraged to do so assertively in order to engage in the discussion.

For team leaders, familiarity with Belbin team roles can be helpful when chairing meetings, particularly meetings that are not face-to-face. Team leaders can draw on the communication skills used typically by the Coordinator to facilitate effective team working using a mix of "seeking" and "giving" behaviors. Equally team members who are looking to be more assertive in team meetings can look to use their team role strengths more confidently and to positive effect.

In the following case study, Diana Danziger, an organizational psychologist, describes how using Belbin team roles can help individuals and teams to understand themselves and to appreciate their own and each other's different strengths.

Case study: Team roles and team effectiveness

Diana has used both the Belbin Team Role Self-Perception Questionnaire and the 360 Belbin Team Role Questionnaire with teams in organizations to help them work together more effectively and assertively. Typically people complete the questionnaire prior to a team event at which the theory of team roles is explained, including the kinds of behaviors associated with each role. They are then given an opportunity to look at their personal feedback and to make sense of it on their own before sharing their feedback with others in the team.

At large team events (between 50 and 100 people) people are invited to form groups of eight with people with whom they may not have worked, but with whom it would be useful for them to network as they may be working together in the future. Also people are invited to choose those people who they may have had electronic or telephone contact with but not actually met face-to-face. Once in the groups people use their feedback as a way of getting to know each other better. In doing so all participants are given the opportunity to connect more deeply with themselves and engage more fully with the other people.

Team members are encouraged to use the feedback to help them be more creative and productive and to explore how they can learn from each other. Within the teams people identify at least one other person who has a team role strength that they would like to learn more about. They inquire of the person how she or he behaves in this role, and how she or he draws on these behaviors or communication skills in different situations. In this way people learn about one another's strengths and at the same time find out more about how they could do things differently. As a team everyone then discusses how, with their increased awareness, they can use their strengths to be more effective and productive.

One of the benefits of using Belbin team roles with teams is that team members often identify that they could be more effective if they asked more questions of each other (seeking behaviors), rather than making statements (giving behaviors), including asking for help from each other as and when needed—and this not being seen as a weakness but as a strength. The feedback process facilitates engagement between team members and an increased awareness of shared responsibility for making the team more effective. This necessitates a recognition of the leadership potential in each of the nine team roles, and the need for people to take the lead at different times during a meeting, project, or team activity, irrespective of whether they are the formal leader in the group.

Diana uses Belbin team roles alongside other personality and psycho-metric questionnaires, in particular the Myers-Briggs Type Indicator. The combination of the Belbin Self-Perception Questionnaire and the MBTI helps people explore their preferences and their communication behaviors. The process of personal reflection combined with group discussion helps team members to develop greater self-confidence, appreciate their differences, and work with their differences rather than against each other.

In teams where there has been a breakdown of communication Belbin team roles can be used to help people look at the range of team roles and their different strengths, and what might be getting in the way of them communicating and working together. Equally, Belbin team roles can be useful in a situation where a line manager and employee are experiencing conflict. For example, a coach can discuss each person's strengths and communication behaviors (initially separately with each person) which can facilitate them having a conversation in which they are able to "depersonalize" their differences using the shared language of Belbin and their knowledge of the different team roles. In this way the downward conflict spiral is transformed, through dialog and engagement, and through both people listening, questioning, and reflecting back what each has heard, leading to a more effective and assertive working relationship. They are helped to understand and respect their differences, and explore how they can work together effectively.

CASE ANALYSIS: STRENGTHS AND BEST SELF

Belbin team roles give people a language with which to talk about their differences—and in particular their strengths. People are encouraged through working with team roles as part of a team-building event to transfer their learning into the working environment in which they may be part of several teams, some of which are virtual teams. With their new awareness people can use their strengths with more confidence and, when needed can draw upon strengths associated with their less well-used team roles.

Recognizing that strengths can become "allowable weaknesses," and that this is most likely to happen when people are in a not-OK life position, for example when they are feeling stressed or under pressure, helps people to be more tolerant and accepting of each other. With this knowledge people are better able to self-manage and manage their relationships with each other more effectively. They are encouraged to be their "best selves," to be confident in their strengths, and at the same time to recognize that others have different combinations of strengths and to be curious about how they can work together assertively and effectively.

> To build a well-balanced team demands that there is a reasonable supply of candidates, adequate in number and in diversity of talents and team roles.
>
> (Belbin, 1993: 113)

12 The Learning Cycle and Learning Styles

Introduction

The learning cycle model is used widely in organizations in the design of learning experiences for individuals, including coaching and leading others, and in the design of training programs. It is linked to what is known as "experiential learning," literally learning from experiences, and provides people with a way of thinking about how they learn and the process of learning, rather than focusing attention solely on the "what" of learning or doing.

The theory is particularly useful when thinking about the design and delivery of learning and development in organizations, and in creating true learning organizations in which people are engaged in learning and development every day. In this chapter the learning cycle and the different learning styles are explored and summarized in relation to developing assertiveness.

The case study illustrates how the learning cycle was used in the design of a leadership development program aimed at helping leaders to become their best, assertive, and authentic selves through greater awareness of their physical, intellectual, emotional, and spiritual energies.

Positive self-belief and learning

For many people their experience of learning is associated with being at school, of school reports, and of "doing well" or "not well" in different subjects. For those people who did not do well in particular subjects, or at school in general, the experience can have a long-lasting negative impact on their self-esteem. There are those people who leave school,

118

and go on to be hugely successful in a subject not offered to them at school.

Sir Ken Robinson (2006) gives the wonderful example of a young girl who was taken by her mother to an educational psychologist in order to diagnose the causes of her lack of concentration in class, and who, left on her own in the room, started to dance to the music on the radio. The educational psychologist responded by saying, "Gillian isn't sick. She is a dancer." She needed to move to think. Gillian Lynne became a star dancer, a stager, and pioneer choreographer—best known for her directing of *Cats* (with Trevor Nunn), and staging for *Phantom of the Opera*.

Many people are themselves unaware of their talents, and lack confidence in their ability to learn, and do not know what will help them become their "best selves" or how to fulfill their potential. Most people can however remember at least one teacher from their school years whom they liked, and whom they feel liked them. Furthermore these teachers believed in them, and their ability to do well. This in turn helped them to believe in themselves, and that they could do well. William Nicholson (2006), a scriptwriter known in particular for *Shadowlands* and *Gladiator*, talks about the importance of having someone "who believes in you to help you become who you are," of being given positive recognition in developing positive self-belief.

Providing opportunities for people to discover "the power of who they are" is very much part of developing assertiveness in organizations. Increasingly people are recognizing that "it is never too late to learn," and that every experience can be a learning opportunity.

Using the theory of the learning cycle and different learning styles to help people become their "best selves" and to appreciate difference

People learn in different ways, and an appreciation of these differences can help leaders, educators, HR professionals, and coaches in the design and development of learning experiences. Irrespective of whether people have completed the Learning Styles Questionnaire (Peter Honey Learning, www.peterhoney.com) most people know the kind of experience from which they learn best. Helping people to learn how to use these experiences to enhance their learning and to move around the learning cycle greatly facilitates them in feeling confident in themselves and in their ability to learn from experiences. Equally recognizing that people have different styles and different strengths assists leaders in identifying experiences that people are more likely to find motivating. At the same time encouraging people to step out of their preferred way of learning can lead to them learning from new experiences. For example people whose preferred style is that of Activist, of "doing," can be challenged and stretched by learning from a different kind of learning experience such as being asked to observe and reflect. This again helps them to move round the learning cycle and to increase their self-awareness, and in turn their self-confidence as well as to appreciate differences in how others learn.

Case study: Learning in practice

The Developing Leadership Commitments (DLC) program was designed by a group of internal and external consultants to Unilever to support leaders initially in developing the Path to Growth strategy (2000–05). The program was further developed in 2005 by a group of consultants including the author, to support the Unilever "Vitality Mission"—"to feel good, look good, and get more out of life." The overall design of the five-day program reflected the learning cycle, and each day also provided delegates with an opportunity to "go round" the learning cycle.

Vitality was seen as being closely related to the physical, intellectual, emotional, and spiritual intelligences or energies, and the importance of feeling alive and vital in each of these areas. At the start of the program delegates reflected on how they looked after themselves in each of the four energies, and what kinds of things depleted their energies. They were encouraged to pay attention to their energy during the week, and to regularly "check in" with themselves how they were feeling physically, intellectually, emotionally, and spiritually. They were shown techniques to help them energize as well as to relax, particularly at the end of the day when many people reported that they found it difficult to "switch off" from work-related activities. Delegates were also provided with a journal in which to keep a record of their learning experiences, and to note anything that particularly related to them from other people's sharing of experience.

During the first two days of the program delegates worked together in small coaching groups focusing on their leadership, and how they could be their best and most vital self in all that they set out to do during and beyond the program. They responded individually to three questions:

Who do I want to be as a leader?
Who do I not want to be as a leader?
What are my personal leadership commitments, and how am I going to work on them this week?

These questions helped delegates inquire within, to reflect on their "best experiences" of themselves.

Physical, intellectual, emotional, and spiritual energies or intelligences

Delegates identified how they felt in each of the four energies when they were being their "best and vital self." Statements made by delegates in response to the question, "How do you feel physically, intellectually, emotionally, and spiritually when you are your 'best and most vital self'?" included:

- I am passionate in all that I do.
- I am willing to take risks.
- I dare to dream.
- I enjoy a challenge.
- I inspire others.
- I am good at listening to others.
- I work well under pressure.

Story telling

Delegates shared personal best stories of when they had experienced themselves being their most vital and authentic self as a leader, and received feedback from their colleagues as to how they could draw on these strengths in order to be their authentic and vital self in everything that they did. The process of reflection, of making connections and plans, facilitated people in moving round the learning cycle.

Personal leadership commitments and business simulation

Having made personal leadership commitments, delegates then entered into a two-day business simulation in which they were encouraged to be their "best" authentic and vital selves—in their relationships with each other, with people in other groups, in their tasks and achievement of business goals. At the end of each day there was an opportunity for them to reflect on their personal leadership commitments and the extent to which they had been able to live them with vitality.

The final day of the program gave people opportunity to reflect on their experiences during the week, to receive feedback, and ask questions in order to look at ways of leveraging their strengths back in the working environment in order to be their best and vital selves as leaders.

CASE ANALYSIS: THE POWER OF STORY TELLING

This program draws on the learning cycle as an overall framework to facilitate delegates in developing greater self-awareness and awareness of others. In particular it involves their truly knowing who they are when they are being their best selves, and how to create situations in which they can lead from this place of integrity and authentic connection. Story telling is used as part of the process to assist delegates in engaging with their emotional energy and passion, and to make an emotional connection with their colleagues through their story.

Annette Simmons in her book *The Story Factor* (2002) writes about the importance of knowing "who I am," and "why I am here," and being able to tell stories that illustrate and give others a bigger picture with which they can connect at an emotional level. "Who I am" and "why I am here" stories are powerful ways of connecting with people, referred to by Annette Simmons as "pull strategies."

> The pull strategy of story taps into the momentum living in your listeners rather than providing momentum for them.
>
> (Simmons, 2002: 109)

To work they must be real stories based on personal experience. Telling these stories requires people to be their personal best and authentic self, to be respecting of self and at the same time of others, to be in an I'm OK: You're OK life position, and to have the courage to tell their stories. Stories that "move round" the learning cycle powerfully illustrate people's learning from experience, including from mistakes and from doing things differently.

Vitality is integral to developing greater self-confidence, positive self-esteem, and feelings of self-worth. It is integral to developing assertive relationships that are honest, trusting, and for which people have energy. Assertive relationships are characterized by their vitality and energy; they are "bigger" relationships in which people act with integrity and enjoy the respect of each other, and in which they can have the conversations that they need to have.

Part IV

Multicultural Differences, Differences of Sexual Orientation, and Gender Difference

13 Multicultural Differences

Introduction

Assertiveness is about feeling safe and secure, and having "the right to belong." For many people the experience of being different is difficult and undermining of their self-confidence. People feel a lack of recognition for who they are and do not feel included. All organizations are multicultural, and the need to work with difference is vital to valuing, attracting, and retaining people, and to developing truly inclusive and assertive organizations.

In this chapter the interrelationship between personal, national, and organizational cultures is explored, and the "target and non-target" approach (www.visions-inc.com) to working with multicultural differences is offered as a method for facilitating people in developing greater awareness of and responsibility for their differences, and for developing truly assertive organizations in which everyone feels safe and secure, valued, and respected.

The first case study illustrates how working with the target and non-target approach can help people to think about difference, to take responsibility for difference, and to talk about difference. The second case study illustrates the importance of sharing experiences within ethnic minority groups, and in particular with women from these groups, in helping them to find their voice and be assertive.

Personal, national, and organizational cultures

The way people work together in organizations is hugely influenced by their personal and national cultures. Their personal culture is made up of values, beliefs, and attitudes that people adopt from their parents, and their education—from their life experiences and to a small extent their genetic make-up. The national culture is made up of social and religious values, attitudes, and beliefs. The personal and national cultures are passed down implicitly and explicitly from one generation to the next. Similarly the organizational culture is made up of values, beliefs, and attitudes that are passed on, often invisibly, by people within the organization. These values, beliefs, and attitudes inform how people behave towards each other, and what is acceptable and unacceptable behavior. For many people reflecting on their values, beliefs, and attitudes, and the impact of these on their behavior, is a vital and valuable part of their personal and professional journey.

An assertive organizational culture is one in which people can feel safe and secure in their difference, respecting of difference, and respected for their differences. In an assertive organization people are able to build assertive relationships with each other, and to have open and honest conversations with each other, in which they are curious to understand themselves and each other better. It is one in which everyone takes responsibility for understanding and working with difference.

The target and non-target approach

The target and non-target approach is a way of navigating and working with difference. It helps people to think and talk about difference, and to look at prejudices, paranoia, fears, and ignorance that lead to many of the "isms" listed in Table 13.1.

Table 13.2 shows the criteria that need to be present to create the relationship between target and non-target groups.

Both target and non-target groups tend to blame and complain about the other group, or the system, in order to justify their own behavior towards the other group; both are dysfunctional and non-assertive. Neither takes responsibility for their own behavior, and underlying the behavior of both groups is the fear of difference, and the unknown. It is important to emphasize that the target group's behavior never ever justifies the behavior of the non-target group. Most often the non-target group's behavior is a projection by members of the group of unacknowledged, hidden, repressed, and denied parts of themselves. For example, if a white person judges that a black

Table 13.1 Main target and non-target groups

	Target	Non-target
Racism	Black people, people who are not white	White people
Sexism	Women	Men
Homophobia Heterosexualism	Lesbian, gay, bisexual, transgender, intersex people	Heterosexuals
Xenophobia	Everyone who is different	People who are the same
Ageism	Older people	Younger people
Religious prejudice	Catholics Muslims	Protestants Christians
Classism	Working class	Upper class
Anti-Semitism	Jews	Gentiles

person is cruel, it is likely that the white person fails to acknowledge he or she can also be cruel.

The criteria of target and non-target groups described in Table 13.2 help, for example, white people to understand that while they may be persecuted as white people, they are never a target group purely because they are white. All non-target groups see the target group as "less than," and as inferior in some way to them; they adopt a position of I'm OK: You're not OK—"I am more than you, you are less than me." The target group, being in a position of economic and/or political vulnerability, absorb the persecution and oppression in order to survive.

The case study that follows shows how the target and non-target approach can be used as a way of working with difference and of helping people to "act with grace across ethnic, cultural and linguistic lines" (Hughes, 1994: 83).

Table 13.2 Criteria that need to be present to create a relationship between target and non-target groups

Target group	Non-target group
Targeted for a long, long time by non-target group	Targeting for a long, long time
Do not have economic and/or political power	Do have economic and/or political power
Are not in control of the environment in which they are being targeted	Are in control of the environment in which they are targeting
Usually in the minority, but not always	Usually in the majority, but not always
Are targeted simply for being in the target group	Target people because they are in the target group

Case study 1: Assertiveness and awareness of difference

Robert Taylor is a solicitor and lecturer at a London university, and leads and facilitates groups; Yvonne Taylor is a leader, facilitator, and counselor working with people in developing multicultural awareness.

Assertiveness means that people of both non-target and target groups truly accept their differences, honoring them and not using them as "weapons of prejudice." People from both groups deny their differences rather than accepting and honoring each other. Robert Taylor describes making a "fatal mistake" in a group made up of black and white men, saying to a black man in the group, "I don't see you as a black man in this group, I see a man." The man challenged Robert to see him, to see his blackness and their difference. By denying the difference and identifying with the man, Robert mistakenly thought he was being "non-racist." It is a mistake that non-target groups of people often make in an attempt to be "non-racist," or for example, "non-sexist"—when a man says to a woman colleague, "I don't see you as a woman, I see you as a professional colleague." In this moment he denies both of them their difference; and if she accepts his statement she also denies their difference.

Assertiveness, responsibility and choice

A key aspect of assertiveness is taking responsibility, and in particular taking responsibility for the choices that we make. Both non-target and target groups have their own work to do, raising awareness of their differences within their non-target or target group before they can work together.

> The work is very much about the non-targets accepting that they are responsible for their behavior of targeting the targets and that the targets are not to blame. For the targets it is to stop denying their differences and to accept that they are indeed different from the non-targets and to celebrate their uniqueness and to stop trying to be like the non-targets. In any event the non-targets despise the targets for trying to be like the non-targets.
>
> (Robert Taylor, interview, 2006)

Robert makes it clear that we all have our own work to do: "When a white man says to a black man: 'Please can you help so that you don't see me as a racist,' the black man might justifiably say: 'Don't ask me to pick cotton for you, do your own work.'" The "work" that people have to do in their non-target and target groups comes before people can truly work together. Being aware of and taking responsibility for differences comes first. This involves acknowledging similarities of experience within one's own group, working with the knowledge of what it means to be in this group, and taking responsibility for one's role in the "ism."

> If you have a black skin you are target—like it or not; if you have a white skin you are non-target, like it or not.
>
> (Robert Taylor, conversation, 2006)

Through questioning, supporting, and challenging each other it is then possible for people to have a dialog with people from different groups about their differences, to really listen, see, and honor each other, and explore the values they share, to enjoy assertive relationships with each other in which both can feel trusting and safe.

True understanding and compassion

True understanding of and compassion for each other as people is possible when we take responsibility for who we are, as a non-target or target person. Only when people have taken responsibility and are able to accept and honor their differences can they truly see each other as human beings, and find their common humanity. Connecting with another person who is different means taking risks, letting go of assumptions, and asking questions.

Robert gives the following examples from his work as a university lecturer and facilitator of groups, he asks: "I see you are black, how is it for you doing this course?" and: "How do you feel being on this course?" He asks people how they would like to addressed, rather than categorizing using a label which may not be right for them. In all his work Robert encourages people to feel their difference, to experience and to connect with their own history, and their experience of being in a target and/or a non-target group.

People in a non-target group can be unaware of what is getting in the way for someone else in their group; it is only when they connect with their own experience that they can realize how unsafe it maybe for someone from a target group to speak their truth and be assertive. Once people have connected with their own experience, they are able to connect with others, to recognize their humanity and find common values. Creating a safe physical and emotional environment in which people can truly be themselves is the challenge for everyone: individuals, groups, and organizations who are committed to honoring diversity and assertiveness.

Yvonne Taylor leads multicultural workshops that give people an opportunity to: "come together with their differences and relate to difference and honor it." She describes her work with both target and non-target groups as "helping people to understand and respect themselves, and each other and ultimately to see, hear, and feel the human being in each." In all her work she creates a safe space in which people can voice their fear and, with awareness, move towards a greater understanding of their own uniqueness and respectful connection, leading to assertive relationships with each other.

CASE ANALYSIS: COURAGE AND COMMITMENT

Working with multicultural differences individually, as members of target and non-target groups, and as multicultural organizations, involves a commitment from everyone to learn from each other's experiences, and from mistakes. Sometimes mistakes are made unwittingly through a lack of knowledge of another person's cultural values and norms. Something that is taken for granted as being acceptable behavior in one culture may cause huge distress for someone from another culture. Equally something that is very humorous in one culture may be experienced as very improper in another, and cause offence. Learning about each other's differences is key to developing assertive relationships in which people can question their own assumptions and check out assumptions with each other.

It takes courage and commitment to talk about difference openly and honestly. By denying difference we fail to see and hear each other. Providing opportunities for people from target and non-target groups to meet, initially separately and then together, helps to create an assertive organization in which everyone is valued and respected for their difference. Through the process of exchange people are empowered and connected to themselves, to each other, and to the humanness in us all.

It is particularly important that non-target groups put multicultural diversity firmly at the top of their agenda if they are to build truly assertive and multicultural organizations. All too often in the working environment it is people from a target group, for example an ethnic minority group, who feel the need:

> To constantly explain and justify their differences in order to feel more accepted, and to educate people around them on who they are and "where they are coming from".
> (Kirit Patti, senior recruiter, correspondence, 2007)

Kirit Patti goes on to describe how, for many years, she felt that she could not bring her whole self to work, in particular her feisty and passionate self, for fear of being seen as aggressive and "overly emotional." Not until she was in a working environment in which this side of her was recognized, by a Sikh man, was she able to truly be herself. She describes being seen for who she is, and being able to bring her whole self to work, as "a huge comfort."

Case study 2: Trusting and empowering from within

Indu Khurana is founder of Sunai, and describes her work with women as being about helping them to develop greater self-confidence, positive esteem, and

*assertive relationships in the working environment. "Sunai" means "to hear"
in Punjabi and Hindi, and is about listening at a deeper level—listening to the
whole person at the physical, intellectual, emotional, and spiritual level. Indu
discusses the particular challenges for women from ethnic minority groups to
be assertive, and the importance of her work in helping them to be heard and
to find their voice.*

Indu founded Sunai in 2001 out of a deep passion for living her vision
and her values in her work and life. In founding Sunai, and giving her
company the name "Sunai," she was making a commitment to live her
values in everything that she does. She describes this as learning to trust
her intuition and to speak her truth: "It's in every cell of me now and life
is so much easier for me" (Indu Khurana, interview, 2005).

Indu believed, and believes, that she can make a difference. It is this
belief that has led her to work primarily with women who struggle with a
lack of self-confidence and find it difficult to be assertive in the working
environment. She identifies with this struggle from her own past experience. In developing her own self-confidence and assertive relationships,
she is keen to help others, especially women, to do the same.

Women, organization, and culture

Indu has worked and works with a range of organizations in the corporate, public, and voluntary sectors, and has made a number of
observations with regard to women behaving assertively and feeling
self-confident. There would seem to be some confusion around what
assertiveness is in the public and voluntary sectors. Assertive behavior is
often confused with aggressive behavior, with women thinking that
they are being assertive when in fact their behavior is interpreted as
aggressive. This, she noted, seems to be less true of women who have
higher positions in the organization and more status.

Indu has observed that some Asian women find it especially difficult
to be assertive unless they are in a higher position and have more status
within the organization. The women are not used to having a voice and
to speaking their truth at home, and often feel awkward about doing so
at work. Some of the women are not sure either how to do this—or what
their truth is—because it is so deeply held within them. Indu helps the
women, through "listening deeply," to reflect on what really matters to
them in their lives and to speak their truth.

Women have the opportunity on the assertiveness courses to
practice giving voice to their feelings and thoughts, to expressing their
needs, and asking for what they want. The courses are all held in

supporting and nurturing environments, which help the women to feel safe and secure. It is hugely challenging for the women to confront some of the values and beliefs with which they have been brought up, especially that of keeping quiet and not speaking up. They fear being judged by each other and the community for being different and for speaking out. It is not their place to do so. Being given a place where they are actively encouraged to "find their place" and to "speak their truth" is challenging as well as empowering. It requires a shift in self-perception and perception of each other, to take their place in the world, accept that they rightfully belong, and that their needs and wants matter. "Being accepted rekindles their inner flame," Indu commented (Indu Khurana, interview, 2005).

Indu has also observed in her work with organizations that some African and Caribbean women struggle with being assertive in the working environment. In their efforts to behave assertively and to state their needs and wants, they are perceived as being aggressive rather than assertive.

The courses in assertiveness help women think about what assertiveness means, and where assertiveness comes from within themselves. The women are helped to draw on their own inner resources, to give voice to their "inner woman," to empower and trust her. In the groups there are often women from Asian, and African-Caribbean backgrounds who together share their experiences and are empowered through being encouraged to give voice to their feelings and thoughts about themselves, and to support each other. The women explore and clarify what matters to them by way of values and beliefs, and their needs and wants. They then look at the ways in which they can communicate these assertively—using "I" statements, addressing the other person as "you," listening all the while to their intuition, and having the courage to speak their truth and to be their "best selves."

CASE ANALYSIS: CHALLENGE AND COURAGE

Indu works with women who are target group members as women and as members of ethnic minority groups. It can be hugely challenging for women to question some of the values and beliefs that they have been brought up with, in particular about what is expected of women. It takes courage to overcome some of the fears about being different within one's own cultural group, at the same time as being different from those in the majority.

Many women experience a conflict between the values and beliefs—religious and cultural—of their parents and their own. This can make it difficult to be their "best selves," to feel comfortable and at home within themselves physically, intellectually, emotionally, and spiritually, and able to enjoy assertive relationships in which they can be open and honest. Being heard and accepted by other women in a group is a powerful and transformational experience for most women. Being accepted by other women helps women to accept themselves, to be less judgmental of each other and of themselves. It is encouraging of courage.

14 Differences in Sexual Orientation

Introduction

Assertiveness is about bringing the "whole self" to work and being able to be true to oneself without fear of being judged negatively and discriminated against. For many people in minority sexual orientation groups the experience of being open and able to speak their truth about who they are can be a difficult and challenging experience. The feeling of being different from others, and of uncertainty about whether it is safe to disclose one's sexual orientation, is a common experience for many people in minority sexual orientation groups.

Fear is the biggest block to assertiveness and to developing assertive relationships. People who are living in fear do not perform to the best of their ability and for much of the time they are hidden and silent. People can only be their "best selves" in organizations where diversity is truly accepted and people are respected for who they are. Thus developing an assertive organizational culture in which difference is truly respected is vital to people's being themselves and to their, and their organization's, well-being.

This chapter explores assertiveness in relation to the particular challenges facing people who are lesbian, gay, bisexual, and transgender (LGBT) in being able to be authentic in the workplace—the fear and ignorance of others, and overcoming feelings of fear. The case study illustrates through an individual's journey how being able to be open, to live and work without fear, people are not only self-empowered but also empowering of others to be who they are—their "best selves," and to fulfill their potential.

The challenges to people being true to themselves

One of the biggest challenges to be being authentic in the workplace is the fear and ignorance of those in the majority. Many people react to differences in sexual orientation out of fear and ignorance—fear of questioning their own sexual orientation and fear of others' differences; and ignorance based on "false knowledge," for example: "all gays are pedophiles." This "false knowledge" feeds people's fears.

Fear can lead to stereotyping and bullying, in particular aggressive and offensive behavior. Homophobic bullying is common in education and organizations throughout the world where religious and cultural values and beliefs can make life miserable for many people struggling to be true to their sexual identity. Ben Summerskill, chief executive of the campaigning charity Stonewall, invited heterosexual readers of *Report* magazine (February 2005) to, "Imagine how you'd feel if, in an entire education career from 5 to 21, you'd never once read a set text in any language that featured a heterosexual character."

The right to be treated with dignity and respect in relation to sexual orientation at work is recognized by most organizations, and legislation that supports people's rights to be treated with respect is reflected in policies, mission statements, and the values of many organizations. Translating these values into actual behaviors and ways of doing things in organizations is key to the success of everyone accepting, respecting, and celebrating difference in order to create a truly assertive organization.

Concealing their true identity can be, for some people, the only option open to them in the work place. The combination of keeping oneself hidden and of living in fear of being "found out" represents a huge cost to the people themselves and to the organizations in which they work. Performance suffers as the person suffers in silence, feeling anxious and unable to join in informal conversations and activities that might lead to unwanted self-disclosure. Dr Fionn Stevenson, reader in sustainable design at Oxford Brookes University, comments, "It takes enormous energy when choosing to conceal one's identity. It wastes energy" (correspondence with author, 2006).

Supporting people in being true to themselves

Meeting with people who have had similar experiences of being in a minority sexual orientation group, and sharing personal stories, is hugely affirming and validating, not least because within these groups there will also be differences. Fionn Stevenson describes the experience of being the same, and of being different:

> One of the most powerful moments in my life was attending a gay festival in the US where everybody was gay—but also black, young, old, white, poor, rich .... I suddenly felt full of emotion, normal and real; I was somewhere totally safe but still full of difference.
>
> (Fionn Stevenson, correspondence with author, 2006)

A powerful way of working with difference is to provide people with opportunities for greater awareness by reflecting upon their values and beliefs around sexual orientation, their own and others'. Through listening to others and having conversations with each other, people are helped to appreciate and validate each other for who they are, and to develop truly assertive relationships with each other—in which both people feel I'm OK: You're OK. Fionn Stevenson adds, "Being able to be real, to be authentic, is the desire of all minorities, I think—to feel secure in oneself, and to be accepted for who one truly is" (correspondence with author, 2006).

In the United Kingdom an increasing number of organizations are joining Stonewall's Diversity Champions program (www.stonewall. org.uk/workplace). In 2005 KPMG, the global professional services company providing audit, tax, and advisory services to multinational companies, became the 100th organization to join the program, and in 2007 it was joint eighth in the Stonewall Index of best employers for gay and lesbian people. Stonewall works with organizations to promote lesbian, gay, and bisexual equality in the workplace based on the belief that "people perform better when they can be themselves." Dr Ashley Steel, a KPMG board member, is a role model internally and externally to the firm, as a senior woman within the firm who is also gay. She describes being a member of Stonewall's Diversity Champions program as sending: "an incredibly strong message to KPMG's lesbian and gay staff, that they are a valued part of our firm. It also reminds all staff that we work in a diverse environment which is good for business" (Steel, 2005).

In the following case study, Amanda Gutierrez-Cooper, project manager, LGBT Strand, Diversity and Citizen Focus Directorate, Metropolitan Police Service (MPS) describes her individual journey from living and working in fear to feeling safe and secure in who she is; feeling empowered to speak her truth and to speak on behalf of others about equal rights for all, irrespective of sexual orientation.

Case study 1: Living and working without fear

Amanda Gutierrez-Cooper joined the police service 15 years ago following a 10-year career in the army and two years in retailing. When she joined the army aged 19 she was already aware of her sexual orientation as a lesbian but unaware of the homophobia that she would experience within the army. She did however find many women like herself, most of whom were living and working in fear of being found out and dismissed. Amanda describes her experience of being interviewed by a psychiatrist and brigadier, who questioned her about her sexual orientation, as "very frightening."

> I was not able to be myself. I denied myself for fear of running the risk of being seen. They were horrific times. People were named and booted out. If I had been able to be myself I suspect that I would have been a whole lot more efficient.
>
> (Amanda Gutierrez-Cooper, interview, 2006)

Nevertheless Amanda was successful and did get her commission in the army. At that time she didn't question the homophobic culture of the organization. She says, "I didn't bang on the closet door—I would have lost my job. I was good establishment material. I did what I was told. I didn't question " (Amanda Gutierrez-Cooper, interview, 2006).

It was during her career in the army that Amanda first told her mother that she was a lesbian. While her mother and the rest of her family were not thrilled, nor understanding, they were accepting of her. Despite this she felt however that her relationships were taken less seriously than those of her heterosexual sister.

Amanda left the army aged 29. She worked for a couple of years as a department manager for a retailer, and realized that she was not suited to retailing but that she had good people skills. The experience helped "civilianize" and to "de-institutionalize" her, and gave her the opportunity to explore the London gay scene, although she chose not to disclose her sexual orientation at work, and stayed "closeted."

It was a natural step for Amanda to go from the army into the police service. She had a number of friends who were police officers, and felt welcomed by the police—stepping into Hendon Police Training College was like "coming home." It was safer during this time for her to stay "closeted" at work while continuing to be on the gay scene outside of work. Of the trainees on her course Amanda was not only one of the oldest but also one of the few women, another of whom shared with her that she was a lesbian. Amanda was alarmed about why the woman had shared this information with her, and advised her to keep it to herself. However after some weeks into the training the woman—who was used to being open about herself and her sexual orientation—publicly announced that she was lesbian. Amanda remembers feeling very frightened and walking away from the woman out of fear. Happily they have shared this experience and how it impacted on them, which has helped them remain friends to this day.

At that time, 1991, sexual orientation had only just been included in equal opportunities regulations and it was very early days. It was not until her two-year probation period was over and then some three years into her service that Amanda "came out," in 1994. Although she was aware of people knowing that she was lesbian, it was not until she took her partner to a big team Christmas party that she came out, and knew it was the right time to do so. "Once you come out, you carry on coming out, there is no going back in," she says (Amanda Gutierrez-Cooper, interview, 2006).

In 1996 Amanda moved to work with one of the territorial support groups—policing large events including demonstrations, protests, hostage situations, and supporting specialist operations. They were known for their macho culture, in which it was difficult enough to be a woman, let alone a lesbian woman and one who had "come out." Amanda was on the receiving end of homophobic ridicule as well as sexist humor, and her old fears returned. She became anxious and suffered a number of stress-related symptoms and was not able to work at her best.

Subsequently Amanda passed the sergeant's exam and was promoted to become an acting sergeant. This was a turning point for her and her career within the police service. By now she was in her mid-thirties, a sergeant with some rank, and for the first time felt that:

> People liked me for who I was. I felt valued. I moved to a busy inner London station and a very challenging environment. My colleagues were fantastic. I was given a great deal of responsibility that gave me confidence to be myself. I was operating on my own terms and was open about myself.
>
> (Amanda Gutierrez-Cooper, interview, 2006)

In 2003 Amanda joined the Diversity and Citizen Focus Directorate. By now she was much more politically aware, and very much conscious of the lack of rights for LGBT people within the workplace—for example the lack of pension rights and benefit packages available to same-sex couples that were available to heterosexual couples. Amanda felt empowered by the deputy director to whom she was a staff officer. The deputy director gave her opportunities to look at and do things differently, to meet the right people, to establish herself and her credibility as an ambassador on the LGBT front. "I felt valued, trusted, and empowered," she says, and had a belief in herself that "I can tackle the big things" (Amanda Gutierrez-Cooper, interview, 2006).

She was not only invited to represent the directorate on many occasions, but also asked to be one of the founding members of the Commissioner's LGBT Focus Group. Since 2005 she has been project manager for the LGBT Strand Team.

In the United Kingdom the Civil Partnership Act was passed on 17 October 2004 and came into force in December 2005, meaning that same-sex couples who register a civil partnership have the same rights as heterosexual couples. Amanda had joined the LGBT Strand Team during the run-up to the legislation coming live in December 2005. She is passionate about equal rights for same-sex couples and discovered that the MPS was ill-prepared for the legislation, and its impact on staff and service users. She took responsibility for unraveling the 500-page legislation and what it might mean for the MPS by way of pension rights and survivor benefits, and other employee benefit packages.

Amanda gathered information from Stonewall and from the Department of Trade and Industry (DTI), and worked with her HR colleagues to draw attention to all the paperwork that needed to be changed for both staff and service users. Through the Crown Prosecution Service (CPS), Amanda wrote a leaflet for operational staff and officers informing them of the changes under the legislation and its impact on service users; the leaflet written for the MPS is now being used by other services. For Amanda it is the very best example of making something happen, of changing something—and of it having a huge benefit for staff and users of the service.

> I am passionate about LGBT issues. If there is a diversity hierarchy then LGBT can fall in the lower half and not be seen as high as other diversity issues. It takes passion and vision, not being afraid of standing up and being counted.
>
> (Amanda Gutierrez-Cooper, interview, 2006)

Amanda is keen to see the same kind of robust legislation applied to "goods, facilities, and services"—for example, schools—where homophobic bullying is commonplace. She knows that many young people feel invisible and unable to share their sexual orientation for fear of feeling unsafe and being bullied.

Education is an area that Amanda believes is very important to LGBT people, in particular the value of having personal development courses that are specifically for LGBT women which will give them an opportunity to be open about themselves and to be able to truly integrate the learning into their lives. They cannot do this if their identity is hidden.

From being afraid to speak her truth and being hidden for many years, Amanda is now very much a force for change within the MPS and the wider community. She works with external partners to raise awareness and understanding of LGBT issues, giving people necessary information in order to ensure that everyone is treated with dignity and respect for who they are. Amanda knows that there are a lot of lesbian, gay, bisexual, and transgender people in the MPS and in the community it serves, and that it is vitally important to respect them and their choices. She believes that data monitoring is important and that people need to be given a choice by their organization whether they disclose their sexual orientation. However she is committed to making the MPS an environment in which people can choose to share their sexual orientation with others without fear or prejudice.

CASE ANALYSIS: SPEAKING ONE'S TRUTH

Amanda's story of her journey from being hidden and silent to being seen and heard for who she is, highlights how confidence in oneself and in one's abilities comes through having the choice and the courage to "speak one's truth." The support given to Amanda by her line manager in the Diversity and Citizen Focus Directorate was crucial, and shows how being trusted and valued by another person helps empower people to be their "best self." Through being given encouragement and opportunities Amanda was able to "speak her truth," and through doing so empower others within the MPS to deliver a better service to the diverse community that the MPS serves.

15 Gender Difference

Introduction

An increasing number of organizations are committed to gender diversity and to providing learning and development opportunities for women and men to explore—separately and together—values, beliefs, and behaviors that inform people's thinking, assumptions, and expectations of each other. Through this process people are encouraged to be true to themselves, to feel confident in who they are, and to find ways of communicating with each other that are flexible and assertive, and I'm OK: You're OK—respecting and valuing difference.

Assertive communication and negotiation hinges on awareness of self and others. By increasing awareness of different styles of communication, women and men can be more effective in their communication with each other, and more open to possibilities of thinking and feeling differently about themselves and each other. A gender-aware organization is one in which people are encouraged to learn from each other and to better understand how perceptions of each other, as women and men, are influenced by our cultural backgrounds. With this awareness people can create an assertive organization in which gender differences are acknowledged and explored, and stereotypes challenged. In all communication exchanges people say something about their gender, cultural background, values and beliefs, and about the relationship.

This chapter explores gender differences in relation to culture, styles of communication, and leadership, and how these differences impact on the different ways in which women and men typically perceive each other, communicate, and negotiate. The first case study looks at the importance of treating people with respect through valuing diversity, in particular appreciating differences between women and men in the workplace. In the second case study the value of women meeting and talking with other women about their experiences of being in the minority is well illustrated. The case study looks specifically at a leadership training program for senior women designed to increase the number of women leaders at senior levels in the organization.

Gender difference and culture

Gender is one of the most significant areas of difference in our lives. While there are physical, biological, and neurological differences between women and men, gender differences are very much determined by the cultures within which people grow up, early childhood role models, and the expectations that people have of each other as women and men. What is appropriate behavior in one culture for women and men can be considered inappropriate in another culture. The values and beliefs that people bring to their relationships are often communicated implicitly, rather than explicitly. People make sense of their experiences through attributing meanings, and making assumptions, based on data that they have selected from the environment that serves to confirm their values and beliefs. People can be unaware of how their values and beliefs, personal and cultural, underpin their behavior. Through questioning these implicit values people become aware of their biases, and prejudices, and are able to embrace different perspectives.

Gender difference and styles of communication

Women and men have different communication styles and conversational rituals, and an understanding of these differences is helpful in developing a flexibility of style that is assertive. Given that women and men's experience of gender roles is influenced by the culture within which they grew up, it is not surprising that language reflects these differences. The five dimensions of gender difference, drawn from the work of Deborah Tannen (2001a, 2001b), are particularly helpful in the understanding and developing of assertiveness, and assertive relationships between women and men. They are:

- marked and unmarked
- uncertainty and certainty
- general and specific

- invisible and visible
- feelings and facts.

Marked and unmarked

In the English language men are "unmarked" and women are "marked." Women are differentiated from men, and from each other. "Unmarked" words are usually "male," and are the norm, while "marked" words differentiate from the "norm." Deborah Tannen gives the example of form filling. In the English language women are often given three options—Ms, Mrs, or Miss—whereas men have only one option—Mr— and are undifferentiated. Whichever choice a woman makes, she communicates something about herself and in this way is "marked."

For example, in many cultures women mark themselves out differently from other women in how they dress. Even in those cultures where women choose or are forced to wear a burka, there are differences in burkas that "mark" women out from each other. There are many examples of roles that are "gender bound" and stereotyped, and it is often only after a thorough inquiry into the implicit values and beliefs underpinning a job role that the role is "gender freed" and made possible for both women and men. Examples include those professional roles that are typically associated with men, such as a doctor. When people talk of a woman in such a role they often talk about a "woman doctor."

Uncertainty and certainty

Women tend to downplay "certainty" and appear more uncertain than they really are in order to restore a balance in the dialog and to appear equal while being in authority. Men downplay "uncertainty" and appear more certain than they really are in order to maintain or restore the "upper hand." This can give rise to women being perceived by men as lacking in confidence and having doubts about their competence, while men can be seen by women as being arrogant, dominating, and controlling. Equally those men who are more concerned with maintaining and restoring balance in the dialog or relationship can be seen as lacking in confidence and competence. Women who express themselves with certainty are sometimes criticized for being aggressive and "uppity."

General and specific

Women tend to start out in a conversation by being more general and to move towards the specific during the discussion. Men tend to start out by being more specific and to stay specific throughout the discussion. Again misunderstandings and judgments about each other mean that women can think that men are in fact being general like them, and that men can mistake the general for the specific, thinking that women are like men.

Invisible and visible

Women tend to get on in a planned way, quietly getting on with the task at hand, while men tend to go for the "big show," meaning that they are more visible and get more recognition for their achievements. This has implications for women in that they are more likely to talk about their work and to network with people that they know and like, and not to network upwards in their organizations. Men are more likely to network upwards and thus to get recognition for their work from more senior people.

Feelings and facts

When a woman talks to a man about a problem she is not necessarily looking to him for a solution. Rather she is talking about how she feels and what she thinks right now about the situation. The man, keen to solve the problem, doesn't necessarily hear how she feels, and may dismiss the problem altogether. This can lead to conflict, the woman feeling "not heard" and the man feeling discounted for his solution to the problem.

Gender difference and leadership

Assertiveness is often misunderstood and confused with aggressiveness. What is perceived as assertive in men can be experienced as aggressive behavior when expressed by women. There is an expectation that women are more indirect in their communication and that men will be direct. Hence when women are direct in their style of communication they are judged as stepping out of line with what is expected of them. Likewise men whose communication style is indirect can be judged as "not being confident enough." Deborah Tannen relates direct and indirect communication styles to differences in authority and power, and not specifically to differences between women and men. Assertive leadership is underpinned by an I'm OK: You're OK life position, one in which women and men move between being direct and indirect in their communication style depending on the situation and the relationship.

Gender difference and assertive negotiating

Given the five dimensions of gender difference described above, and the dimension of indirect and direct communication, it is not surprising that negotiations between women and men can be difficult and challenging. Research by Linda Babcock, Sarah Laschever, Michele Gelfand, and Deborah Small (2003) highlights how women from an early age are not brought up to ask for what they want and need. Instead they concede to the needs of others.

Indeed when women do ask for what they want and need they can be perceived by others (women and men) as being aggressive, whereas a man asking for exactly the same thing would not be seen as aggressive, simply as asking for what he wants and needs. This leads women to feel dispirited and demotivated to such an extent that they may choose to leave their organization rather than negotiate for what they want or need. It is not only when asking for more money and a pay rise that women can be at a disadvantage, but also when asking for and negotiating other needs and wants such as flexible working hours. Women do not have a template for negotiating their needs and wants in the same way as men.

Linda Babcock and her colleagues suggest a number of things that leaders can do to create a culture in which gender difference is truly valued and people are encouraged to understand and appreciate differences. They are shown in Table 15.1.

Case study 1: Gender diversity

Respect for each other and for individual differences has contributed to the diversification of business at DuPont. The company prides itself on the wide range of business areas and countries within which it operates. It employs people in those countries to work in the businesses, and respects their different ways of doing things. Each of the 20 or so businesses and joint ventures has its own particular style and market demands. There is a flat organizational matrix structure in which people enjoy an individual identity while being part of the DuPont collective identity and culture.

There is a huge respect for difference in DuPont in the areas of ethnicity, sexual orientation, disability, age, and gender. While the company respects difference in all of these areas, 90 percent of senior

Table 15.1 Creating a culture in which gender differences are truly valued

- Tell women employees they must ask for what they want and need.
- Inform female reports about the benefits of negotiating.
- Give men and women comparable raises for comparable achievement.
- Recognize that many women have a style that is less assertive than men's— and don't leave them out because of it.
- Monitor their own track record for advancing female employees.
- Walk the talk: Create a workplace in which men and women are rewarded equally.

Source: adapted from Babcock et al. (2003).

management is male (2005). This is not due to a lack of respect for women: on the contrary it would seem that the lack of women in senior positions is due to a mix of traditional and contemporary views about women, as well as about what senior roles and responsibilities require of the individual.

Traditional and contemporary views of senior roles and responsibilities

The requirement to work long hours, to jump on a plane, to be away from home several days and nights a week and to work on international assignments limits the range of people who might apply for these jobs. The requirements are not peculiar to DuPont, and many companies are in a similar situation. The rules of entry to the top layer of senior management are such that only people who are single, without caring commitments, or have a support system in place at home (nanny, house husband, house wife) can take up the jobs. The challenge to DuPont and to many other organizations is to change the rules of entry and thus open up the top layer of senior management to a much more diverse group of women and men. Lynn Powell, former work environment manager, DuPont HR Europe, describes her experience of working in DuPont:

There are very rare examples of disrespectful behavior towards women in DuPont. However, reality shows that there are not enough women in senior leadership roles. Women can and do reach the topmost levels of DuPont but what we need do is to change the rules of working so that everyone can be part of working together.

(Lynn Powell, interview, 2006)

Traditional and contemporary views about women

Research into gender diversity in DuPont showed that the major barrier for women advancing their careers in the organization is the importance to them of personal and family commitments and responsibilities. The barrier, it would seem, needs to be lifted if gender diversity is to be manifested in a greater balance between women and men in senior positions. This means:

- changing the rules of entry to senior positions
- challenging the attitudes and behaviors of women and men towards each other
- introducing support systems for women and men so that they can enjoy promotion and acceptance into senior positions at the same time as choosing to enjoy personal and family time.

DuPont has introduced a number of systems that support both women and men in their personal and professional development. These include the following.

The WorkLife policy allows employees to request flexi-time, flexi-place, unpaid leave of absence, and compressed working hours. Both women and men take up the policy. (See Chapter 18 for more on flexible working.)

A mentoring scheme for women helps them to develop greater self-confidence, to understand the unwritten rules of progressing within a corporation, and to get feedback on how they are perceived.

A workshop on "Strengthening women in management" encourages women to assert what they want, to step up into their leadership, and to give voice to their true aspirations. This means:

- stepping out of their safety and comfort zone
- feeling confident and behaving assertively
- overcoming any fears that they might have about being judged as "difficult" or "awkward" by others.

The workshops also provide a great opportunity for the women to network with each other across businesses which otherwise operate independently of each other.

CASE ANALYSIS: SAFETY AND RISK

Safety has been and is critical to the success of DuPont a company that deals with chemicals. As with most people and organizations, its positive characteristics can also have a negative, or shadow side. Ensuring safety at all times can mean that people become fearful of risk, and in particular fear raising issues and concerns which may lead to feelings of safety being threatened. Issues and concerns that might, if raised, cause conflict are avoided, leading to a general avoidance of conflict and lack of assertiveness.

The biggest challenge for DuPont as a company and culture based on safety is possibly to allow itself to feel unsafe emotionally through questioning values and beliefs that have provided a backbone of safety and security for the company.

DuPont employees are in a strong and powerful position to engage in this inquiry, given the high level of respect that they enjoy in their relationships with each other. Through building on their strong sense of respect, employees are encouraged to talk openly about their feelings and thoughts, and to engage with each other in meaningful dialog about their differences, in particular the values and beliefs that inform how they interpret experiences. They are able to build assertive relationships with each other through acknowledging differences in perception of what women and men should or should not do.

Case study 2: Working with senior women leaders

In 2003 Eve-olution, a consultancy committed to gender diversity in organizations, and MSA Interactive, a provider of 360 performance review, teamed together to design a 360 review for senior women leaders in organizations. Through Eve-olution's work with senior women in organizations and through surveying women within organizations, the team was able to identify five key categories of competencies for inclusion in the 360 performance review.

In 2003 the Equality and Diversity Department of a leading global financial services company invited Eve-olution to carry out a training needs analysis. This was done with a small focus group of experienced senior women who also had responsibility for increasing the numbers of senior women in the company. The goal of the training needs analysis was to ascertain the key development areas for women that would enable and empower them to work at senior executive level and above, thus meeting the company's objective to increase the representation of female senior executives globally.

The focus group identified a number of key development areas as being critical to senior women feeling enabled and empowered to take their careers to the highest level within the company:

- greater self-awareness, of values, choices, strengths, and ways of promoting the self
- increased self-confidence and confidence in one's ability to perform to high standards
- networking with others
- influencing others
- leading and coaching dynamic teams
- making high-level presentations.

Eve-olution worked closely with the Equality and Diversity Department in designing a five-day program that would meet the identified needs of the senior women and the objective of the company to increase the number of senior women at the senior executive level. The five workshops of the program addressed each of the stated learning and development needs. They were:

- The whole professional woman
- Assert yourself and coaching your team
- Negotiating for success
- Personal branding and building relationships
- Senior presentation skills.

Each workshop developed and furthered the learning of the previous workshop/s. The 360 performance review related to the competencies covered in each of the workshops. The women were able to identify their strengths and work on how to leverage them back in the workplace, as well as identifying areas for improvement and what they needed to do to develop in these areas.

Many of the women on the program particularly enjoyed and appreciated the opportunity not only to focus and reflect on themselves, but also to network and to connect with other senior women in the company. The power of developing assertive relationships with each other through open and honest communication helped people to feel valued and respected for both who they were and what they did.

Together the women developed a working group that was inclusive and in which they were trusting of each other. Delegates recognized through open discussions that there was much they had in common by way of their experiences of being women leaders in the company. Some of the women under-valued their contribution as women leaders and lacked confidence in their ability to influence and to network with others.

The workshops, combined with the focus on their personal 360 performance review, helped participants to identify the values and the behaviors that they brought to their roles, to feel confident in their abilities, and to recognize key areas for development. Many of the women reported feeling an increase in their self-esteem and courage to pursue their values, aligned to their objectives and the objectives of the company. They felt a renewed commitment to the organization and to outstanding performance.

CASE ANALYSIS: GENDER AWARENESS

The program proved to be valuable in helping meet the financial services company's objectives of encouraging and supporting senior women leaders in the organization by providing:

- development for women
- encouragement and support of women "being themselves," finding their individual and collective identities as women leaders
- a learning environment in which women could explore their differences and similarities of values and respect each other.

For many women in senior positions, meeting with other women in their organization or from other organizations is a rare opportunity. They may have heard about each other but not actually have met with each other prior to a program. Attending an all-women program can be difficult and challenging for women for a number of reasons. They may have to deal with negative comments from colleagues about attending an all-women program. Some women may have reservations about being in an all-female group based on their experiences and perceptions of women as competitors and not to be trusted.

The experience of the five-day program described in the case study is an example of women finding that there are huge benefits to sharing experiences, learning from and trusting each other, and becoming more confident as women leaders. For women, recognizing and valuing themselves and each other as women is an important part of developing diversity in organizations. Seeing themselves as women, and different from men, and valuing this difference is a vital part of women being truly assertive, respecting themselves and others—women and men.

16 Working with Multicultural Differences

Introduction

Assertiveness is about open communication, and is a language of respect and inclusivity. Building assertive relationships in which people can be open and honest with each other, freely sharing their ideas and developing each other's ideas without fear or prejudice, is key to business success. Through working together, and connecting with each other, people get better results and are more creative. Providing forums in which people can be supported in being open and honest with each other is empowering. People are recognized for who they are, and are able to bring their "best selves" to their work and the overall success of the business.

Assertive relationships are those in which everyone feels respected and recognized for their multicultural differences. The more diverse the make-up of a group, team, or network, the more opportunity there is for developing assertive and inclusive relationships. Through working with each other people increase not only their self-awareness, but also their awareness and understanding of each other.

It is only when people feel safe enough to be themselves, to know that they can take risks, and make mistakes without fear, that people are able to be assertive. Safety is developed through people interacting with and understanding each other, in particular understanding their multicultural differences and similarities. Being willing to give and receive feedback is key to raising awareness and learning together. This requires people having the courage to "speak their truth," in other words to share their experiences of what it is like to be who they are. Organizations committed to developing assertive relationships and to full inclusivity provide opportunities for people to engage with each other, to learn about their differences from each other in a supportive environment.

This chapter wonderfully illustrates through the case study the importance of organizational commitment to working with multicultural differences, and of open communication, and offers a number of ways of facilitating diversity and inclusivity.

Case study: Diversity and inclusion

Lynne Fisher, former managing director, diversity and talent management, for the Corporate and Investment Bank of Citigroup in Europe, Middle East, and Africa (EMEA) describes how diversity and inclusion have become a way of doing business at Citigroup and how Citigroup has become a champion for diversity and inclusion. Anouschka Elliott, CFA and vice president, global banking, describes how the firm is committed to recruiting people from diverse backgrounds, and also the rapid growth and evolution of the "Empower Hour" at Citigroup.

In 2000 a forward-thinking and visionary leader of the Fixed Income Division at Citigroup requested diversity and equality awareness training for his division. He had noticed that women and minority groups were not progressing in the business as fast as men. In the same year Lynne Fisher, supported by the same business leader, organized a European Women's Conference for the 90 most senior women in the business.

At this conference a set of recommendations were made, including the setting up of a London Office of the Diversity Function. Lynne stepped into this role and was able to build on her success of implementing the awareness training and the European Women's Conference. Lynne firmly believes that for diversity and inclusion truly to be embraced, it has to be business-led. This is certainly the case in Citigroup, where diversity is seen as central to business success, as well as key to achieving the goal of Citigroup to be the most respected global financial services company.

In her new role, Lynne initiated a diversity program which started with five "breakthrough" teams made up of ten individuals from across the business with diverse and varied backgrounds. All of the teams had a mix of women and men, ethnic backgrounds, businesses, and countries. Four out of the five team leaders were women. Each team had a senior sponsor whose role was to guide, lead, and coach the teams and their leaders. The five teams each had a goal to move the diversity agenda forward in one of five areas:

- recruitment of women
- retention of women
- career development of women
- work–life balance, including sabbaticals
- respect and inclusion in the workplace.

These teams were known as "100 day task teams," since the teams were given 100 days—three months—in which to set a goal and deliver results by way of implementing diversity in their area.

During the initial three-month period external consultants were brought in to help facilitate breakthrough thinking as a methodology in all the teams. Key to breakthrough thinking is picking indicators of success that can be shown in a short period, and looking for opportunities to experiment that don't need to draw on more resources. All the teams were successful and the way of working was also hugely successful, so much so that the methodology has now become the way things are done within Citigroup beyond just the diversity agenda. The diverse make-up of the teams and the positive leadership demonstrates that diversity works, promotes creativity and breakthrough thinking, and provides cross-business networking opportunities.

The team focusing on respect and inclusion in the work place developed a respect index which was used to survey the attitudes and behaviors associated with respect of two different business groups. The same groups were surveyed twice using the respect index. The index encouraged people to think about the extent to which their own behavior towards others was respectful and inclusive, and how they perceived others' behavior towards them in terms of respect and inclusion. Throughout the company, people's behavior has become more inclusive and respectful of each other.

In 2002, following the success of the 100 day task teams, Citigroup Difference was formed, providing a background framework for diversity within Citigroup in EMEA. Citigroup Difference is made up of a Senior Diversity Committee led jointly by a senior business head and Lynne Fisher. Since its formation four employee networks have been formed within Citigroup Difference, each with a different focus:

- Citigroup Women—focus on gender
- Citigroup Roots—focus on race and cultural diversity
- Citigroup Pride—focus on sexual orientation
- Citigroup Parents—focus on family and work–life balance.

Each of the four networks has a business sponsor, a core steering group of between 10 and 12 people, and is co-chaired by two people who lead the group. These groups report to the Senior Diversity Committee. The four groups are made up of as diverse a group of people as is possible, and each has a thriving membership of volunteers. All the groups focus on recruiting, retaining, and developing staff, and on ensuring that the groups of people they represent are respected, valued, and included.

Citigroup Parents has the largest membership, with over 1000 members (2005). The group organizes and runs sessions for parents every two weeks on a range of topics that are of interest and useful to working parents: for example, managing the teenage years, choosing a nanny, nutrition, choosing a school, and elder care. The sessions acknowledge that people lead hugely busy working lives and are at the same time dealing with issues outside of work that are important and demanding of their time and attention. The Citigroup Parents members can also ask questions and share information with each other on the web.

In 2002 the Diversity Office formed a team that created the "Empower Hour," which takes place in the middle of the day and to which people can take their lunch while being inspired, motivated, and energized through discussions on a wide range of topics by internal and external speakers. Internal speakers are usually from within the senior management team, who are fully committed to the Empower Hour.

In early 2004 following the huge success of the Empower Hour for women, both in learning from the speaker and in networking with each other, it was decided to move the Empower Hour from the Citigroup Women employee network to the Citigroup Difference overall diversity group, and to open it up to men. All the sessions are highly interactive and are attended by between 70 and 100 people.

The Empower Hour happens twice a month, and speakers are invited to talk about their careers focusing on one of the core themes:

- assertiveness
- leadership
- communication.

The format is flexible. However, typically speakers talk for 45 minutes and are then open to questions. Following the hour they are available for further conversations.

Having such senior internal speakers sends a powerful and positive message that personal and career development is important to

Citigroup. Empower Hour provides an informal opportunity to network and to learn from senior people about their career development.

(Anouschka Elliott, interview, 2005)

At the end of every Empower Hour attendees are asked to complete a feedback form. This helps the Empower Hour Team determine the theme and goals for the next year. The theme in 2004 was Achievement and Development; in 2005 Getting Empowered and in 2006 Influence and Impact. The key measure of the success of the Empower Hour is the number and mix of people attending the sessions.

The Empower Hour Team is made up of eight people, all of whom volunteer for one year and are then able to continue for a further year. The team seek to reflect the diversity within the bank by having members from across the business and a gender mix.

The team has had a lot of interest from Citigroup employees in other countries who would like to be able to listen to the Empower Hour via a conference call line. The Empower Hour Team have declined these requests in order to keep the spirit of the Empower Hour confidential and informal. It has encouraged others to create their own Empower Hour. Anouschka Elliott comments, "It is vital that the Empower Hour is driven from within. The employee networks in the UK have progressed because of people taking ownership for them. We have a real interest in empowering people to move forward" (Anouschka Elliott, interview, 2005).

In 2003 a subcommittee of Citigroup Women focused on recruitment, in particular the recruitment of pre-university students, and designed a number of activities to attract young people. The pilot involved an open day for 30 girls from five targeted schools. The program has subsequently been run on an annual basis.

The majority of the girls who attended the pilot had no knowledge of the banking world, and the day helped demystify banking and gave them an opportunity to ask questions and to think about banking as an option for them. It was extremely valuable in opening the choice of banking as a career.

(Anouschka Elliott, interview, 2005)

While Citigroup Women's initial focus was on gender within Citigroup, and on women in particular, by 2004 the group's focus had also turned outwards towards women in the wider community. The group decided to form a partnership with Camden Women's Aid, London, and to live and develop their values through partnering with this group of women. Women's Aid is a national voluntary organization that helps women and children who are being physically, emotionally, and sexually abused in their own homes, and campaigns for the right for everyone "to live in safety and to have a future without fear" (www.womensaid.org.uk).

Citigroup Pride focuses on sexual orientation, ensuring that lesbian, gay, bisexual, and transgender (LGBT) people are respected and included. Each group within Citigroup Pride has its own specific goals. The groups have worked with their HR partners to ensure that policies are respectful, and in particular that the language used in policies is inclusive of different sexual orientations. The group has also produced a booklet that explains the benefits available and reassures people that requests will be treated sensitively. Citigroup Pride as a group has used a number of techniques to help raise awareness of the different LGBT within the company, to further sensitivity not only to each other as employees but also to customers with different sexual orientations.

One of the techniques used, and found to be very successful in helping raising awareness and sensitivity to sexual orientation, has been "fishbowl" training. This involves a group of people from the Pride group sitting in a circle in the middle of the room, and an outer group of people sitting observing and listening while they talk about how it feels to be gay or lesbian in the organization. The groups then change over, and then form one large group to share their experience of what they have learnt about themselves and each other. The fishbowl has been used successfully to give lesbian and gay individuals an opportunity to be heard. This, like the breakthrough thinking methodology, is a technique that is used more and more in Citigroup for raising awareness of issues, increasing understanding and sensitivity towards people and difference.

Citigroup has become an employer of choice, financial service provider of choice, business partner of choice, and neighbor of choice, through living the values of diversity and inclusion in everything that it does. The company has experienced a huge culture change, and become a place where people are respected for who they are and what they do. People are promoted on merit; customers needs are met because employees understand and share their diverse background and differences; people want to do business with Citigroup because they know they will be respected and valued; and communities welcome working with Citigroup because of its involvement with and development of the communities.

CASE ANALYSIS: OPEN COMMUNICATION

In a survey into what constitutes an "employer of choice," "Open commu-nication" was found to be the highest-rated single factor—followed closely by 'See the results of my work" (WorkChoice Survey, 2005). Meeting employees expectations, based on the reputation of the company for open communication, is what Citigroup does, through ensuring that working together is extended not only to all employees, but to suppliers, customers, and the communities in which it operates globally.

Open communication is assertive communication, and it is a key factor in the success of all groups, teams, and businesses. Each of the employee networks has two chairs that co-chair the core steering group and lead the way forward. They receive coaching and mentoring on team leadership, which benefits not only the employee network but also the individual's team leadership development.

Open communication is central to employee engagement. Employees who feel engaged with the company and feel that the company is engaged with them are more motivated and productive, and have higher levels of commitment to the company. The employee networks at Citigroup facilitate employee engagement; likewise the Empower Hour sessions, use of the fishbowl technique and other forums for open discussion all help build employee engagement and open assertive communication.

The fishbowl technique gives people an opportunity to communicate openly about how they feel with people who belong to the same target or non-target group, to be heard by each other and the other group, and to listen to their experience of being in that group. The groups then change over and repeat the same process, finally meeting as a whole group. (For more on target and non-target groups, see Chapter 13, pages 125–31.)

The process of engagement between people is also one of becoming more engaged with oneself, through developing self-awareness at the same time as developing greater awareness of others. In this way the 'open window pane' of the Johari Window (see page 42) is enlarged through people sharing their experiences, being heard, and listening to others' experiences. With this awareness people can choose to change, to reflect on their attitudes and beliefs, while relating with more under-standing to each other.

Part V

Assertiveness and Diversity in Organizations

17 Making the Business Case for Diversity

Introduction

The business case for diversity and assertiveness is huge; people perform better and make a bigger contribution to the success of the business when they feel valued and respected for who they are and what they do. Diversity goes hand in hand with inclusivity and the building of assertive relationships. People who feel safe, and know that they can live and work without fear of discrimination and prejudice, feel more secure and confident in themselves. They are more likely to engage fully in their endeavors if they know that they will be respected for their contribution and the difference that they can make by truly being who they are. People need to feel respected, valued for their unique contribution, cared for, and to feel that what they do has meaning and purpose.

Embracing diversity is crucial for organizations if they wish to maximize the potential of their workforce in productivity, engagement, and commitment. Recognizing that diversity is about the way we do things with each other every day opens up possibilities for people to work together more effectively, leading to greater productivity.

In this chapter the key success factors of the business case for assertiveness and diversity are outlined. The case study highlights the business case for assertiveness and diversity in organizations, and the importance of committing to and celebrating diversity and inclusivity.

161

Key success factors for the business case for assertiveness and diversity

Engagement and commitment

The engagement and commitment of senior business leaders to diversity and inclusivity is one of the keys to the successful development of assertive relationships within organizations. Business leaders who demonstrate that they value difference and are inclusive in their approach inspire others to do the same. Communicating the engagement and commitment of business leaders to all employees is vital to the success of any diversity initiative or strategy.

Communication and education

Helping raise the awareness of employees to issues of diversity through education and the provision of opportunity for reflection and discussion about differences, including prejudices, helps people better understand each other. Through communication and education people are helped to make connections with each other, and at the same time to raise their self-awareness and to be more connected. Through developing strong connections people are helped to release their creative energy and to work together more effectively.

Dialog and celebration of success

Feedback on how people feel and think about diversity, their experience of being included, valued, and respected for who they are, is vital to the success of any organization. Only through feedback can issues be addressed and people learn from their experiences. Rewarding and celebrating business success that is directly linked to "bringing people in" from different backgrounds demonstrates both internally and externally that "diversity means business success."

In the following case study, Geoff Glover and Kamaljeet Jandu describe how Ford is driving "Unity in Diversity" through a belief in the business case for diversity, the development of assertive relationships, and an assertive global organization in which everyone is included and valued for their difference.

Case study: Driving diversity

Ford believes that diversity and "Unity in Diversity" is the right thing to do—that there is a strong moral case for valuing and celebrating difference, as well as the need for legal compliance and a compelling business case. Ford has identified six key factors that together ensure that "Diversity Works." They are:

- the business need
- diversity strategy
- leadership commitment
- organizational awareness and understanding
- organizational commitment
- impact evaluation.

The company culture at Ford recognizes that "Through difference there is additional strength"(Geoff Glover, former HR manager, Ford Southampton Assembly Plant: all quotes from interview, 2005). Progress on diversity-related issues was made part of the company's business plans at every level in 2000. All Ford Britain departments and plants have diversity councils comprising local managers, employees, and trade unionists, acting on equality and inclusivity in their teams. The changes effected have been recognized externally, making Ford Britain Business in the Community award winners in 2005 (highly commended for their holistic and inclusive approach to diversity) and 2006.

The business need

The strong business case at Ford for diversity and inclusivity is under-pinned by developing relationships that are engaging, that connect with and have impact on driving the diversity agenda forward in society as a whole. Table 17.1 gives the business case for diversity at Ford.

Geoff Glover comments, "Product quality has improved; the number of vehicles produced has increased, overall productivity has improved, and work practices have changed."

Diversity strategy

"Diversity at Ford is not simply a project but a way of life," says Kamaljeet Jandu, former diversity manager, Ford Britain (email, 2005). Ford's diversity strategy is fully supported by the Diversity Council, a group made up

---

Table 17.1 The business case for diversity at Ford

■ Engaging and connecting with an evolving customer base: people buy products from a company with they can identify with, that understands their needs, and exceeds their expectations.

■ Engaging and connecting with employees and prospective employees: people are attracted to a company that they know will treat them well, that will respect them for who they are, as well as valuing their competence and the skills that they bring. People are more likely to stay with a company in which there are opportunities for them to develop professionally and personally.

■ Engaging and connecting with company success: people like to work for a company that is successful and in which they can feel confident of success in the market place. Ford is keen to involve all employees in that success, and for them to know that they are an integral part of corporate success.

■ Engaging and connecting with good corporate citizenship: people increasingly choose to buy from, invest in, and work for a company that is committed to diversity and inclusivity in everything that it does. Ford has a strong sense of responsibility towards the communities in which it operates and serves, and to driving the diversity agenda forward in society as a whole.

---

of three key stakeholders: trade unions (representing both the hourly paid and the salaried), line managers, and employees who neither have a line management position nor are members of a union. Membership is rotated, and the members are ambassadors for diversity within Ford. The four key elements to Ford of Britain's diversity strategy are:

■ Drive organizational diversity.
■ Unleash employee potential.
■ Raise company profile.
■ Broaden consumer base.

Leadership commitment

There is total commitment from the global senior leaders at Ford to diversity and inclusivity. All of them recognize that there is a strong business case for diversity making a difference to business success. The diversity strategy and vision is fully approved of and supported by the global senior leaders. As leaders of the business they are role models for diversity and inclusivity in everything that they do as people.

All senior leaders and managers have diversity-inclusivity performance objectives alongside their other performance objectives. This communicates a strong message to everyone that "Unity in Diversity" is a specific, measurable, achievable, realistic, and time-oriented (SMART) objective like any other key performance objective.

Ford as a company believes in celebrating difference, acknowledging and rewarding people who have contributed to business success and made a difference, through promoting a socially inclusive environment. Under the annual Chairman's Leadership Awards for Diversity (CLAD), employees are given an opportunity to nominate people at all levels of the company—individuals, groups, and teams—who have made a difference in six main categories:

- individual: most inspirational role model
- individual: making a difference
- team: most inspirational role models
- team: making a difference
- most inspirational employee and resource group
- most inspirational diversity council.

Organizational awareness and understanding

Key to the success of the strategy is communication, and raising organizational awareness and understanding of diversity and what it means for people. One of the innovative ways used by Ford Britain is theater. The play *The Challenge*, written and performed by the Garnett Foundation, wonderfully illustrates how people's fears, insecurities, hurts, losses, and lack of confidence get in the way of being able to engage and to enjoy assertive relationships with each other, and to work together.

The play vividly illustrates the impact and cost of exclusion, and the absolute imperative for inclusion, respect, and dignity. Following the performance the audience break into small discussion groups with members of the cast, to talk with each other about the impact on them of the play, and to relate it to their own experience, and what they can do as individuals and as a group to take responsibility for diversity and inclusivity in their lives.

The European magazine, *Diversity @ Ford, Valuing Difference, Creating Success*, is published quarterly and communicates to everyone within Ford that diversity is a business issue that Ford takes seriously. Communication is key to the success of helping people to increase their awareness of diversity and to take responsibility for their behavior and actions.

Ford helps raise awareness and understanding of diversity and inclusivity issues globally through linking up with other organizations, and its employees taking opportunities to speak at conferences, and sharing their experience of the "distance traveled"—and still to travel:

> Diversity and inclusivity are a journey. We have a come a long way, and we still have a way to go. Not everyone is on the same journey but there are enough people who are passionate about and committed to where we are going to drive diversity forward.

(Geoff Glover)

Organizational commitment

As part of Ford's organizational commitment to diversity through inclusivity, the company seeks to meet all employees' expectations and needs:

> Diversity involves each and every one of our Ford employees, dealership staff and customers. It is about engaging people on an individual basis, treating them with the respect and dignity we all deserve while, where appropriate, also understanding, meeting or exceeding their individual needs and expectations.

(www.ford.co.uk)

The "Dignity at Work" policy sets down standards of behavior, and these are communicated to all employees through training sessions. Training is also given to "Dignity at Work investigators." These are people whose role is to listen to complaints about transgressions of behavior, and to handle the complaint in a respectful way, modeling the Dignity at Work policy behaviors.

Policies and procedures are regularly reviewed. A Diversity Master Schedule is created annually using a business process with which people are familiar for setting targets and monitoring progress on key business issues, such as quality, safety, and cost. The current situation is analyzed and the desired situation is defined. Actions are then discussed and agreed on how to realize the targets, and people are given the responsibility and accountability for delivering these actions. Again this sends a clear message to everyone within the company that "Unity in Diversity" is as vital to the success of Ford as any other aspect of their business.

Ford of Britain also has a process tool in place, the Diversity Equality Assessment Review (DEAR), which is used by Operations to measure progress in diversity in six areas: policy planning, selection, developing and retaining staff, corporate image, corporate citizenship, and auditing.

Ford is committed to the learning and development of not only its employees, but also their families and the communities in which it operates all over the world. The recognition of people's learning and development needs as whole people—physical, intellectual, emotional, and spiritual—and extending this to their families and communities sends a powerful message that they are valued and respected.

One example of this is in the United Kingdom, where through "learn direct status"—online learning—people (employees, their families, and members of the community) are able to learn and develop interests in areas that are not computer-linked, while those wishing to learn more computer-based skills can do so through the UK Online Centre. Some computers have been modified so that people with disabilities can use them. Others may wish to improve their literacy and other essential skills, and are assigned to a learning program to assist them in developing more confidence and competence in these skills areas.

Commitment to employees as "whole" people includes running campaigns that address general, specific, and topical physical issues and concerns. For example in the United Kingdom, one campaign highlighted the importance of sun protection. Other campaigns include encouraging people to exercise and eat a well-balanced diet.

The provision of access to an employee assistance program (EAP) provided by ICAS (see Chapter 20) and of flexible working practices acknowledges that people have different needs at different times in their working lives.

At Ford people's different spiritual paths are acknowledged and respected in a number of different ways, including the provision of facilities for prayers and a multi-faith employee group which represents all the different religions and faiths. This communicates to people that they are valued, and that their values and beliefs matter to the organization, and importantly that different religions and faiths can and do live side by side in people's lives.

Impact evaluation

Perceptions are key. Ford regularly undertakes "perception surveys" to assess the impact of the Diversity Strategy and Vision within the company, and to find out what matters to employees on issues of diversity, inclusion, equality, and work–life balance. The perceptions of employees are key to how the company is perceived by people outside the organization, locally, nationally, and globally. The majority of employees within Ford believe that diversity matters, and that they have a role in making diversity and inclusivity happen.

The diversity message is communicated to all the companies with which Ford operates—this includes suppliers, agencies, and dealerships. People know what to expect from Ford by way of behavior. They can expect to be treated with respect, to be listened and responded to, communicated with, and involved in the processes.

CASE ANALYSIS: COMMITMENT AND ACKNOWLEDGMENT

The approach to diversity at Ford is inclusive. It seeks to ensure that everyone is valued for who they are, and is treated with dignity and respect. Ford's commitment to its employees is underpinned by a commitment to diversity and inclusivity based on a commitment to them as "whole people." The "Unity in Diversity" mission is for everyone in the company to feel valued and respected, and to know that they can make a difference to the company by way of their contribution to and participation in the success of Ford. Ford wants people to give of their creativity, to share their ideas with each other, and to commit to the company.

Ford's acknowledgement and commitment to diversity and inclusivity by rewarding and celebrating people who make a difference to "Unity in Diversity" is vital and instrumental in creating a culture in which difference is celebrated and people can be their "best selves."

18 Meeting the Work-Life Balance Needs of Employees

Introduction

Giving people choice over how and when they do their best work is an important part of developing assertive relationships and assertive organizations, and of respecting difference. People have different demands and commitments during their lives, and being recognized as a whole person with commitments and responsibilities inside and outside of work makes a huge difference to people.

There is growing recognition within organizations that, for people to give of their best, they need to be given opportunities to manage their lives and work differently and more effectively. One of the ways in which organizations demonstrate their commitment is by offering people flexible working arrangements that help them manage their home and work lives more effectively.

In this chapter flexible working practices are explored in relation to finding out about and meeting employees' work–life balance needs, the importance of developing assertive relationships in which people can negotiate their needs successfully, and of educating people about the benefits of flexible working. The case study powerfully illustrates how meeting the work–life balance needs of employees helps develop assertive relationships and impacts on greater productivity and overall business success.

Flexible working practices

Flexible working refers to a range of working practices, some of which are full-time and others part-time. They allow employees an opportunity to take responsibility for managing and integrating their working lives with their personal, family, and social lives. They include:

- part-time working
- flexitime
- compressed working hours
- term time working
- working from home
- job sharing.

Identifying work–life balance needs

Finding out what people's work–life balance needs are, and responding to them, demonstrates to employees that the organization is committed to, and understanding of, them as whole people. Employee surveys, face-to-face interviews, discussion groups, and focus groups are methods of seeking feedback that give people an opportunity to share their experiences and needs. Discussion groups and focus groups facilitate the development of assertive relationships by encouraging people to be open with each other as well as to understand and respect each other's differences. Responding and acting upon the feedback is vital to the feedback process, and can lead to organizational culture change.

Assertive relationships underpin the success of flexible working

The success of flexible working and work–life balance programs depends very much on the relationship between employees and their line managers, the area in which they work, and the extent to which their organizational culture supports and encourages diversity.

> Having a manager who is prepared to be supportive, who sets the tone and has thought through the benefits and challenges of flexible working, and who is prepared to say "Yes" or "No" according to the needs of the business is key to the success of flexible working.
>
> (Sarah Bond, head of diversity, KPMG, interview, 2005)

The relationship between full-time employees and those working flexibly is crucial, and requires understanding and a willingness to work together and to communicate fully—and regularly—with each other. To work in partnership with each other is necessary for flexible working to work. This means that people need to develop assertive, I'm OK: You're OK, relationships with each other, in which they can be open and honest, and in which there is a high level of trust. They must sort out issues and concerns as they go along, deal with any conflicts as and when they arise, as well as negotiate ways of making flexible working work for everyone.

Educating people about flexible working

Many employees feel somewhat apprehensive when it comes to requesting flexible working. This can be for a number of reasons, but one main reason is that they fear being seen as less committed to their work and/or fear that they will not be considered for promotion. Organizations have a responsibility to make clear flexible working options available, and to provide training and development for line managers and employees in how flexible working can work for them.

Fear on behalf of both employees and line managers is usually what gets in the way. This can be fear of change and that the new way of working might fail. Giving people time and opportunity to voice their fears and concerns, and looking together at ways of making the flexible working arrangement work, are important steps in any work–life balance program. Focus groups which facilitate open discussion between those who work full-time and those who work a flexible working option help people to share their experiences—positive and negative—and together to look for ways of working together more effectively and with more understanding.

> Managing flexible working can seem difficult at first but in practice a lot of people are already out of the office a lot of the time—for example seeing clients. People manage and can be managed whether they are seeing clients or working from home.
>
> (Sarah Bond, interview, 2005)

In 2005 KPMG formed a network of "flexible working champions" to further support people in understanding flexible working as an option. These were people managers who were already excellent at managing people, and who were well placed to champion flexible working. They receive training and support in managing flexible working, and share best practice across the firm.

The costs of not paying attention to work–life balance needs

The costs to organizations of not paying attention to the work–life balance needs of employees are huge, impacting on the overall productivity and success of the organization. "With parents acknowledging that family unfriendly conditions like long hours negatively effect their morale and productivity, organizations may wish to examine the business case for work–life balance measures" (Swan and Cooper, 2005: 26).

Employees who work longer and longer hours are less able to take care of their physical, emotional, intellectual, and spiritual well-being. They have less time to enjoy personal space and relationships outside of work; less time to exercise and eat well, less time to really be true to who they are. Many people feel that they rush from one thing to the next thing without pause. People who are rushing often find it difficult to slow down, and to connect with what they need—physically, emotionally, intellectually, and spiritually. They become disconnected from themselves and from others.

> Long hours on the job are making us unproductive, error-prone, unhappy and ill. Doctors' offices are swamped with people suffering from conditions brought on by stress: insomnia, migraines, hypertension, asthma and gastrointestinal trouble, to name but a few. The current work culture is undermining our mental health.
>
> (Honoré, 2004: 5)

The long hours culture impacts hugely on people's work–life balance, and can be excluding of people. This may be because they have responsibilities outside work that make it impossible for them to work full-time, let alone take on overtime. The diversity of the organization is affected, as those with responsibilities of caring for others are excluded from jobs that are associated with long hours and large amounts of traveling.

The benefits of paying attention to work–life balance needs

The benefits for both employees and their organization of encouraging flexible working are huge. People who feel valued and respected for who they are and what they do feel more positive about themselves and their organization. They are more likely to perform better, give more of themselves, and put more energy into their work. They are less likely to suffer from stress and stress-related illnesses, as they are living the life they choose and doing the job that they really want to do for an organization that values them. When people are encouraged to look after themselves physically, intellectually, emotionally, and spiritually, and are given time and recognition for doing so, they are more productive and creative.

In the case study that follows, Chris Ward, commercial director of MSN UK, the online media business of Microsoft, describes how Microsoft has met the work–life balance needs of its employees and promoted not only greater diversity and inclusivity, but also greater productivity at MSN.

Case study: Work–life balance

At Microsoft, we know that our people are our most important asset. We encourage them to create the most comfortable work–life balance for them. Providing services and facilities that help people combine and carry out their commitments—both at work and at home.

(www.microsoft.com, 2005)

Microsoft as a company—of which MSN is part—wants to be the best employer in the world, and is committed to finding out what the needs are of its employees, to meeting them, and to addressing any problems and putting them right. Reputation is key to the company. Chris Ward says, "We have built a reputation as a great employer. We recruit fast, and we are attracting talent because we are a great place to work" (interview, 2005). Across the company an annual employee survey gives people the opportunity to give open and honest feedback on what they want more of, less of, and would like to the company to do differently.

"Without feedback we wouldn't have identified the problem [of work–life balance]," Chris Ward says (interview, 2005). Feedback in 2001 showed that staff were hugely committed but felt that the company was not recognizing the high levels of stress and pressure that they were under. In particular people felt that there was a lack of recognition of their lives outside the working environment. As a result of the feedback Microsoft invested in and hired a consultant, Suzy Black, in 2002 to work with a group of 10–12 people across the business to pilot a wide range of flexible working options that would recognize and meet people's need for a more balanced life. People volunteered for the different flexible working options. Productivity was measured, and feedback on performance was collected from managers and customers over a period of two months.

The pilot was hugely successful, with both performance and productivity increasing in relation to people managing their lives in a way that worked for them and their particular circumstances. Research carried out at the end of the pilot revealed that:

- 81 percent of employees feel they provide a better service and can better meet business objectives as a result of flexible working
- 61 percent have learnt more efficient working practices
- 84 percent report feeling more relaxed at home.

From this a flexible working policy was developed and a work–life balance program made available to all employees. The success of this program has been widely recognized. MSN UK was awarded the "Innovation Employer of the Year" award by Working Families in 2004. The scheme is used as a global best practice throughout Microsoft, and MSN UK has evangelized the benefits to many major UK companies.

Workshops enabled people to share their experience of working a flexible option, and those working alongside them, and those managing people who were working flexibly to share their experiences—in particular what was working well for them, less well, and what they would like to do differently to make it work better—for them, the team, and for productivity. "Providing people with the opportunity to share their experiences has helped build the program into everybody's everyday life," (Chris Ward, interview, 2005).

The work–life balance program has challenged and transformed the culture at MSN and Microsoft, which had been based very much on "presenteeism"—that employees had to be "seen to be doing," and that if they were not seen around they were not being productive. Through the work–life balance program, the workshops and the support of senior management, people realized that it was possible to work more effectively when they were living more balanced lives, and choosing when, for them, was their most effective time to be productive. Learning to trust each other has been a vital part in the shift in culture and the acceptance of flexible working within Microsoft.

The success of the work–life balance program is that it has been built from the bottom up with the full support of senior management.

(Chris Ward, interview, 2005)

Employees have been further enabled to work from home through the latest technology that is available to them:

- the fastest broadband connection and wireless at work, and at home should they require it, all funded by MSN
- the latest mobile devices and smart phones to enable effective mobile working
- the latest software from Microsoft (www.microsoft.com, 2005).

Within MSN UK, 80 percent of the people work flexible working hours—a figure that is consistent throughout all departments, including sales, product development, and marketing. Chris Ward describes his own working hours: "I start at 09.30, which gives me a chance to get my children ready for school, and sometimes to take them to school, which is very important for me" (interview, 2005).

People who choose work flexible hours feel that Microsoft respects them as a whole person, with commitments inside and outside work. They feel that their values, what matters to them, are recognized and respected by the company, and they are seen as whole people who live full and committed lives. Likewise those people who do not choose to work flexible hours feel respected for their choices and commitments. The work–life balance program works for everyone: for individuals, the teams within which they work, the business, shareholders, and customers—many of whom are involved and interested in the work–life program.

> Greater diversity through people working flexibly is good for retaining people, good for attracting new people, and good for commercial business—our productivity has improved.
>
> (Chris Ward, interview, 2005)

Crucially the work–life balance program has not only had a positive impact on staff, it has helped drive commercial success too. The introduction of the program coincided with a record breaking financial year in 2003–04 for MSN UK.

> Our commitment to achieving meaningful work–life balance for our staff is not just about creating healthy people, it's about creating a healthy business. Our staff morale, productivity and talent retention increased as a result of flexible working, all in a year when we grew revenues by 150%.
>
> (Gillian Kent, managing director, MSN UK, email, 2005)

CASE ANALYSIS: COMMITMENT TO PEOPLE

People feel proud to work at MSN. They are committed to making the business a success, and committed to each other as people working together to create both a healthy work–life balance and outstanding performance—to be the best in terms of both people and performance. Reputation matters at MSN, and having the reputation as a company that supports work–life balance while achieving great results is important to MSN for attracting, retaining, and developing people.

Feedback is key to the success of the MSN work–life balance program: feedback by way of people and performance. A combination of feedback from employees and commitment from senior leaders in the business to responding to the feedback led to the huge changes around work–life balance, and to a culture change—to a different way of doing things.

The feedback that people gave to each other early in the pilot groups helped the company develop a work–life balance program that has changed attitudes towards flexible working. Feedback in the form of year-on-year results showed that the company has become fitter and healthier, as have its employees.

Employees at MSN feel respected and trusted. They are empowered to work in the way that best suits them and to give of their best. Giving people responsibility for and choice of when they work has made it possible for people to both live their lives more fully and be more fully present in their work. People feel confident, and feel that they have the confidence of their colleagues to do a good job. They enjoy assertive relationships in which there is mutual trust and respect, and a recognition that they know how best to live and lead their lives.

19

Corporate Ombuds

Introduction

In this chapter the Corporate Ombuds is described, and in particular how the provision of it complements other channels of communication and services for employees. The Corporate Ombuds facilitates the development of an assertive relationship between employees and the organization, one in which there is opportunity for employees to be open and honest about work-related concerns that are impacting on their performance, and in some cases on other people's performance and that of the organization.

The case study illustrates how the Corporate Ombuds at a global technology company is an integral part of the organization's code of ethics, supporting assertiveness, honesty, and transparency at every level of the organization worldwide.

Corporate Ombuds

Most large organizations have channels of communication to which employees can turn when they have issues and are experiencing conflict. These channels of communication range in the United Kingdom from the person's line manager, through Human Resources (HR), to a trade union and employment tribunals. Some international organizations have a Corporate Ombuds, also known as a Corporate Ombudsman, who offers an informal, neutral, and confidential channel of communication to all employees. The term "Ombudsman" originates from the Swedish, meaning "representative," and is a person whose role is independent of the establishment.

A Corporate Ombuds complements the more formal channels of communication in that discussion is informal and "off the record."

Formal and informal channels of communication for managing issues

Employees are typically encouraged to manage issues with their line manager, and if this cannot be achieved then a member of the HR or Personnel team will become involved. When the issue is between employees and their line manager, employees will usually approach a designated member of the HR team. There are, however, occasions when people for a variety of reasons would prefer not to involve HR, and look for a less formal route. Table 19.1 shows the kinds of issues that people may take to the Corporate Ombuds.

The Corporate Ombuds complements other channels of communication. It does not replace any of the other resources or services that employees have access to. For example, in organizations that offer employee assistance programs, personal issues will usually be addressed through workplace counseling (see Chapter 20). Table 19.2 highlights the differences and complementarities between HR and Corporate Ombuds.

The chief executive of an organization appoints Corporate Ombuds, and it is to her or him that they report, entirely independently of the

---

Table 19.1 Issues that people can take to the Corporate Ombuds

---

■ Interpersonal, for example:
  Conflicts between people that are impacting on their work performance and commitment, including alleged bullying and harassment.

■ Performance management, for example:
  People feel undervalued, discounted for their contribution, excluded from relevant meetings/discussions/information circles. They feel that their performance appraisal has been unfair/biased/poorly done, leading to demotivation and unhappiness.

■ Career development, for example:
  People feel unable to talk about career development concerns with their line manager or HR specialist for fear of being seen as unhappy.

■ Personal issues, for example:
  People are dealing with the break-up of a significant relationship, death of a close family member or friend, illness of a partner, child, or parent, which is impacting on their work performance.

Table 19.2 Differences and complementarities between Human Resources and Corporate Ombuds

Role and responsibility	Human Resources	Corporate Ombuds
Part of management structure	Yes	No, independent of management
Can provide true confidentiality and informality	No, usually need to file a complaint when made	Yes, with exception of potential suicide, harm to others including the organization
Neutrality	No, have to protect and represent interests of company	Yes, have no vested interest or agenda, neutral
Testifying in court	Yes	No, assert the Right of Privilege re confidentiality
Protect company	Yes, directly	Yes, indirectly by providing a resource for people to bring issues and concerns forward anonymously
Defend and advocate on behalf of management, conduct investigations	Yes	No
Record keeping and documentation	Yes	No, any notes taken are destroyed when relationship is closed
Interrelationship between HR and Ombuds	Can refer to and help Corporate Ombuds by providing information about other resources; changes in company policy and management actions that might be impacting on employees	Can refer to HR and assist HR's effectiveness by identifying key and emerging themes before they become huge problems

Source: inspired by and adapted from Bensinger et al. (nd).

line management structure. Structural and functional independence are critical for Corporate Ombuds to be able to perform their role and responsibilities with integrity, in particular to be impartial. The Corporate Ombuds is free from interference, control, and limitation by anyone in the organization with the exception of the chief executive. The form of reporting to the chief executive is usually in the form of "key findings" and "emerging themes," and any recommendations are based solely on a review of facts and the law. The key roles and responsibilities of the Corporate Ombuds are shown in Table 19.3.

Table 19.3 Key roles and responsibilities
of the Corporate Ombuds

- To provide independent, confidential, and informal help to users of the service by way of listening to their issues and exploring options available to them.

- To explore with users of the service the pros and cons of different options.

- To assist in reconciling conflicts; this may involve as well as listening and exploring options, exploring the option of mediation. Mediating can only happen when the user of the service has decided on this option and is willing to invite the other person/people involved in the conflict to mediate, and the other party is willing to be part of the mediation process.

- To help avoid recourse to formal grievance processes.

- To help users of the service to make sense of the organization's policies and procedures in relation to their issue/s.

- To refer users of the service to the appropriate resource or other service, for example, employee assistance program, medical center, Human Resources, and/or other issue resolution channels within the organization.

- To identify "emerging themes" that may impact on a whole department or the whole organization.

- To recommend creative ways of implementing system changes.

- To be a resource when policies and procedures are being reviewed, amended, or developed.

- To help identify any gaps between the stated goals and values of the organization and the actual policies and procedures.

- To ensure that the Corporate Ombuds is advertised widely within the organization.

Taking an assertive course of action through exploring options

Typically people arrive at the Corporate Ombuds feeling very "stuck" physically, intellectually, emotionally, and spiritually. They may be "stuck" in one particular feeling, for example of anger or fear, and are unable to think through their options. Indeed many people turn to the Corporate Ombuds feeling that their options are either "flight" or "fight," both of which are potentially I'm not OK: You're not OK, lose: lose courses of action. People who take the "flight" option lose their position and job, and the organization loses valuable and talented people. Those who take the "fight" position risk losing their position and job, and the organization its reputation and large sums of money. Faced with these options people can feel disempowered and unable to make any shifts in their thinking. The Corporate Ombuds, through listening, asking questions, and reflecting back to people what she or he has heard, helps them to assess what truly matters to them, what it is that they most need and want, and how best to go about achieving this outcome. In some situations this might mean that people choose to take no action whatsoever; in others it may be that people feel empowered to have the necessary conversation, for example with their line manager.

Case study: Ethical principles and practices

In this case study Andrea Doane, manager issues communications, and Steven Cordery, Corporate Ombudsman, United Technologies Corporation (UTC), describe how having a clear code of ethics that encourages honesty and transparency as a way of doing business and behaving in all relationships is supported by having channels of communication in place that ensure the code of ethics is practiced.

UTC has a rich history of pioneering innovation, and its businesses are worldwide market leaders. In addition to developing cutting-edge technology and providing services to the building systems and aerospace industries, UTC has established a culture of corporate and social responsibility, of honesty and transparency in all that it does. Its business practices are governed not only by economic results, but also by social and environmental impacts. Both profitability and responsibility are pursued with discipline and focus:

> We do this with great products and product innovations and a relentless focus on productivity and cost reductions whilst at the same time

meeting high standards of corporate citizenship. Good companies can do both, and UTC does.

> (George David, chairman and chief executive officer,
> UTC, 2004 *Corporate Responsibility Report*)

UTC's commitment to corporate responsibility is expressed in the Corporate Principles which underpin the Code of Ethics that have guided the company since 1990. The fundamental values expressed in the Code of Ethics inform and influence UTC's business activities. In particular, the code provides leaders and their employees with a framework for decision making. The core values expressed in the code are an integral part of UTC's identity as a company. "Our ethics and principles help define our brand as a corporation," says Andrea Doane (interview, 2005).

When employees need to raise a concern, there are a number of communication channels available to them. They can contact a business practice officer (BPO), use the 'DIALOG' program or contact a Corporate Ombudsperson. Employees at all levels of the company are responsible and accountable for compliance with the code.

The Code of Ethics underpins the Standards of Conduct applied to all relationships as outlined in the UTC Corporate Principles (see Box 19.1).

BOX 19.1 UTC CORPORATE PRINCIPLES

UTC is committed to the highest standards of ethics and business conduct. This encompasses our relationship with our customers, our suppliers, our shareowners, our competitors, the communities in which we operate, and with each other as employees at every organizational level.

Source: www.utc.com, 2005

The UTC Code of Ethics goes above and beyond legal compliance, sets standards higher than international law, and is published in 29 different languages (2005). In addition to enforcing compliance, it also requires integrity, fair dealing, and avoiding conflicts of interest. It is reproduced in Box 19.2.

BOX 19.2 UTC CODE OF ETHICS

Our Customers

We are committed to providing high quality and value, fair prices and honest transactions to those who use our products and services. We will deal both lawfully and ethically with all our customers.

Our Employees

We are committed to treating one another fairly and to maintaining employment practices based on equal opportunity for all employees. We will respect each other's privacy and treat each other with dignity and respect irrespective of age, race, color, sex, religion or nationality. We are committed to providing safe and healthy working conditions and an atmosphere of open communication for all our employees.

Our Suppliers

We are committed to dealing fairly with our suppliers. We will emphasize fair competition, without discrimination or deception, in a manner consistent with long-lasting business relationships.

Our Shareowners

We are committed to providing a superior return to our shareowners and to protecting and improving the value of their investment through the prudent utilization of corporate resources and by observing the highest standards of legal and ethical conduct in all our business dealings.

Our Competitors

We are committed to competing vigorously and fairly for business and to basing our efforts solely on the merits of our competitive offerings.

Our Communities

We are committed to being a responsible corporate citizen of the world-wide communities in which we reside. We will abide by all national and local laws, and we will strive to improve the well-being of our communities through the encouragement of employee participation in civil affairs and through corporate philanthropy.

Source: www.utc.com 2005

Business Practices program

The Code of Ethics is supported through UTC's Business Practices program, which reinforces ethical standards in corporate policy, training, assessments, and investigations. Business practice officers (BPOs) implement UTC's Corporate Principles worldwide. They:

- offer perspectives on cultural differences by region in order to reconcile any conflict between the code and local custom
- provide appropriate direction and support for employees in all locations. investigate allegations
- conduct training
- facilitate communication.

If any breach in the Code arises, the DIALOG program and Corporate Ombuds service offer employees a secure channel of communication to voice their concerns.

The DIALOG program

In 1986, UTC created its confidential DIALOG program, a two-way written communication channel. Although open communication is encouraged among all employees, certain situations require a degree of discretion. For these circumstances, the DIALOG program is an alternative outlet for employees to anonymously ask questions, raise concerns, make suggestions, register complaints, and report any suspected wrongdoing within the company. Employees can submit confidential reports, which are processed by one of the DIALOG program administrators (DPAs) worldwide.

The DIALOG program is carefully administered by the DPAs through two main communication channels, paper and electronically. Paper forms are available for employees to submit to a confidential address. Since 2003, employees can also use eDIALOG, an encrypted secure website which guarantees confidentiality. Upon the submission of an enquiry the DPAs ensure that employees cannot be identified by senior management, and edit information on reports accordingly. For example employees might have given particular information about themselves in their original enquiry that could potentially mean that they were identifiable—such as time with the organization and department in which they work. The DPA takes this information out of the message without detracting from the importance of the issue being raised, or the question being asked. Once confidentiality is established, inquiries are sent to senior management and responses are reported back within 14 calendar days.

DPAs have a key role in ensuring that written communication between employees and senior management is concise and respectful. They are also trained to contact the Ombuds when an issue is complicated, unclear, or cannot be answered within the 14-day target response time. Employees can also contact Corporate Ombuds regarding legal issues at any time, either directly by telephone or through eDIALOG.

The Corporate Ombuds

The Corporate Ombuds oversee the entire Ombuds/DIALOG program on a full-time basis, and represent three geographical areas: Asia Pacific; the Americas; and Europe, the Middle East, and Africa. The goal of the Corporate Ombuds is to create an open atmosphere for employees, and also help the company meet expectations of external stakeholders, customers, and communities in which UTC operates with regard to the Corporate Principles and Code of Ethics.

> Gaining trust as a Corporate Ombuds is important. People sometimes check out the level of trust by raising a smaller issue, they try and test out the system. Once they have done this, and understood how the system works and that it can be trusted, any fears that they might have had are allayed, they raise the more serious issue.
>
> (Steven Cordery, interview, 2005)

Since the establishment of the program, it has fielded more than 60,000 DIALOG employee inquiries and handled more than 10,000 Ombuds cases (2006). Each report is carefully reviewed; management often enacts policy change as a result of employee input. Since 1998, 42 percent of issues brought to the Ombuds/DIALOG program have resulted in change, 36 percent were reviewed without a change, and 22 percent of issues raised did not request change.

CASE ANALYSIS: SUPPORTING HONESTY AND TRANSPARENCY

At UTC, everyone is responsible for ethics and compliance, as outlined in the Code of Ethics. All employees are trained to interpret the code, and are encouraged to implement its principles in the workplace. Through training in "living the Code of Ethics" and giving employees the responsibility to apply the code in their relationships with colleagues, suppliers, customers, and communities, UTC has created an assertive organizational culture in which honesty and transparency are the governing principles.

The provision of the Ombuds/DIALOG program at UTC gives all employees who use the service an opportunity to be heard—to be given recognition—and to reflect upon the impact of their own behavior, and the behavior of others. It offers people a safe and secure environment in which they can discuss openly and honestly their feelings and thoughts about their situation. Through a process of exploring their options people are helped to be really clear about possible courses of action, and to choose the one that is best for them and is supporting of their "best selves." People usually feel empowered through the combination of reflection and exploration to take a course of action that is assertive. While it may involve a hitherto unimagined option—such as talking directly with a line manager—many people choose to deal with issues differently and more directly.

20 Workplace Counseling

Introduction

Organizations have a range of communication channels and support services that are based on respecting people for who they are and what they do. Most of these services provide employees with an opportunity either to communicate with the organization about concerns and issues, or to discuss in confidence their personal issues with a professional counselor or advisor. The services are offered to employees on the premise that people need to communicate, to be listened and responded to, in order to be effective in their work performance and in working together. The provision of a counseling service is an acknowledgement by that the organization that people will, from time to time, experience problems that may impact on their effectiveness and indeed happiness at work. Organizations that acknowledge the "whole person"— employees' physical, intellectual, emotional, and spiritual well-being —recognize that people need help from time to time in order to be their "best selves."

In this chapter the development of workplace counseling and employee assistance programs (EAPs) is described; the costs of not providing these services are outlined, and the benefits of providing them to employees and their organizations are highlighted. The first of the two case studies illustrates how the provision of a worldwide EAP underpins the commitment of a global organization to employee safety—physical, emotional, intellectual, and spiritual. The second case study shows how short-term workplace counseling can help a person shift from a non-assertive to an assertive attitude and behavior, benefiting not only the employee but also those with whom she works.

187

The development of workplace counseling and employee assistance programs

The EAP model first evolved in the United States in the early 1940s in response to the post-Prohibition situation. Dr Michael Reddy, chair of ICAS, an EAP provider, describes the process as:

> essentially a *managed care* process (identification of need, assessment, referral and aftercare) built, via the supervisor, into the organisation's *performance management* processes, and supported by a climate of *government legislation* which favoured a treatment approach to drinking problems, including the provision of appropriate counselling.
>
> (Reddy, 1994: 60–78, original italics)

Over the years the EAP model has evolved and developed in response to the needs of organizations. However the primary purpose remains that of offering employees a support service, available when they need it, to help with personal issues and concerns that may adversely impact on their work performance. In this way an EAP is different from, and complements, a Corporate Ombuds, which offers employees a channel of communication in which they can primarily explore work-related issues and concerns that are adversely impacting on their effectiveness at work (see Chapter 19).

An EAP is usually set up and paid for by the organization, for employees and their closest family members, offering them a confidential counseling and advice service that is accessible by telephone 365 days a year and 24 hours a day. Users of the service are also offered face-to-face short-term counseling.

The success of an EAP depends very much on the organization working in partnership with the EAP provider, as is illustrated in the first case study. How the EAP is perceived and the extent to which it is used by employees depends on how workplace counseling is viewed within the organizational culture, and that in turn is influenced by the national culture in which the counseling service is being offered. To encourage take-up of the service the EAP needs to be coordinated and advertised alongside other policies and practices that are concerned with supporting employees' physical, emotional, intellectual, and spiritual well-being.

There are a growing number of EAP professionals internal and external to organizations. The US EAP Alliance is a forum for all leading employee assistance professionals in the United States. In 2002 the

European Assistance Employee Forum (EAEF) was formed, and by 2005 there were over 60 employee assistance member professionals drawn from 23 countries.

The costs of not providing workplace counseling

In 2005 PPC Worldwide produced a Research Report, *Milestone or Millstone?*, looking into the kinds of personal issues and concerns that people experience as impacting negatively on their work performance. The report revealed that there are a number of life events that are difficult for people to manage alongside work. The most difficult for both women, and their partners, are miscarriage (95 percent) followed by the death of someone close (94 percent), serious illness (93 percent), and infertility problems (88 percent).

The findings show that reduced productivity as a result of a reduction in performance during difficult personal times costs business around £15 billion a year. Fifty percent of people felt that if they had been supported during these difficult personal times they would have coped much more effectively. Instead many people resort to supporting themselves through unhealthy eating, drinking more alcohol, and smoking more than usual. The consequences of this can include low self-esteem, absenteeism, sickness, lateness to work, mistakes, and the taking of unnecessary risks.

The research findings are in line with Working Families research into *Time, Health and the Family: What working families want* (Swan and Cooper, 2005: see page 10), in relation to coping with stress brought on by the lack of time to balance home life with work life.

The benefits of providing workplace counseling

EAPs provide employees with emotional support during difficult times, and help them to be able to continue to work effectively and safely while experiencing difficulties. The ability to deal with adversity helps people to feel more positive and assertive. In spite of a life event being so difficult, with support people know that they are able to manage themselves effectively. This in itself is a huge boost to self-confidence and relationships. It makes asking for help during difficult times an important strength, and gives the message to employees that there is strength in vulnerability. It is acceptable to ask for help, and better to do so during a difficult time before it becomes too difficult to manage. In this way EAPs have a preventive role. They encourage employees to use the service when they need it and not to discount a personal difficulty as being insignificant, since this can be the beginning of a downward negative spiral leading to greater personal difficulties.

Research into the effectiveness of workplace counseling strongly suggests that it "has a beneficial effect on psychological symptoms and well-being, and on sickness absence" (McLeod, 2001: 21). Further "evidence-based" research into people's attitudes towards work, in terms of satisfaction, productivity, and commitment, needs to be done in order to measure the effectiveness of workplace counseling at an organizational level. Nevertheless people's experience of workplace counseling would suggest that that there is a potential link between people feeling more empowered through the counseling and feeling more positive and committed in their work and to their organization.

In acknowledging that employees' personal difficulties matter and providing support to people during difficult times, organizations send a positive message to their employees that they are recognized as being more than their work. Through giving this kind of recognition people feel valued and respected for who they are by their organization. This helps in the developing of assertive organizations in which there is openness and trust, people are helped not only to "be themselves," but also to be their "best selves."

Case study 1: The employee assistance program

Thomas Spiers, employee assistance program manager, EMEA region, DuPont, describes the importance of workplace counseling in ensuring the safety of all employees.

DuPont has grown from being primarily an explosives company 200 years ago into a company that has focused for the past 100 years on delivering science-based solutions in all areas of people's lives.

The success of DuPont is the people:

> Their commitment to excellence, innovation and making the world a better and safer place is a key reason for our success.
>
> (www.dupont.com, 2005)

Given this, it is no surprise that the company offers employees a range of services to support them in their working lives. The EAP provided by ICAS in partnership with DuPont is designed to give employees more resources, and in particular to ensure safety. The DuPont culture is one of ensuring safety in all things and at all levels. The EAP service supports employees in taking better care of themselves emotionally as well as physically, intellectually, and spiritually.

People are more likely to take unnecessary risks when they are feeling negative about themselves, or when they are feeling stressed and distressed within themselves, and consequently take less care of safety for themselves and others. Thomas Spiers cites people working hurriedly, who are not really present in what they are doing: for example, putting up a ladder but not displaying the safety sign alerting others to what they are doing.

The EAP was first introduced to the company to support the safety of employees, and as a preventive measure, through providing people with a service that they can use when they are feeling unable to manage, stuck, stressed, and distressed. Since then it has been introduced and rolled out throughout the world. The utilization rate varies across the world. In Europe between 5 and 29 percent of employees use the service (2005), with between 28 and 29 percent of employees in Southern Europe making use of the telephone advice line, suggesting that people are more comfortable with non-face-to-face counseling and advice. In Northern Europe there is higher level of face-to-face counseling and advice, and a lower utilization rate. In Africa the EAP is, in the words of Thomas Spiers, a "stomping success," with high utilization rates. Employees in Central and Eastern Europe view their safety needs as being more physical than emotional, spiritual, or intellectual. They are concerned with feeling safe physically and with their need for physical security. The company aims to have an overall worldwide annual utilization rate of 12.4 percent (2005), while always pressing for higher utilization through advertising the program and educating people about what it can offer to them and their families. Apart from in Italy and Spain, where the service is available to employees' sons and daughters up to the age of 25, the service is available to children up to the age of 18 in the rest of the world.

The DuPont/ICAS counseling approach varies from country to country, depending to a certain extent on the training and background of the counselors and the national culture. For example, in the United States and the United Kingdom the approach is more integrative and humanistic than in Germany and Switzerland, where the training and background is more psychoanalytic. The principles however are the same: to provide employees with a service that enables them to access resources within themselves with which they can make a difference and make different choices.

It is an approach that is developing of self-esteem and assertiveness. Through the EAP people are encouraged and helped:

- to reflect on their experience, to tell their story, and to explore how they might address their issues and concerns
- to generate a range of different options including the possibility of feeling and thinking differently about their situation
- to make different choices and decisions based on exploring options
- to explore the resources that they have within themselves for moving towards their desired outcome
- to reflect on their beliefs and values about themselves, to look at those that are self-limiting which have led to rigid thinking and feeling about themselves and others
- to feel confident in their abilities to sort out difficult and challenging situations
- to feel comfortable about asking for help so that they can—with the help of another person—help themselves.

A key aspect of the change process is movement. Thomas Spiers, describes this as "A process of becoming more open and flexible, of having more resources to look at things differently and enabling people to see things for what they are" (interview, 2005). In line with the majority of providers, the DuPont/ICAS EAP offers employees an initial series of between six and eight sessions. Sometimes people require fewer sessions, sometimes more. For people who require more sessions the company is looking into being able to offer medium-term psychotherapy through the company's private insurance scheme.

CASE ANALYSIS: SUPPORTING CHANGE

The EAP at DuPont encourages people to consider that they have the solution for their situation within themselves, and that with help they can resource that solution and move forward. The approach is similar to that of existential time-limited therapy, which states that values and behaviors can become rigid and fixed but that, with help, people can become more flexible and open, embracing new ways of interpreting experiences that are more positive and beneficial to them. (See Chapter 2, page 19, for more on making positive shifts.)

The counseling helps people to make the shift in their thinking and feeling, to move towards a more flexible and less rigid position. The shift referred to by Thomas Spiers, from rigidity to openness, is both intra-personal and inter-personal. It is intra-personal in that people are supported in making changes to how they feel and think about themselves, to become more positive, assertive, and flexible. It is inter-personal in that people are better able to deal with conflict, and to make a shift towards the positive and upward spiral in their relationships with others. (See Chapter 6, page 60.)

The EAP at DuPont is a resource for people when they most need it to help them re-resource themselves, to develop positive self-esteem and assertive relationships in which there is open and honest communication.

Case study 2: Workplace counseling

This case study is based on the experience of a counselor working with a client. The names of the client and her colleague, and some of the details, have been changed, and the identity of the organization is not given, in order to ensure anonymity.

Jess came for short-term counseling wanting practical help on how to deal with a colleague, Susan, whose behavior she found aggressive and defensive. During the first session Jess disclosed that she also felt that at some level her colleague would make a better job of running the department than she, and described herself as "not being good enough." She felt that the best thing that could happen would be for one of them to leave. This "flight" response to a difficult situation was, she said, typical of her. At work she frequently felt unable to manage her feelings of low self-esteem, and would hide in the toilet until she was able to "pull herself together again."

As she talked about the working relationship with her colleague she looked away from the counselor, avoided eye contact with her and appeared to shrink into the chair, getting smaller and smaller. She spoke quietly, regularly ringing her hands, and readily bursting into tears, sobbing quietly to herself. The counselor explained to Jess that one of the ways in which they could work together would be for Jess to practice being more assertive with her in their working relationship during the counseling.

During subsequent sessions Jess talked more about her family, and the messages that she received in particular from her father, but also from her mother. The main message was "Be successful," and that only through being successful in exams would she and her siblings be deemed "good enough." She did not feel loved or valued for who she was as a person. She was never able to be "good enough" for her father, no matter how successful she was in her exams and at school. She never felt that she really belonged in her family, nor to herself.

Jess was very keen to change her behavior and to change her under-lying attitude about herself. She became aware of how frightened she was of conflict between people, in particular of others being angry with her. The memory of her father being angry with her for "not being good enough" permeated her whole being. She was able to see how this expe-rience, and the messages from her parents, had influenced how she was in the world.

Jess cowered from the possibility of conflict in relationships, making herself smaller—if she could have, she would have become invisible. She felt powerless in relationships, wanting to change, but at the same time fearing the consequences. She found her anger difficult to express; instead, she easily burst into tears, feeling hopeless, very small and child-like. She frequently compared herself with other people and found them to be better and more able.

Jess realized that the challenge she had to face was one of growing up, finding her own feet, and standing on her own feet. The counselor and Jess took some practical steps to help her to do this. This included Jess standing during one session, with both feet on the ground, breathing deeply and talking to the counselor about those things she really enjoyed doing. She was encouraged by the counselor to make eye contact with her as she spoke about the things that she enjoyed, and to express her pleasure using her hands. The counselor encouraged Jess to use "I" statements and to be aware of stepping into her own power as a woman.

In the penultimate session Jess practiced "stepping into her woman" in a role-play. In this role-play she "played" herself as "the woman I am today" and spoke to her "little girl" (in the form of a small chair with a cushion on it). Jess acknowledged the little girl's feelings, her fears and anxieties about not being good enough, admired her for her courage, and appreciated her for being a wonderful, playful, successful girl. She told her "little girl" that now she was going to be taken care of by Jess, the woman, and that she was now a mature and successful person, devel-oping more resources and enjoying relationships with others in which she was valued for who she was, and not solely for what she did. As a woman she said that her feelings were really important, and that she was learning ways of expressing them that were positive and constructive, in particular her angry feelings.

In the final session Jess focused on what "feeling OK" meant to her, and identified some positive self-affirmations that she would be able to use when she was feeling insecure in relationships and/or situations. These included:

I am a powerful and successful woman.
I have positive and creative relationships with my work colleagues.
I respect myself and others respect me.

She noticed that she no longer felt so angry with her parents, in particular her father, and realized that during the counseling she had made a shift in how she perceived her father. She understood that underlying his aggressive and defensive behavior was a very insecure man, full of fears both of failure and of success. Jess experienced a feeling of forgiveness towards her parents, and an acknowledgement that they had done the best they could with the resources that they had available to them at that time. This was the first time that she had felt some sense of separation from them, and a feeling of growing up and becoming who she really was.

Jess herself commented on how different she felt as she walked into the counseling room. She felt taller and more sure of her footing. She looked at the counselor and made appropriate eye contact at the beginning, during, and at the end of the session. She sat differently in the chair, more comfortably and with an open body posture. She had stopped ringing her hands, and used them much more to express what she was saying. Most importantly she recognized that she could choose how to interpret situations, and that she was responsible for her own choices of interpretation. She chose to see her working relationship with Susan much more positively and constructively; and saw that she had been given this gift by way of a challenge to be more assertive and creative in this relationship.

CASE ANALYSIS:
FROM NON-ASSERTIVE TO ASSERTIVE BEHAVIOR

Early on in life Jess made the decision that she was "not OK." The messages from her parents, particularly her father, were that in order to be "OK" she had to be successful in her accomplishments, and that she was "not OK" unless she achieved this. No matter how hard she tried, nor how well she did in school and in her exams, she was never going to be good enough for her parents. She internalized these messages and lived her life from this "not OK" life position. From this position she compared herself with others, and always found herself to be lacking in some way or other. Other people were better than her, more successful, and had a right to be themselves in a way that she had never experienced.

Her working relationship with Susan had become a symbiotic relationship in which Jess anticipated that Susan would put her down, ignore, and/or dismiss her. This had happened on a number of occasions in the working environment. The challenge for Jess was to look at her own life position of I'm not OK: You're OK in relation to Susan, and to make a shift from this position into the I'm OK: You're OK position.

She was helped to make this shift in a number of ways through the counseling, and to move from the passive life position to an assertive life position. She experimented during the counseling sessions with different ways of behaving verbally and non-verbally, and in ensuring that "what" she was saying was congruent with "how" she was expressing herself. The use of "I" statements had a profound impact on Jess. She stepped into herself, and most importantly for her, began to experience herself as a woman "in her own right" and not as the frightened and angry little girl.

As Jess made the shift from I'm not OK: You're OK into I'm OK: You're OK, so too did her relationship with Susan shift. In the "not OK" position she expected Susan to discount her and to put her down. At some level she invited Susan to discount her. The You're not OK discount confirmed Jess's negative self-limiting beliefs. In making the shift she invited Susan to join her in being I'm OK: You're OK, and to work things out together.

21 The Power of Assertive Relationships

Introduction

Assertive relationships have the power to transform people, and to create organizations that are truly inclusive and respecting of difference. They are relationships that are based on a high degree of self-respect, mutual respect, and regard for each other. Integrity, openness, and honesty are values that underpin assertive behavior. Those organizations that are committed to developing people and performance have clear values and beliefs that are translated into observable behaviors. People know what the values are and what is expected of them by way of behavior, and know what to expect from others. Indeed an increasing number of organizations include these observable behaviors in people's performance appraisals. The behaviors are for the most part based on how people manage themselves—physically, intellectually, emotionally, and spiritually—and how they manage and communicate in their relationships with others. The focus is on both what people do and on how they do it.

This chapter highlights the importance of having clear values that are understood by everyone in the organization, and the importance of developing assertive relationships for business success. The case study illustrates how through having a clearly communicated and understood set of values and beliefs people are empowered to develop assertive relationships and "do good business with each other."

Values and beliefs

Many organizations espouse values of integrity, openness and honesty, respect, and trust—the values that underpin assertive relationships. For

197

global organizations the values provide an important and central part of their identity, and give them a strong market presence. These values give the organization its edge, attracting and retaining employees, customers, partners, and shareholders.

The challenge for organizations is how to live the values day to day, and to appreciate that living these values through behaviors will be challenging for people. People need to feel supported, safe, and secure to be able to behave assertively, "to speak their truth." Equally people need to be responsible and accountable for their behaviors, to really take on board that they are responsible for their behaviors, thoughts, and feelings, and to recognize that they can make a difference through their own actions. Every interaction is an opportunity for people to live the values of the organization: for example, to "behave with integrity." This requires people to be aware of their individual power to make a difference, and to know that they have the power to influence the behavior of others through their own behavior.

Assertiveness is about people bringing their "best self" to everything that they do. To behave with integrity means bringing awareness of the four energies—physical, intellectual, emotional, and spiritual—to every situation, and to be "integrated." In order to build strong connections, strong relationships, with others, people need first to have a strong connection with themselves.

This applies equally to organizations. For organizations to be and do their "best" they need to operate with integrity in all that they do—to be connected internally in order to connect externally with the environments and communities within which they operate. They need to make explicit their values through clearly defined assertive behaviors, and to provide learning and development opportunities aligned to the values of the organization to help people be their "best selves." Organizations depend upon people being in relationship with each other; the more assertive these relationships, the greater the business success and the stronger the organizational identity.

Case study: Shared values and beliefs

This case study illustrates the importance of having clearly defined values, including that of integrity, and of developing assertive relationships. Neil Sherlock, KPMG partner, public affairs and vice-chairman, KPMG Foundation describes how the "Global Code of Conduct" has made a true difference to the way in which people think, feel, and behave within KPMG, the impact that this has had on perceptions internally and externally as well as on KPMG's excellent reputation in how it does business and conducts relationships.

KPMG is a global professional services company providing audit, tax, and advisory services to multinational companies. The KPMG Global Code of Conduct gives all employees and partners of member firms clear guidance as to what is expected of them by way of values and behavior, irrespective of their title or position with the company. The Global Code of Conduct is what gives KPMG member firms worldwide a shared identity, and communicates to clients, subcontractors, and the communities in which they operate a clear understanding of what they can expect from KPMG employees and partners.

At the heart of the KPMG Global Code of Conduct are the values that define "the KPMG Way," the core of which is referred to as "Performance with integrity." Table 21.1 lists the values as defined in the Global Code of Conduct.

The values and behaviors that are "the KPMG Way" embrace diversity, and make for an organizational culture that is inclusive of multicultural differences, and that enjoys assertive, open, and honest working relationships. People are respected for who they are and for what they do. They are supported in developing their knowledge base and skills, and encouraged to widen and deepen their experiences through working in different environments, and also through actively engaging with different communities.

The responsibility for performing with integrity, honoring the values

---

Table 21.1 KPMG Global Code of Conduct: Performance with integrity

- We lead by example.
- We work together.
- We respect the individual.
- We seek the facts and provide insight.
- We are open and honest in our communication.
- We are committed to our communities.
- Above all, we act with integrity.

Source: KPMG International, *KPMG Global Code of Conduct: Performance with integrity*, 2005 (online) www.kpmg.com

and behaviors, is that of each and every individual within KPMG. Senior management have the further responsibility of leading by example through being:

■ a role model to others
■ open and honest in their relationships
■ personally accountable for their own integrity shortcomings as well as those of the people they lead.

Everyone has a responsibility within KPMG to understand that respecting difference is key to people being able to be their "whole" selves at work. People who are able to be true to themselves at work have more energy and are able to give of themselves fully—bringing out the best not only in themselves but also in their relationships with others.

> Through enabling people to be themselves people are more likely to join KPMG and to remain with us. If you're not hiding who you are at work you're more likely to put all your energies into work, and be your "whole" self in the workplace.
>
> (Sarah Bond, head of diversity, KPMG, interview, 2005)

Relationships are central to making the right decisions. People are more likely to make the right decisions when they have a good relationship with the people with whom they are doing business. People do good business when they have good relationships with each other—internally and externally.

> There is more chance of our getting it right if people are getting it right with each other, in their relationships with each other. We maximize our chances of making the right decisions because of our underlying philosophy and the recognition that we give to people who live the values in everything that they do. We minimize getting it wrong and maximize getting it right through our relationships with each other, and through working together.
>
> (Neil Sherlock, interview, 2005)

The Global Code of Conduct has an "Ethics Checklist" against which employees and partners can ensure that they are behaving with integrity—following the legal, professional, and ethical standards that apply—and making the right decision, for which they are responsible and accountable. There is an important acknowledgement that employees and partners may at different times need help, and they are encouraged to seek advice and further guidance in performing with integrity.

Neil Sherlock is very clear that "the KPMG Way" has made a difference to how people work with each other and how they do business with each other internally and externally. He comments, "The Global Code of Conduct is what binds us together. It provides everyone with a framework and a common identity wherever they are. It empowers people to challenge and to speak up—even if people are senior to them" (Neil Sherlock, interview, 2005).

The Annual Values Survey confirmed his experience, and while there are areas for improvement, the vast majority of employees and partners feel that huge progress has been made and that the Global Code of Conduct gives a clear message of what is expected of everyone within KPMG and what people can expect from KPMG by way of values and behavior.

Neil makes very clear his commitment to the strong moral and business case for greater diversity and inclusivity, for openness and transparency in relationships and in working practices. "Diversity of experience, and diversity of mind is key. There is a business and moral case for embracing diversity and for making a difference through making a contribution to and engaging with all communities" (Neil Sherlock, interview, 2005).

As a professional services business, KPMG is all about people and about engagement with people, internally and externally. KPMG takes diversity seriously, and as part of this, encourages people to open their hearts and minds to new, different ways of feeling and thinking through engaging in open discussion. Employees and partners are challenged to question their values and beliefs, and supported in reflecting upon them, talking with each other, and increasing their awareness and acceptance of similarities and differences.

KPMG recognizes and rewards people who uphold the values and beliefs of the company through their behavior and in the way they do business globally. Employees and partners are given training and coaching in "Performance with integrity," and the behaviors that reflect the values are measured and recognized in each person's performance appraisal. Likewise recruitment and promotion are aligned with all of the values and behaviors that make up "the KPMG Way."

Supporting people in developing assertive relationships and understanding of diversity takes place in lots of ways in the firm. Interventions include the introduction of an online training program for all people managers to help them better understand why diversity really matters, and the business case for people being themselves at work. Throughout the year information is given about different religious festivals and celebrations, explaining the significance of the festivals and their content.

In 2005 the KPMG board formed a subgroup to take forward the strategy on diversity and inclusion. The fact that the board created a subgroup sent a powerful message that diversity really matters and is key to the success of KPMG, since it does not usually form subgroups. Within the subgroup there are diversity champions for race, gender, disability, and sexual orientation. Each of the diversity champions has run open forums for people in these groups, encouraging them to share their experiences so that the board, and the company as a whole, can better understand their experiences and what the firm needs to do to recruit and retain talented and diverse people. Following these discussions strategies have been developed to deliver on the suggestions made by people in the firm. The consultation process itself has been key to furthering understanding, as it has supported open and honest communication, and encouraged understanding of difference through dialog and the sharing of experiences. People in the groups felt listened to by the board, and that the company really does want to understand and meet their needs.

Other projects for promoting diversity and assertiveness within KPMG include a mentoring program in one area of the business which initially set out, in 2005, as a women's mentoring program. The program, like all initiatives within KPMG, was a direct response to a consultation process. Focus groups were held on diversity, and many women felt that there were a limited number of senior roles available to them. It was hugely successful for those women being mentored and for the mentors, and had a positive impact on the business, so much so that it was extended to include men.

CASE ANALYSIS: IDENTITY AND INTEGRITY

Assertiveness is about feeling secure and safe, feeling self-confident, and having a strong identity. KPMG as a global organization has a strong identity, which is summed up in "the KPMG Way," which stands for integrity in all that it does. People not only seek to join the firm as an employee but also enjoy doing business with KPMG because it has a reputation for being open and honest. KPMG has defined itself by how it does business, and is clear that assertive relationships make for strong leadership and a strong market presence.

People are encouraged to deepen their understanding of themselves and each other in order that they can appreciate and truly respect their differences and sameness. Providing information about differences, for example religious festivals, helps people to understand and appreciate others, and to respect each other.

The commitment of the most senior people in the firm to the "KPMG Way" is vital. The leaders at KPMG lead by example. In particular they are open and willing to make changes in response to feedback. As members of the board the senior leaders at KPMG fully support diversity and assertiveness in relationships. They themselves are diversity champions to employees both internally to and externally of the firm.

22 360 Review Feedback

Introduction

360 review feedback is an effective way of developing assertiveness in organizations. In particular it works through supporting people in developing greater self-awareness and in taking responsibility for their learning and development, and a greater understanding of the impact of their own behavior on others. In this way 360 review feedback fits well with the Johari Window (see page 42), and supports—through the process of giving, receiving, and asking for feedback—people in being open and honest with each other. It gives people a framework and a language with which they can talk about their behavior with each other.

360 review feedback gives people information about themselves, and it is their responsibility to choose how they respond to it. In an assertive organization people use the feedback to leverage their strengths, address their weaknesses, and develop stronger, "bigger," and more assertive relationships.

In this chapter the 360 review process is explored in relation to developing assertiveness in organizations. The case study shows how one organization has successfully introduced 360 review feedback to support the development of assertive leadership and an assertive organization where developing open and honest communication, and a commitment to learning, are central.

The 360 review process

The very introduction of a 360 review process into a team or department is encouraging of assertiveness. People are asked by the person being reviewed to complete a questionnaire. This is significant, and a gift for the person, as those who respond must take the time to consider their experience and perceptions of the person. For the individual completing the review it encourages self-awareness through reflection, and an invitation to do an honest self-assessment.

The 360 review process offers people "all-round" feedback, also known as "multi-rater feedback." Usually it includes the individual's line manager, peers, direct reports, sometimes customers, and occasionally her or his family and friends. The review can be aimed at a particular group of people in the organization, for example senior leaders or line managers, a department, or team. This is in recognition that different competencies are associated with different roles and functions, while there may be some areas that are overlapping. Some 360 reviews give people the option of making "free response" comments, such as:

- What would you like to see the person doing more of/less of in order to be more effective?
- What do you value about the person?
- What would you like to see them doing differently?

When a whole team or department uses the 360 review process, over a period of time, people become more comfortable and engage more fully in the process of giving, receiving, and asking for feedback. It becomes the way of helping establish a learning and development culture. Having received 360 review feedback, people are encouraged to have more conversations with each other, to check the feedback out, and ask for support from each other. They become more comfortable with giving and using the feedback to improve their effectiveness.

Sometimes 360 review feedback is designed to measure a particular competency, or set of competencies, associated with living the values of the organization—for example, observable behaviors associated with openness, honesty, inclusivity, and diversity can be measured. It can help in developing assertive relationships characterized by a high degree of openness, honesty, and trust because it:

- encourages individual reflection and increased self-awareness
- provides individuals with a range of perceptions on their behavior
- helps identify strengths that can be leveraged and further developed
- helps identify areas that need to be developed for the current role

- encourages dialog between people, where the person receiving the feedback talks about the feedback with others
- develops openness and trust between people where the feedback is shared
- provokes curiosity and interest in the person completing the questionnaire for someone else
- promotes self-confidence in individuals through receiving positive feedback from others.

Key to the success of any 360 review process is the involvement and support of line managers. It is usually the line manager who agrees performance, learning, and development objectives with direct reports for the coming year. Linking the 360 review feedback to this discussion can be enormously helpful in facilitating a discussion around the feedback, focused on what people need to do in order to be their "best selves." The feedback can further help in facilitating more open and honest discussions, and thus the development of a stronger and "bigger" relationship between people and their line manager.

The advantages of linking the 360 review feedback to people's learning and development objectives, rather than to the formal performance appraisal system, is that they feel more comfortable about being more open and honest, in both their self-assessment and the assessments of others.

Feedback from 360 review process

Feedback from the 360 review gives people an opportunity to explore, in particular, differences and similarities in their self-perceptions and the perceptions of others; their areas of strength and those for development. The value of having at least ten or more people complete the questionnaire for people is that they receive a range of feedback from others, and ideally a mix of feedback from their line manager, peers, and direct reports.

360 review feedback is about perceptions, and different people often have different perceptions of the same behavior. Feedback can say as much about the person giving the feedback as the person receiving it. Even though 360 review feedback is given anonymously, people are encouraged to take responsibility for their feedback, and to be willing to have conversations with the reviewers about the feedback. People receiving the feedback have a choice whether they make changes in their behavior as a result.

One of the most useful aspects to the feedback is where people's assessment of themselves is very different from that of others. This can be for a number of reasons. People may, for example, have assessed themselves as doing less well in most areas, and this might highlight a lack of positive self-belief, while others see them as doing well in the same areas. Equally people may assess themselves as doing really well in a particular area only to discover that others have assessed them as not doing well. This may be because they are not communicating what they are doing to others, or they have a view of self that is at odds with the view of others.

Some people discover that their behavior is different depending on the people with whom they are interacting. For example, people may behave assertively with their peers and non-assertively with their direct reports. Again this can be hugely revealing for people, giving them the opportunity to reflect on values, beliefs, and attitudes that may underlie differences in behavior towards others.

Where there is broad agreement in how people are seen by others, and they agree with the feedback, it can be affirming of their competencies and those that are important for their current role. (Some 360 reviews give people the opportunity to rate the competency in relation to the relative importance in the person's current role.) The 360 review feedback can highlight an area that is important and that requires development, and people can use this feedback to focus on what they need to do in this area.

It can be useful to combine the 360 review with a psychometric questionnaire such as the Myers-Briggs Type Indicator (MBTI) so that the person can relate the behavioral feedback to her or his "MBTI type," and preferences.

The following case study illustrates how the introduction of a 360 review process at EMC has led to the development of an assertive organization in which feedback and coaching have become part of the way things are done.

Case study: Developing an assertive organization through 360 review feedback

EMC is a leading global technology company that partners and innovates for customer success by providing integrated technology solutions for information lifecycle management (ILM). In 2000, after a time of rapid growth in terms of numbers and staff, EMC Germany responded by creating the role of training manager and a local Training Department, with the full support of senior management. Management training had happened prior to the creation of this role on an international basis, albeit occasionally and sporadically. In 2001, when EMC experienced its first financial losses, there were also people losses in the form of redundancies. However a decision was made to further invest in training and development, despite and because of the difficult situation, since the managers in the company needed to learn new skills to deal with the people issues that arose during this difficult time.

Gisela Banken, training manager, EMC Germany, described the process of getting people to buy in to management training as follows:

> It was challenging at first to get participants for the training. However little by little we had successes of single projects, mainly working with line managers' requests and the outcome being successful for them, leading to others asking for training.
>
> (Gisela Banken, interview, 2005)

At the beginning of 2002 it was decided to introduce a 360 review process internationally, starting by training HR professionals in using this management development tool. A sales manager was selected from Germany to participate in the pilot. He really benefited from the 360 feedback, and requested that all his team went through the process. This was the beginning.

Initially internal coaches were used. However this was found to be less effective than using external coaches because the HR professionals did not necessarily have sufficient time for the coaching, nor did they have training in coaching. They also had the challenge of being in the double role of neutral coach and internal HR professional. The most important reason, however, was that there was little follow-up to the process once participants had received their feedback.

Gisela Banken proposed a pilot process that was rolled out for all the direct reports of the customer service director in Germany using external coaches. This was hugely successful and very well received, and afterwards it was rolled out on a quarterly basis for all the EMC people managers in Germany (about 100), with ten participants going through the process each quarter. By the beginning of 2006 everyone had completed the process, and the company decided to implement the process as a permanent feedback tool. This means that all managers now receive 360 review feedback every two to three years. Table 22.1 shows the six phases of the 360 review process in Germany.

Table 22.1 360 review process, EMC Germany

	Phases	Method and goals
1	Briefing	Conference call briefing for all participants about the 360 feedback process
2	Online feedback process	Self assessment Assessment from feedback givers
3	Analysis meeting with coach	Meeting of external coach with participant to make sense of 360 feedback and to identify areas for development Create draft individual development plan (IDP)
4	Development meeting with coach and manager	Discussion of feedback results and draft IDP Finalize the IDP
5	Individual coaching meetings	Three or four coaching meetings of one and a half hours, allowing approximately three to four weeks between meetings
6	Closing meeting with manager (sometimes coach present)	Review of IDP and of achievements and areas for ongoing development Agreement of next steps

Source: adapted from EMC (2003).

The 360 review feedback process

The 360 feedback behavioral items were based on the 16 EMC management competencies. These are:

- Operational command of the business
- Results driven
- Recognize global implications
- Leadership
- Fosters teamwork
- Creates a positive climate
- Attracts talent
- Manages people

- Influence
- Communication
- Initiative
- Adaptability
- Customer responsiveness
- Accountability
- Problem-solving
- Technical/functional expertise.

Assertive leadership within EMC

The management competencies listed above are all part of developing an assertive organization and developing assertive leadership. These competencies were further reinforced by EMC's Leadership Conference, held in 2004 and again the following year. The conference was mandatory for all people managers. In the first year Ten Principles of Leadership were identified for everybody in the company:

- Our behavior is aimed at bringing success to customers, clients, employees and shareholders.
- We assume responsibility for our own department *and* the whole company.
- We assume that this responsibility is beneficial to the business as well as to employees.
- We take responsibility for the consequences of our actions.
- We expect full commitment and dedication from everyone.
- We ask and enable employees to show courage and initiative as the basis of our success.
- We expect everybody to be dedicated to their personal development all the time.
- Our relationships with each other are determined by trust, respect, and feedback.
- We behave the same way as we expect our employees to behave.
- We commit to measure ourselves against the fulfillment of these principles.

These principles were then reviewed at the conference in 2005 alongside the drive to become more of a matrix organization in which cross-functional, assertive communication is key. Other measures that were taken to establish a leadership culture, characterized by coaching and feedback, included:

- management training for all people managers on performance management, change, and coaching
- support for all people managers in living these principles in the form of training on how to write individual development plans (IDPs)
- training for all people managers in both matrix workshops and cross-functional team work.

CASE ANALYSIS: BUILDING TRUST AND RESPECT

Since the losses in 2001 EMC has once again returned to profitability and impressive growth by focusing on growing the business through its people. This is hugely important for a company like EMC, which has a growth strategy that includes the acquisition of small companies, each of which might otherwise "do its own thing" rather than join the drive to ensure that people "do things together and succeed together in business." The formation in the German subsidiary of a Training Department with a training manager dedicated to the development of people and the business through improved communication has been a tremendous success story for EMC Germany.

The buy-in of senior management to the initial introduction of 360 review feedback was very important in sending a message to all employees that they mattered and that the process was important to the success of the business. What is particularly noticeable about the success of the management training in EMC Germany is the way in which it has been built on success and word of mouth, from the initial training given in response to individual managers' requests, through the sales manager from Germany participating in the first 360 feedback process, to the roll-out of the various training courses that support the Principles of Leadership.

At an individual, team, and organizational level EMC Germany is engaged in the business of learning and development, and growth. The annual Leadership Conference was an opportunity for presentations and reflections on the success of interventions and actions taken during the previous year, and mirrors the process that individuals themselves go through in learning from the 360 review feedback process, planning for success by way of IDPs that are reviewed and developed on a continuous basis.

23 Assertive Leadership

Introduction

Assertive leadership underpins assertive organizations, and involves those people in leadership positions truly valuing openness, honesty, and respect of people, and expressing this through their own assertive leadership behavior. People in leadership positions have the responsibility for leading the way in creating organizations that espouse the values of integrity, inclusivity, and diversity. For them to do this, leaders within organizations need to have a strong sense of who they are, and what leading with integrity means to them. This requires bringing their "best selves" to their leadership, being aware of the impact of their behavior on others internally and externally to the organization. Assertive leadership makes for an assertive organizational culture in which people are valued for who they are and rewarded for what they do. Truly assertive leadership requires that leaders within organizations create and maintain assertive organizational cultures in which multi-cultural differences are respected and valued, and in which people are rewarded for what they do.

In this chapter the characteristics of assertive leadership are described and explored. The case study illustrates how an organization can help develop assertive leaders and an assertive culture through providing leadership training and development.

The characteristics of assertive leadership

The characteristics of assertive leadership listed in Table 23.1 are important to leaders within organizations who have the responsibility of, and are accountable for, living and working with integrity. They are based on a valuing and respecting of difference, on inclusivity and the right of people to belong. They are characteristics that many people aspire to and live in their lives. They are, however, vital to senior people within organizations who, in their leadership position, inspire and motivate others to follow them.

Self-awareness and awareness of others

There is no one particular style of assertive leadership; rather, assertive leaders are those people who bring a high degree of self-awareness and awareness of difference to their leadership. With this awareness they are able to choose to behave with integrity in all that they do. They relate to others from an I'm OK: You're OK position, and their behavior is consistently assertive towards others, underpinned by self-respect and respect of others.

Assertive leadership involves a high degree of awareness of multicultural differences, and expressing this awareness of difference through behaviors that reflect values, attitudes, and beliefs that are honoring and respecting of difference. It is vital for senior people in organizations to demonstrate through their own behavior their commitment to making truly multicultural organizations in which everyone is treated fairly and with dignity.

Table 23.1 Characteristics of assertive leadership

- Self-awareness and awareness of others.
- Self-confidence and positive self-esteem.
- Commitment to personal and professional development.
- Self-responsibility, choice, and courage.
- Connection and compassion.
- Congruency of values, beliefs, and behaviors.
- Vision, passion, and communication.
- Learning and development of others.
- Relational and task focused.
- Managing conflict.

Self-confidence and positive self-esteem

Assertive leaders have a strong sense of who they are, and are able to draw on positive and affirming self-beliefs. This inner resource of positive self-affirmations is important particularly at times when, as leaders, they may be in challenging situations, giving them the confidence and courage to "speak their truth."

Commitment to personal and professional development

Assertive leaders are committed to ongoing personal and professional learning and development. They actively seek feedback from others as well as pursuing their career development. In this way they are aware of their strengths, both qualities and skills, and feel confident as people in themselves. They are able to lead from within, with integrity. Assertive leaders are aware of their limitations, and feeling secure and confident, they are able to ask for help from others as and when needed. Equally they are able to delegate tasks that they are not best suited to, and to recognize that someone else may be better suited to the task and developed through doing it.

Self-responsibility, choice, and courage

Assertive leaders take responsibility for their thoughts, feelings, and behaviors. They recognize that they have choices about how they perceive a situation, and how they engage with people. They look to do so with positive intent, and focus on positive outcomes in situations. By taking responsibility for their thoughts, feelings, and actions they are called upon to be courageous: for example, to be honest when they have made a mistake and to speak out when they see or hear biases and prejudices.

Connection and compassion

Assertive leaders are aware of the connection between the four energies, physical, intellectual, emotional, and spiritual, and recognize the importance of managing these energies in order to fully engage with people and with what they are doing, to be fully present as a whole person. Through being connected to their energies and aware of their strengths and vulnerabilities, assertive leaders are able to truly connect with the humanness of others, to appreciate their strengths and vulnerabilities, their similarities and differences. In this way assertive leaders are able to feel respect and compassion for others, and to truly honor multicultural differences. They challenge people to acknowledge and to work with their prejudices and biases, to take full responsibility for attitudes and beliefs that may not be truly respecting of difference and inclusivity.

Congruency of values, beliefs, and behaviors

Assertive leaders are clear about what their values and beliefs are, and that these are based on openness, honesty, respecting and honoring of difference. They take time to reflect on what matters to them, what their passions are, and how best they can fulfill these in all that they do. For most assertive leaders, living their values and beliefs through working in an organization that shares their values and beliefs is important. In order that they can live and work in integrity, and be congruent, they seek to work in organizations in which they can align their values to those of the organization. They are willing to be challenged when their behavior lacks congruency, and are willing to address a lack of congruency between values, beliefs, and behaviors in their organization.

Vision, passion, and communication

Assertive leaders are able to communicate their vision and that of the organization to others, and inspire people. This can be in small ways such as behaving and communicating in everyday ways that are respectful and inspiring of trust. Assertive leaders are also those who inspire and motivate large numbers of people, and whole organizations, through their vision, passion, and behavior.

Learning and development of others

Key to assertive leadership is recognition of people's learning and development, and providing opportunities for them to learn which they may have hitherto not considered. Encouraging people to engage in different learning experiences, not necessarily job-related, can support people in becoming more themselves and reaching for their potential. This is developing of people's self-confidence, and belief in their abilities to learn new and different ways of thinking and feeling about themselves, others, and ways of doing things.

Relational and task-focused

Assertive leaders are focused on the relationship that they have with people as well as the tasks that they are asking them to do or working on together. Thus whether they are giving direction and/or support they maintain an I'm OK: You're OK life position that is encouraging of people being and doing their best, of working separately and together, all the time respecting and honoring difference. In this way assertive leaders are empowering and developing of others, they are aware of people's differences, and seek to empower people to be their "best selves."

Managing conflict

Assertive leaders see conflict as a creative opportunity, in terms of both the task and the relationship. They see the conflict separately from the person, and at the same time work with the person in understanding the conflict and the differences in order to move forward. The conflict may not be resolved, but those involved are given space to be truly heard, and to be recognized for how they are feeling and what they are thinking. Through this process of recognition, of being listened to and heard, people feel more secure, and are able, from this more secure place, to make moves towards understanding each other, even though the conflict in itself may not be resolved. (See Chapter 6 for more on the transformational approach to managing conflict.)

In the case study that follows, Simon Dally (a pseudonym), a senior manager at Nestlé,* describes how the company has developed and supported him in becoming more self-confident and assertive as a leader through training and development.

Case study: Developing an assertive organization through developing assertive leadership

Nestlé is the world's leading food company, with operations in almost every country, including many developing countries. Training and development are a vital part of creating and maintaining the Nestlé culture and underlying philosophy of respecting and caring for people. The company describes what is required of its senior leaders and

---

* The Nestlé name is reproduced with the kind permission of Société des Produits Nestlé SA.

managers regarding people in the Basic Nestlé Management and Leadership Principles:

- A prerequisite for dealing with people is respect and trust.
- Transparency and honesty in dealing with people are a sine qua non for efficient communication. This is complemented by open dialogue with the purpose of sharing competencies and boosting creativity.
- To communicate is not only to inform; it is to listen and to engage in dialogue.
- The willingness to cooperate, to help others and to learn is a required basis for advancement and promotion within the company.
  (source: www.nestlé.com)

These Leadership and Management Principles are all about developing assertive relationships, which are constructive and creative, and based on respect and trust. Within these assertive relationships people can be open and honest with each other; they listen to and seek to understand each other; they are able to work with conflict and to look for opportunities to help and learn from each other.

Given the diversity of people within Nestlé the principles are critical to everyone being respected by and developed within the company. The company is inclusive of all people. People are developed in both technical and people skills in order that they can be the best of who they are. There is huge respect for people in ensuring that training and development meets their particular needs in their particular location.

Nestlé's people principles are translated into training and development so that people know what is required of them, what they need to do in order to fulfill the company's requirements of them, and also to fulfill their personal and professional aspirations within the company. The Nestlé culture is made explicit, as is the psychological contract between company and employee. Employees can expect to be treated fairly and with respect, and are expected to treat each other fairly and with respect, and to foster open and honest relationships with each other.

Simon Dally returned to work at Nestlé following a short period of working for a small start-up company. He had enjoyed ten years of working at Nestlé—a huge global company—and had left feeling the need for change and a challenge. On his return, Simon felt huge relief and a sense of security. He looks back on his 18 months out of Nestlé as being a positive experience in that it made him appreciate even more the Nestlé culture of looking after, respecting, and developing people. Nevertheless, he felt that he had to prove himself in some way, and at the same time was feeling unsure of himself and of how to go about doing this. He was nominated to participate in a development program for senior managers, and says, "The program came at just the right time. I was struggling with settling back in and aware of not leading my people to the best of my ability" (Simon Dally, interview, 2005).

The program was called the Nestlé Leadership Challenge, and was designed to help senior managers reflect on, develop, and practice new ways of leading that would help them in leading the company forward in line with the company culture. The focus of the program was on leadership attributes in particular helping delegates to:

- develop a clear personal vision to drive the strategy of their department/ function forward
- identify practical ways in which this vision can be achieved to ensure departmental effectiveness
- understand better the effectiveness of their personal leadership, and identify areas for improvement and action
- enhance their key leadership skills, including coaching and managing conflict
- co-create a supportive and challenging company-wide network of leaders.

(source: Nestlé UK ManCom, Leadership Challenge program information, 2003)

Simon attended the program for senior managers in 2003. He reflected on the experience two years later as being transformative for him, in particular the feedback that he received from his colleagues via 360 review feedback, the Life Styles Inventory (LSI), and the feedback from fellow delegates on the program whom he had not previously met. (See Chapter 22 for more on 360 review feedback.) He was impressed by the self-disclosure of delegates, and felt encouraged by their personal stories to share his own story, including his strengths and areas of vulnerability. For Simon this was a powerful experience of rediscovering himself and his inner self-confidence. Having felt uncomfortable, insecure, and unsure of himself, he describes himself during the program as "Feeling comfortable in my own skin again. I had felt uncomfortable and unsettled by the feedback, people saw me differently from how I saw myself" (Simon Dally, interview, 2005).

Others saw Simon as a "perfectionist" and his style as aggressive/

defensive. Aggressive/defensive styles "reflect self-promoting thinking and behavior used to maintain one's status/position and fulfil *security* needs through *task* related activities" (www.humansynergistics.co.uk). The "perfectionistic" style is one of four aggressive/defensive styles. "Perfectionists" are described in the LSI as belonging to a group of people who "like to be seen and noticed, and want to prove they are superior to others ... perfectionists believe that people are basically incompetent and not to be trusted, they have difficulty delegating work" (LSI, 1990: 99).

Simon recognized himself in the description, and in particular his experience of delegating to others, which he found difficult. Simon had described himself as having a more passive/defensive style. The passive/defensive styles represent: "self-protecting thinking and behavior that promote the fulfillment of *security* needs through interactions with people" (LSI, 1990). The program helped Simon to become more aware of his security needs, in both the short and longer term, and how he could meet these needs in a positive and creative way.

The feedback from his colleagues, and the encouragement from the facilitators and delegates during the program, helped Simon to trust others and to give them more responsibility. This has allowed him to focus more on himself, on his leadership challenge and commitments. Key for Simon was trust, and developing a more positive set of beliefs based on self-acceptance of his needs and what mattered to him—his values, in particular security and satisfaction from achievement. Simon was able to identify how important this was to him, and to develop a set of commitments to himself that would enable him to fulfill this need and at the same time to develop a more assertive and positive style of leadership. He says, "The program helped me to reflect on my leadership attributes and to acknowledge myself for my strengths, and for my vulnerabilities" (Simon Dally, interview, 2005).

Simon became aware of the importance of inspiring confidence in others, and that if he was not able to inspire confidence in others he was not doing what was required of him as a senior manager within Nestlé. He became aware that "The only way I can inspire confidence in others is if I am feeling confident and congruent—comfortable—in myself" (Simon Dally, interview, 2005).

Following the program Simon sought feedback from colleagues and engaged with them in giving, receiving, and asking for feedback. For a period after the program he met with his "buddy coach," with whom he reflected on what he had learnt on the program and what he had put into practice.

CASE ANALYSIS: ASSERTIVE LEADERSHIP THROUGH TRAINING AND DEVELOPMENT

The training and development helped Simon to better understand what self-confidence, positive self-esteem, and assertiveness really meant for him as a leader within Nestlé. Feedback from others was vital to his developing self-confidence and positive self-belief. Through the feedback he was encouraged to reflect on his own behavior and the impact that it had on others. He was given the opportunity to walk in other people's shoes and to see how he was perceived from where they were standing.

Simon acknowledged when he reflected on the program that a significant learning had been recognizing that he had choices, most importantly choices about how he interpreted his experiences. When he first attended the program he had low self-esteem and negative self-beliefs. This had had a downward-spiraling effect, causing him to feel a loss of self-confidence, which in turn caused him to feel insecure and unhappy in himself, and unable to be effective.

The power of the positive feedback to transform how he felt about himself helped Simon to reconnect with himself and others positively. In particular he reconnected with what mattered to him by way of his values and beliefs, and realized he could meet his needs more effectively through making positive choices. He was empowered to make the shift from thinking and feeling negatively to thinking and feeling positively. Simon has returned to and used the positive and affirmative feedback from his colleagues on the program to boost his self-confidence, in particular their appreciation of his honesty and openness. He has used this feedback, as an inner resource, to remind him of his strengths and skills as an assertive leader.

The program enabled him to explore his insecurities and uncertainties and to clarify what he needed in order to "feel comfortable in his skin" and to be a truly assertive leader within himself, confident in his values and beliefs, and in his relationships and work at Nestlé.

24 Coaching

Introduction

Coaching helps develop assertiveness and assertive relationships by giving people the opportunity to develop greater self-awareness and effectiveness. It supports people in their learning and development, and helps create organizations that are inclusive and assertive.

Many organizations have introduced coaching programs as a way of providing people with opportunities to further their learning and development. Coaching can be formal or informal. Formal coaching is provided either by a coach external to the organization, or people within the organization who have been trained in coaching. Informal coaching happens between line managers and their direct reports every day, as people are directed and supported in their work.

Coaching dramatically increases people's chances of change, improvement, and breakthrough. Without exposure to the alternative perspectives offered by a coach, people are often left to make progress alone, and this can be incredibly difficult for them. Coaching has a positive impact on people's self-esteem, interpersonal effectiveness, and business success.

This chapter outlines the purpose of coaching, and explores the importance of the coaching relationship in developing trust, openness, and mutual respect. It describes coaching and experiential learning; and the relationship between the coach as leader, and leader as coach, in relation to developing assertiveness in organizations. The first case study shows how focusing on strengths can make a powerful difference to people's self-esteem, and the second how experiential learning can help people to reflect on their interpersonal behavior and develop greater self-confidence and assertive behavior.

The purpose of coaching

The purpose of coaching is on learning and development: in particular helping people to focus on their strengths and skills and realize their potential. Focusing on strengths and on how people can use their strengths to be more authentic and effective in their work helps them to be their "best selves." Coaching helps people build positive self-esteem, to tap into their strengths, and draw on their inner resources. It helps people recognize that they are self-responsible and that they have choices.

The coaching relationship

The coaching relationship is an assertive relationship, one in which there is trust, mutual respect, and openness. The coach helps people to develop greater self-awareness and responsibility for the choices that they make. The coach does this through listening and asking open questions, reflecting and giving feedback, challenging and supporting people to enquire within and reflect on their experiences. This helps them to connect more strongly with themselves, to be aware of their choices, and to explore and clarify ways in which they can become more effective through drawing on their strengths.

The coaching relationship provides an opportunity for commitment and accountability to be experienced and lived. Personal commitment to coaching is a two-way process: both the coach and people being coached need to ensure that they honor their agreements to each other by way of, for example, meeting dates and times. There is a commitment on the part of the coach to stay focused and to ask questions that facilitate the person in moving forwards through reflection, and on the part of the person being coached to commit to this journey of exploration and development.

Accountability for actions and results is part of everyday business and organizational life. Being accountable for one's actions, and taking responsibility in relationships with others, go side by side in creating an organization that is assertive, inclusive, and thrives on difference.

All of the coach's skills are used to help people to:

- develop greater self and other awareness
- take responsibility
- deepen their learning from experience
- improve their performance.

Regular commitment to the coaching helps people to:

- stay focused on their development
- report back on how they are getting on
- ask for feedback from others in between coaching
- achieve their individual, team, and organizational goals
- create a learning and development organization.

The coaching relationship provides people with an opportunity to be open and honest, to have meaningful conversations in which they are able to talk openly about their strengths and vulnerabilities. The experience of being open and honest in the coaching relationship encourages people to develop more openness and honesty in their relationships with others.

Coaching and experiential learning

Knowledge and understanding of the learning cycle and the different learning styles can assist the coach in helping people to learn from experience and to leverage their strengths. People can also be encouraged to step away from their preferred style into a different style that challenges, stretches, and surprises them. (See Chapter 12 for more on the learning cycle and learning styles.) Coaches themselves will potentially be more effective if they have knowledge and understanding of their own preferred learning styles, and particular bias for one or more styles. This can lead to an exploration of difference in styles within the coaching relationship.

During the coaching it is likely that the coach will help people to review experiences, reflect, analyze, and apply their learning to the next action. At each stage the coach is facilitating people to reflect on and learn from experience, to increase self-awareness, build self-confidence and greater effectiveness.

Coaching and leadership

For many senior people the coaching that they seek is focused on their leadership of others, and in particular on how they can be a better, more effective leader at a personal, team, and organizational level. Being a leader of people is recognized as being about coaching. The effective leader is an effective coach.

Increasingly, people who have direct reports will be required to both lead and coach their people towards greater effectiveness and success.

They are also likely themselves to be led and coached by their line manager, and so have the experience of giving coaching to others and receiving coaching from another.

Case study 1: Strengths through coaching

Jenny Rogers is a highly regarded and experienced executive coach, and author of Coaching Skills: A handbook *(2004). In this case study Jenny first describes the essence of her strengths approach, then gives an example of how she used it to help a client develop greater assertiveness and effectiveness.*

The essence of Jenny Rogers' approach to coaching is to focus on people's strengths, on their plusses rather than their deficits. Many people are referred for coaching following feedback from others through a performance review or 360 review feedback. In most cases the feedback has highlighted an area where the person could improve on performance, an area in which he or she is in some way lacking. Areas for development are often those where the person is perceived as needing to develop greater effectiveness in order to be ready for promotion to the next level, or another more senior role within the organization. People are often puzzled by the feedback with regard to their weakness or deficits, particularly when in most other areas they are performing extremely well. Their weakness is seen by others—usually their line manager—as something that needs to be addressed in order for them to achieve greater success be that promotion or a pay increase. By contrast Jenny prefers to work with the person's strengths, and to help them explore how they can achieve greater success. Jenny summarizes her approach as "Helping people to identify what their strengths are, where and how they can use them and what is holding them back from using them" (Jenny Rogers, interview, 2005). She goes on to say that:

> Very often people hold back from being assertive because of negative messages they heard as children—often constantly repeated precepts and advice from parents such as "People like us don't ..." or "Keep your head down then you'll be safe ..." or "Who'd be interested in what you've got to say?" These messages are intended to be positive— for instance, to keep the child safe, but when they are carried over into adult life they can be seriously restricting.
>
> (Jenny Rogers, interview, 2005)

It is these negative messages that get in the way of people asserting and communicating what they want and need in a direct way. Jenny works with people to uncover the negative voice, and helps them overcome this barrier to their personal and professional effectiveness.

Asserting strengths for positive personal impact

Gabrielle was a senior manager in a large organization. She was referred for coaching by her line manager who had given her feedback that she needed "more personal impact," and that she was not making the contribution that she was capable of or making the most of her talents. Gabrielle had been in her current post for three years and felt that it was time to move on. However she had not been successful in her applications for other posts, and had received feedback that she was "not making the necessary personal impact" at the selection stage.

Gabrielle had seven coaching sessions: six of them with Jenny, and the fifth session with an image consultant, Jennifer Hayes. Following the initial session, in which Jenny helped Gabrielle explore the feedback that she had received from colleagues, she completed two psychometric questionnaires (MBTI and FIRO-B); a conflict styles questionnaire (Thomas-Kilmann Conflict Mode Instrument); and the "Rolls-Royce" of 360 Review Questionnaires—the structured telephone interview in which the coach asks a number of people, chosen by the client, a series of questions (see Rogers, 2004).

In the second and third sessions Gabrielle made sense of all the feedback with Jenny, linking the feedback from the different sources to messages that she had received from her parents as she grew up—which were "Keep your head down" and: "Fit in." Gabrielle realized that she had not been drawing on her strengths, and that she had been trying to succeed through focusing on performance rather than people. "Keeping her head down" meant that she had been holding back from asserting herself, and from truly being herself. The feedback from the 360 telephone review confirmed that people wanted more of her, that they wanted her to assert herself—to be herself, and not hide or shy away from situations and people.

In the fourth session Gabrielle used the feedback from the questionnaires and her colleagues to develop her assertiveness in the "here and now" coaching relationship with Jenny. Jenny reflected back the language that Gabrielle was using, both verbally and non-verbally, and Gabrielle was able to use this feedback to present a more centered, present, and assertive self.

Following the fifth session with the image consultant, the sixth and seventh sessions focused on further developing Gabrielle's new found self-confidence and assertiveness, including focusing on "peak experiences" in which Gabrielle had experienced herself being her "best self"—physically, intellectually, emotionally, and spiritually. Through this exploration Gabrielle identified the kinds of experiences and situations that she needed to pay more attention to. This included having conversations with people in the working environment whom she liked and with whom she could talk about her career aspirations. As a result of one of these conversations she joined a new team working in the area of training and development, delivering a service to others within the organization.

CASE ANALYSIS

In the analysis below three key aspects of the coaching linked to developing assertiveness are highlighted. They are:

- identifying negative internalized messages
- seeing weaknesses as opportunities and turning them into strengths
- integrating positive internal messages with a positive external message.

Identifying negative internalized messages

Many people are held back from asserting themselves by absorbing messages that when given were given with positive intention—to protect and/or to motivate the person. The messages are internalized by the person, and serve to hold her or him back from feeling confident in situations and able to be assertive with others. These messages, once identified, can be addressed, and the person can turn the messages round by finding the "gift" within them. The gift can be a challenge to do something differently with the message, to use it for change and development.

In this case Gabrielle had internalized three messages that held her back from asserting herself, and from shining and being her "best self." The message: "Keep your head down" combined with the message of: "Fit in" had kept Gabrielle in a non-assertive place, one in which she held back from asserting herself to others. The coaching helped Gabrielle to become aware of these messages and to turn the messages round. "Fitting in" well turned into getting on well with and a sensitivity towards people, and "Keeping her head down" turned into listening to herself and others, and to speaking her truth.

Seeing weaknesses as opportunities and turning them into strengths

Very often something that is a strength for people can also be a weakness; conversely something that is a weakness can also be a strength. For

Gabrielle her desire to cooperate with people was both a strength and a weakness. It was a strength in that she encouraged people to get on with each other and to listen and take account of the other's points of view; and it was a weakness in that she did not assert her own point of view. The coaching helped her appreciate the need to do both—to listen to and enquire of others at the same time as asserting her own views.

Integrating positive internal and external messages

How people present themselves non-verbally, including how they dress, tells others a story about who they are. Gabrielle "dressed down," and through both her dress and her body posture communicated to others a lack of confidence and assertiveness. The coaching had started with the internal messages and ended with the external messages that she herself communicated to others. Gabrielle was able to integrate her positive belief in herself with her expression of herself through her body posture and how she dressed.

Case study 2: Team coaching using horses as part of the learning experience

Liz Morrison is an accredited coach with the International Coach Federation (ICF), who runs the company Sustainable Tactics Ltd. It specializes in experiential and action learning, including using horses, based on neuro-linguistic programming and inner game techniques. She describes her work with individuals and teams as helping them realize their potential. The focus of her work is on coaching people to become more aware of their values, and to use this understanding to develop behaviors that are more congruent and aligned.

Liz uses the relationship between horse and handler to help people understand and reflect on their behaviors and gain a greater awareness of who they are. Liz has found that if she helps people identify what really matters to them and what they feel passionate about, they understand their values and so move towards living the life that they want to live.

Liz offers team coaching to corporate clients, giving them an opportunity to work experientially with each other and with horses. A typical team-coaching day takes place at a venue where there are facilities for the team to work separately from and together with the horses. She describes below her work with a senior team on a team-coaching day.

The first session began with an introduction to how working with horses can help people to learn about themselves and transform their relationships with others. During this initial session all team members introduced themselves, including their objectives for the day. Tim, the director and leader of the team, stated that his objective for the day was "To learn how I can use my energy better in the team."

Tim took this objective into his work with the horse in the arena. The rest of the team stood outside the arena, observing him and the horse. Liz invited Tim to focus on his energy around the horse. What he discovered was that when he consciously "dropped his energy," the horse became calmer and quieter. When he was not paying attention to his energy, the horse simply ignored him. When he raised his energy, the horse became very active. Tim's colleagues were amazed at the change in his behavior, the impact that this had on the horse, and vice versa. In the debrief they were able to share their observations with Tim, and had an open discussion about their and his energy needs.

An administrative team member, Claire, was unclear what her change objective was in the team. She described herself as: "I am only the team administrator." Liz invited her to leave out the "only," and to say, "I am the team administrator." Claire took this "question" about her role and her uncertainty about her importance in the team into the arena. Again her colleagues observed from outside the arena. Once in the arena she stood still, and looked unsure of herself in this new and unknown situation. The horse came over to her and started to do a "body search," nuzzling for polo mints in her jacket and having a good "nosey around." Liz asked her, "How are you feeling about this?" Her response was that she did not like it and wished the horse would stop. Liz suggested to her that she let the horse know how she felt, and say, "No. I don't like this." She pushed his head away firmly yet gently, and the horse stopped.

Liz then asked Claire to take the horse through the maze, a series of poles on the ground, which require that the person asks the horse to turn, stop, and turn again a number of times. Claire carefully led the horse round the maze. She was polite and courteous, clear and firm with the horse (who had never done this particular exercise before). She thanked and appreciated the horse regularly as the horse successfully completed each part of the maze.

Helping Claire to be clear about what she wanted to achieve through working with the horse was the first step in developing her confidence. Claire had a tendency to put herself down, to think that she did "not matter," and had described herself as "only" the team administrator. Liz reflected "only" back to her, and in so doing challenged her to think differently about herself.

In becoming aware of the verbal language that she used, Claire became aware of how frequently she put herself down. When she came to working with the horse she was invited to assert herself, to state her boundaries clearly and say what she wanted and didn't want. This was revolutionary for Claire. She succeeded in asserting herself, using positive and mutually respectful behavior at the same time, as staying congruent with her values of "courtesy and politeness" in relationships. She was able to assert herself and to enjoy much more positive relationships with the team.

In the debrief Liz emphasized the power of language to transform. By describing herself as "only the administrator" Claire immediately demeaned herself within the team. She positioned herself in relation to others as less than them. Working with the horse enabled her to see that she could have a positive and harmonious relationship without needing "status."

Claire shared how happy she felt that she had been able to say "No," that she had led the horse in a respectful and caring way that had been clear and firm. She had not realized until this point that she could set clear boundaries in a way that was caring and firm, respecting of herself and the other person. Claire's colleagues commented on the quality of relationship between Claire and the horse—there was clear trust and mutual respect. All were delighted in her new-found clarity and assertiveness. Together as a team they were able to build on this success and consider the quality of their relationships with each other.

CASE ANALYSIS:
CONNECTION, LANGUAGE AND BOUNDARIES

Connection with the self is key to developing assertiveness, and Tim was able to see and feel the connection within himself and with the horse during the exercise. In the debrief he was able to relate this to how he interacted with the team. During the debrief session the team were able to connect with him in a way that they had not been able to previously. Tim became aware that when he was not connected he was listening neither to himself nor to others and what they were saying to him.

Language communicates to people what people think about themselves in relation to other people. The language that Claire used communicated to the rest of the team that she believed herself to be less important than other team members. Her language was non-assertive and undermining of her self-esteem.

Knowing one's boundaries is a key part of being assertive. Claire allowed the horse to "push her around" a bit, and did not like it. With help from Liz she was able to assert her boundaries, and in doing so both feel self-respect and gain the respect of the team.

25 Promoting Happiness at Work

Introduction

Happiness and relationships are closely intertwined. Happiness depends on the quality of relationships that we have with other people, and on how we think and feel about ourselves—our self-esteem. Connection is key to enjoying relationships with others and to happiness.

> The single biggest influence on happiness is something we all have the scope to influence for better or for worse—namely, our relationships with other people.
>
> (Martin, 2006: 4)

In this chapter the importance of happiness is explored in relation to people's well-being. The first case study illustrates how putting the happiness of people alongside business success creates a strong, secure, and assertive organization. In the second case study the importance of individuals' positive emotion and optimism in developing assertive relationships between fundraisers and donors is explored.

Happiness

The economist Richard Layard has made a fascinating study of happiness. He makes a strong case for happiness to be at the top of everyone's agenda—especially the political agenda—to ensure the well-being of society. He defines happiness as "feeling good—enjoying life and wanting the feeling to be maintained," and unhappiness as "feeling bad and wishing things were different" (Layard, 2005: 12).

Feeling good has been linked to electrical activity in the left front of the brain, while feeling bad is linked to electrical activity in the right front of the brain. Equally the link between positive self-esteem and emotional well-being to physical and intellectual well-being has been made. Thus people who feel good about themselves and towards others, I'm OK: You're OK, are more likely to enjoy greater physical well-being, a stronger immune system, and be mentally alert and creative.

When people feel unhappy they are more likely to find themselves lacking certain qualities and skills, and when they compare themselves with others, find themselves even more lacking. This downward spiral of feelings and thoughts about self and others can be very demotivating and isolating for people. It is important to recognize that everyone's experience of feeling good or feeling bad can change, often rapidly. People can swing from being hugely positive and assertive one minute to being totally negative and aggressive the next. Sometimes a small thing can trigger a positive or negative response to a situation.

The "relationship factor"

People who feel secure and confident in their qualities and abilities are more able to connect with others and to build assertive relationships. People who neither value themselves nor feel valued by others are less likely to enjoy assertive relationships with others and to feel part of a community. Assertive relationships are built on trust, openness, and honesty, and are facilitated by having channels of communication in place through which people can communicate and connect with each other informally and formally.

Richard Layard describes happiness as being about relationships: "We are inherently social, and our happiness depends above all on the quality of our relationships with other people. We have to develop public policies that take this 'relationship factor' into account" (2005: 8).

Case study 1: Promoting happiness

In this case study, Ken Temple and Fiona Corner describe the role of the partners' counsellor at the John Lewis Partnership (JLP), a UK-based retail organization. The partners' counsellors help promote happiness at work through encouraging open and honest communication, positive and assertive relationships. All employees at the JLP are partners in the firm, sharing in its profits.

The principles laid down in the JLP constitution of fairness and happiness are summarized in "Partnership Behavior—powered by our principles (PBOP):"

- Be honest.
- Give respect.
- Recognize others.
- Show enterprise.
- Work together.
- Achieve more.

It is through the everyday behaviors based on these principles that partners make a difference in all their actions, creating an assertive working environment in which everyone feels respected and valued, and people are able to be truly themselves and truthful with each other. The PBOP list is all about assertive communication and diversity.

The role and functions of the partners' counsellor

The role of partners' counsellor was established in 1943, and is one of a number of roles that exist to ensure that the principles of the partnership are lived in the day-to-day communication between people. The partners' counsellor is the partnership's Ombudsperson, and is the third stage in the grievance procedure, and the first in cases of unfair dismissal. Individuals take any grievance first to their line manager, second to the HR line manager, and third to the partners' counsellor. The Partners' Counsellor's Directorate also fulfils the function of the appeal office, which Fiona Corner, deputy partners' counsellor, likens to "an audit function across the business." The partners' counsellors report directly to the chairman and are not answerable to the two divisional boards: "They are free to be totally impartial, and speak out on behalf of whoever they decide is in the right" (JLP, 2006).

The key functions of the partners' counsellor are:

- Listening, and providing a confidential channel of communication. "I often feel like a counsellor in the more usual sense of the word, and I'd say that the most important quality for me is the ability to listen—not only to what someone's saying, but how they're saying it, too" (Fiona Corner, JLP, 2006).
- Being proactive in noticing what is going on with people. Identifying what they might "reasonably complain" about and addressing these things before they become big issues and concerns for people.

■ Noticing any dips in people's performance as a result of ill-health, enquiring and offering appropriate support to the person.

■ Paying attention to the collective as a whole, and thinking about those things that would benefit all partners. Noticing what "good heads" of other companies are doing to meet the needs of their employees and acting "to follow their example and provide a sports-ground or a billiards-table or put flowers in the staff dining-room or start music in the workrooms or whatever it may be."

■ Promoting the work of the partners' counsellor.

In 1955 the *Gazette* published a series of anonymous "mini" examples of the kinds of problems people can take to the partners' counsellor, in an effort to reassure partners to talk about their concerns, no matter how small or large, and to do so before they become large.

> We understand that some Partners do not consult the Partners' Counsellor because they think he is not interested in problems of their sort, or they think they should not take up his time with any but very grave and out of the way troubles, whereas he exists of course, to prevent troubles becoming really grave.
>
> (JLP, 1955)

Ken Temple's role as partners' counsellor has variously been described as "defender of the faith," "thought leader," and that of the "corporate conscience." Ken describes the partnership behaviors as being about "good management:" "The behaviors we uphold are not optional, they are the only way we can behave towards each other as co-owners" (Ken Temple, interview, 2006).

Ken's view of management within the partnership is that the managers work for the managed. The manager is, as it were, employed by the team to work on their behalf, and as such is accountable to the team. Managers have the responsibility within the partnership to provide structures and processes for the democratic process to happen, in particular for partners to engage and to communicate with each other, and to live the values through their behaviors.

In his work Ken is always looking for ways in which partners can participate in the democratic process. He describes visiting a branch of Waitrose (the JLP's chain of supermarkets), and eating lunch in the partners' dining room. He noticed that the walls of the dining room were painted an unusual green. He asked the branch manager whose choice the color of walls had been. It turned out that the choice of color had not been that of the partners in that branch, and they had not been given a say over it. Ken suggested that choosing the color of the walls could have been an opportunity for partners to make their own decision. He sees the role of manager being very much that of facilitating the democratic process, and of enabling others to engage in this process.

In his role Ken is concerned with ensuring that the happiness of partners is truly lived through the work that they are doing, that what partners do is worthwhile and satisfying in a successful business. Ken likes the Chinese proverb that describes happiness as:

- someone to love
- something to do
- something to hope for.

Someone to love is about being valued and cared for by people; something to do that is worthwhile in the sense that both people feel satisfied in an exchange within a successful business that makes a profit; and something to hope for is about becoming more of myself than I was last year.

(Ken Temple, interview, 2006)

Ken draws on the experience of Andy Law, author of *Open Minds* (1998), and one of the founders of St Luke's, an advertising company based in London. Andy Law asks the question, "Is my work life making me a better person?" Ken believes that one of the best things about the JLP is "that we do what we do with profit, which means that over 63,000 people have the opportunity to become better people" (Ken Temple, interview, 2006).

Ken asks the question, What does happiness mean in the workplace? On a visit to a distribution center he observed a partner driving up and down the racking, putting large items of incoming stock away and picking out equally large items of stock. The partner was taking stock up and down the racks in his cab, and spending two hours on his own doing this prior to taking a break. Ken reflected on this, and with the worker's manager considered the following questions:

- What does happiness mean for this partner right now?
- For example, can he have a radio?
- What about his work wear? Is it comfortable, warm, hot, cold?
- What about the seat he is sitting on? Is it comfortable?

- At the end of his two hours, how does the conversation go with his section manager? How is he spoken to? Is he thanked and encouraged to have a cup of coffee?
- What's the quality of the coffee?
- What is the dining room like?

The partners and partnership are committed to creating a great place to work, and know that when they get it right true commitment and enjoyment are created. Together the partners strive and succeed in making the partnership something that everyone is proud to be part of, and to engage with each other in making it a very special place to work.

Recruitment is key to the success of the partnership, in particular recruiting partners who are committed to the values and principles of the partnership. Ken Temple says, "The Waitrose mantra of 'Recruit the attitude, Train the skill' is a good guide for the Partnership as a whole" (Ken Temple, interview, 2006).

On a visit to a branch of Waitrose a few months after it had been acquired, Ken had a conversation with the partner at the check-out, who said to him, "We're just beginning to believe that it's true!" He enquired what she meant, and she replied, "Well to start with people were really nice, and they are still really nice to us!"

CASE ANALYSIS: HAPPINESS, ATTUNEMENT, AND ALIGNMENT

The ultimate purpose of John Spedan Lewis was the partners' happiness, to be achieved through the provision of meaningful employment within a successful business. This continues to be the higher purpose and spirit of the partnership, and underpins the way in which the partnership is structured, and the processes, its values, and beliefs as expressed in "powered by our principles" behaviors.

The cooperative culture at the JLP is one in which people are attuned to each other and at the same time aligned to the higher purpose of happiness and business success. Roger Harrison refers to alignment being about will, and attunement as being about love: "Alignment occurs when organization members act as parts of an integrated whole, each finding the opportunity to express his or her true purpose through the organization's purpose" (1995a: 168). Alignment is balanced by attunement, and vice versa, creating a value-driven culture. "As the concept of alignment speaks to us of will, so that of attunement summons up the mysterious operations of love in organizations; the sense of empathy, understanding, caring, nurturance, and mutual support" (ibid.: 170).

In a paper entitled "Organization culture and the future of Planet Earth" (1995b), Harrison describes value-driven cultures as being about purpose (alignment/will) and relationship (attunement/love), and that they are interdependent. Some organizations have more of the qualities of the purpose culture and others more of the relationship culture. The JLP endeavors to combine the purpose and relationship cultures through setting clear goals at the same time as seeking to ensure that partners are engaged in work that is personally fulfilling and rewarding.

All six of the JLP PBOP behaviors are characteristic of the value-driven culture, and have qualities that are reflected in either the purpose/ alignment culture or the relationship/attunement culture. The first three PBOP behaviors fit more closely with the relationship culture, while the second three fit more closely with the purpose culture. The partnership successfully weaves the threads between purpose and relationship.

The two interdependent cultures expressed in the PBOP behaviors under "Work together" are shown in Table 25.1.

In many ways John Spedan Lewis was ahead of his time in focusing on happiness as the ultimate purpose. Happiness is closely linked to positive

Table 25.1 Value-driven and interdependent cultures linked to the PBOP "Work together" behaviors

Purpose	Relationship
Alignment/will	Attunement/mutuality/love
Oriented to the achievement of tasks, goals, and purposes	Oriented to relationship, caring, and connection
Qualities:	*Qualities:*
Idealism, dedication, subordination of personal needs to task "Think of others and put the team first" (PBOP), voluntarism, commitment, focus "Rewards cooperation" (PBOP)	Reciprocity and cooperation "Cultivates harmony" (PBOP), seeking consensus, giving, sharing "Be a friend as well as a colleague" (PBOP), empathizing "Develop empathy" (PBOP), considering the context, looking after stakeholders (all partners)

Source: adapted from Harrison (1995b: 249).

self-esteem and assertiveness. Authentic happiness as defined in the theory and practice of positive psychology (see pages 16–18) is linked with the positive emotion of true optimism, and happiness.

The JLP has a reputation for being fair, based on its values and principles, and lived through everyone's behaviors. The happiness and well-being of employees is enshrined in all that the company does. All partners are recognized and rewarded for their contribution in making the company an outstanding business success and one of Britain's most successful retailers. Relationships between partners are assertive. People know how to behave and what is expected of them, and what they can expect from the company. This helps people not only to feel secure, to know where they stand and therefore to feel more confident in themselves, but also to be able to give of their best and to achieve their potential as individuals and collectively.

In the case study that follows Daryl Upsall explores the importance of individual positive emotion and optimism that fundraisers need to bring to their work in order to keep the "fun in fundraising."

Case study 2: Positive emotion and optimism

Daryl Upsall Consulting International SL is a global network of leading senior non-governmental organization (NGO) professionals, each with many years of experience, who together provide a comprehensive range of services to NGOs, including communications, fundraising, management, strategic planning, recruitment, research, new media, and advocacy.

Fundraising is about asking people to give money for which they get nothing tangible in return. The fundraisers' hope is that people donating money feel good about themselves for giving, and that some of that good feeling is knowing that somewhere in the world someone is feeling better and benefiting as a result of their giving. Fundraisers have to look beyond the here and now to a brighter, better, and bigger future, and be able to sell this future to the donor.

Fundraisers have to be both positive and enthusiastic, as they are selling a product that is emotional. The appeal is an appeal to people's feeling for others, and to their values and beliefs. Feeling positive includes not only feeling positive about the "emotional product" but also believing in it, that fundraising does make a difference in creating a better world for everyone.

Fundraising is about communicating with people. The key skill in the art of fundraising is that of listening to people, of hearing their stories, and when appropriate telling one's own story, which communicates a heart-felt message to people and motivates them to give from their heart to help make a difference. Meeting and communicating with people is a crucial part of being a fundraiser, to talk about different causes, and to talk and listen to "big" and "small" donors from a wide range of cultures and social backgrounds. Thus being sociable and outgoing are both characteristics that serve the fundraiser well in networking with others, meeting donors, leading others with a powerful vision of the future, and making things happen.

The motivation for fundraisers is their positive belief and commitment to changing the world. They truly believe in and enjoy the work that they do.

> The key motivator for fundraisers is wanting to change the world, to make a difference. The second is that of recognition for having done a good job raising money for a particular cause. And thirdly it is saying "thank you," appreciating the donors, and being thanked by them and others. A friend once summed up fundraising when he described it as being all about saying: "Please" and "Thank you." There is a terrific buzz here in the call center where people are asking people please to give their money to a cause and thanking them for doing so. When there is a "verification" by way of a confirmation of a gift there is always a huge cheer from everyone else in the call center.
>
> (Daryl Upsall, interview, 2006)

As well as listening to people and telling well-timed, appropriate, and personal stories, fundraisers need to be prepared, to have done their homework with regard to the people they are going to meet. If they are meeting a person again, remembering things about the person from the previous meeting is vitally important in building the relationship with the person. Keeping up to date with what is going on in the person's organization is part of building the relationship, of establishing a connection with the person. Working globally, the fundraiser needs to be highly sensitive to different cultures, to pay attention to them and be respectful of them, to be fine-tuned to the nuances of cultural difference. This includes dressing appropriately, or greeting the person in a way that is comfortable for her or him. It also means being fully present in the conversation, listening and paying attention to everything that the person is saying both non-verbally and verbally.

The characteristics of optimism, positivism, sociability, and extroversion that are strengths for the fundraiser can be overwhelming and off-putting for others. Creative tensions can occur between fundraisers, program staff, and occasionally finance directors. "Fundraisers can be perceived as being superficial, flippant, and overly optimistic, by those at the 'coal face'" (Daryl Upsall, interview, 2006). For example the fundraiser is focused on the future, on targets for growth, and on spending, while the finance director is focused on the present and on saving money. Daryl is very clear that is really important to have two different people in these roles so that the creative tension can be used to positive effect.

CASE ANALYSIS: POSITIVE EMOTIONAL CONNECTION

Fundraising is about making a positive emotional connection with people, appealing to people's values and beliefs, to what matters to them. To do this with integrity it is important for fundraisers themselves to be very self-aware, and aware of others. They need to be able to communicate assertively with everyone, respecting people's values and beliefs, while at the same time appealing to them.

Fun is an important part of fundraising, of people truly enjoying their work and having fun together. The optimistic nature described by Daryl is an important part of being a fundraiser, and of maintaining self-confidence and assertive relationships with other members of the team, and with potential and actual donors.

26 Conclusions

We live and work in a multicultural world, one in which we are called upon to work together. Assertiveness and the development of assertive relationships in organizations is a way of our working together in which values of openness, honesty, trust, and respect are lived through how we communicate with and do business with each other. Our willingness to work with our differences, to acknowledge rather than deny them, to challenge and support each other, to understand our differences as well as to find our similarities, is the way forward for organizational and business success. Only when we feel valued for who we are and know how to value ourselves can we truly value others. We are able to make stronger connections with each other and to build "bigger" relationships that are assertive and inclusive of difference.

Organizations that truly embrace diversity provide opportunities for people to develop greater self-awareness, awareness of their differences, and to understand each other and work together to achieve outstanding performance. This book has shown that through the courage of individuals, groups, teams, and leaders to develop assertive and inclusive organizations, people are making a difference, and opening up possibilities for people to be their "best selves" in their work and to enjoy "bigger" I'm OK: You're OK relationships.

Appendix 1

Contributors and Readers

Gisela Banken, training manager, EMC Germany
Banken_Gisela@emc.com

Joy Barker, integrative practitioner, counsellor, supervisor, and trainer
j.h.barker@btinternet.com

David Birch, business director, Ashridge Business School
David.Birch@ashridge.org.uk

Sarah Bond, head of diversity, KPMG LLP (UK)
Sarah.Bond@kpmg.co.uk

Tracey Carr, founder and CEO, Eve-olution Ltd
tracey@eve-olution.net

Jo Confino, executive editor, Guardian News and Media
jo.confino@guardian.co.uk

Steven Cordery, corporate ombudsman EMEA, United Technologies
Corporation (UTC)
steven.cordery@utc.com

Fiona Corner, deputy partners' counsellor, John Lewis Partnership
Fiona_Corner@johnlewis.co.uk

Diana Danziger, organizational psychologist
DANZIGER2@aol.com

Karen Davison, principal, Dovetail Partnerships
Karen@dovetail-partnerships.co.uk

Anouschka Elliott, director, client strategy management, Citi Global Banking
Anouschka.Elliott@citigroup.com

Maria Fay, head of Executive Development Unit (EDU), Guardian News and Media
Maria.fay@guardian.co.uk

Geoff Glover, vice president, human resources, learning and development, Volvo Car Corporation (former human resources manager, Ford)
Gglover1@volvocars.com

Amanda Gutierrez-Cooper, project manager, LGBT Strand, Diversity and Citizen Focus Directorate, Metropolitan Police Service (MPS)
Amanda.Cooper@met.police.uk

Kamaljeet Jandu, change management consultant (former national diversity manager, Ford of Britain)
kam@kjandu.fsnet.co.uk

Indu Khurana, personal change management consultant, founder of Sunai
indu@sunai.co.uk

Ian Lock, leadership development consultant
ian@ianlock.co.uk

Phil Lowe, organizational consultant and author
phil@facetofaceleadership.com

Vandy Massey, director, MSA Interactive Ltd
vandy@msainteractive.com

Frances Middleton, business coaching and team facilitation, Deep Blue Associates
fran@deepblue-associates.com

Liz Morrison, professional coach and workshop facilitator
info@sustainabletactics.co.uk

Julian C Mount, specialist in personal and team development, Big Top Business Training
julian@bigtoptraining.co.uk

Stephanie Parry, managing director, Wexford Executive Consulting (former director, people and organization development, EMC, EMEA)
Stephanie.parry1@wanadoo.fr

Kirit Patti, senior recruiter
shinus@hotmail.com

Lynn Powell, former work environment manager, DuPont, Europe
lynnpowellwatts@hotmail.co.uk

Jenny Rogers, coach, consultant, and writer, Management Futures
jenny.rogers@managementfutures.co.uk

Atif Sheikh, Senior inventor at ?What If!, explorer and adventurer
atifs@whatifinnovation.com

Neil Sherlock, partner in charge of public affairs and corporate social responsibility, KPMG
Neil.Sherlock@kpmg.co.uk

Thomas Spiers, employee assistance programme manager, EMEA, Dupont
Thomas.S.Spiers@gber.dupontholding.com

Dr Fionn Stevenson, Reader in Sustainable Design, Department of Architecture, Oxford Brookes University
fstevenson@brookes.ac.uk

Robert Taylor, teacher in law, coach, and facilitator
Robert@acoach.demon.co.uk

Yvonne Taylor, therapist and trainer
YvoTastra@aol.com

Ken Temple, president, Partnership Council, John Lewis Partnership (former partners' counsellor)
Ken_Temple@johnlewis.co.uk

Matthew Turnbull, global learning and development director, Reckitt and Benckiser (former global learning manager, Unilever)
Matt.turnbull@reckittbenckiser.com

Paul Turnbull, learning and development consultant, career change coach, former head of learning and development, Guardian News and Media
paul@career-change-coach.com

Daryl Upsall, chief executive, Daryl Upsall Consulting International
daryl@darylupsall.com

Chris Ward, commercial director, MSN UK
chriswar@microsoft.com

To contact the author, please email her on: anni.townend@mail.com
www.annitownend.com

Appendix 2

Contributing Organizations

Big Top Business Training offers creative learning solutions to clients' specific business needs. They are specialists in personal and team development, communication, and life skills.
www.bigtoptraining.co.uk

Citigroup is a global financial services company and is the leading pan-EU financial services provider, offering clients and customers outstanding service in corporate and investment banking, wealth management, consumer banking, and alternative investments.
www.citigroup.com

Daryl Upsall Consulting International SL is a global network of leading senior non-governmental organization (NGO) professionals, each with many years of experience, who together provide a comprehensive range of services to NGOs, including communications, fundraising, management, strategic planning, recruitment, research, new media, and advocacy.
www.darylupsall.com

DuPont is a company committed to making a difference to people's lives through manufacturing materials that go into a wide range of innovative products and services in food and nutrition, health care, clothing, safety and security, construction, electronics, and transportation.
www.dupont.com

EMC is a leading global technology company that partners with and innovates for customer success by providing integrated technology solutions for information lifecycle management (ILM).
www.emc.com

Eve-olution is dedicated to working in partnership with blue-chip companies and public sector bodies on the increasingly complex challenge of increasing female representation in industry.
www.eve-olution.net

Ford Motor Company celebrated its centennial in 2003. With its global headquarters in Michigan, USA, the company's first operation in Britain was established in 1904. Today Britain is Ford Motor Company's second-biggest market after North America. Ford has been the number one car badge in Britain for 30 years and has led the commercial vehicle market for 41 years.
www.ford.co.uk

Guardian News and Media: in May 1921 to celebrate the *Manchester Guardian*'s centenary, C. P. Scott wrote an article in which he expressed the values of the paper: "Honesty, cleanness, courage, fairness a sense of duty to the reader and the community." These values continue to be lived, and are regularly reviewed and published in "Living Our Values," the social, ethical, and environmental audit.
www.guardian.co.uk

The John Lewis Partnership is a hugely successful employee-owned business. Central to the success of the partnership are the values of its founder John Spedan Lewis of fairness and happiness. He believed that the happiness of his employees was central to their success and the success of the business.
www.johnlewispartnership.co.uk

KPMG in the UK is part of a strong global network of member firms with a presence in over 150 countries and approximately 100,000 client service staff worldwide (2007). KPMG is represented throughout the United Kingdom, with 9500 partners and staff working in 22 locations across the United Kingdom providing audit, tax, and advisory services.
www.kpmg.co.uk

The Metropolitan Police Service (MPS) is committed to equality and diversity. Treating people with respect is vital for police officers and police staff within the organization, and with all service users of the MPS. The MPS has a Diversity and Citizen Focus Directorate within which there is a Diversity Central Team which links up the work of six

Strand Teams: Age; Disability; Gender; Faith/Belief; Lesbian, Gay, Bisexual, Transgender (LGBT); and Race.
www.met.police.co.uk

Microsoft/MSN is a global technology company with a multicultural workforce. MSN is the online media business and provides a wide and varied range of offerings, such as Internet search, email and instant messaging, and sells advertising space within these products so they can be provided free to people.
www.microsoft.com

MSA Interactive specializes in developing and supporting online performance tools, in particular 360 performance reviews. The company provides expertise in feedback systems for development and appraisals, and has worked with some of the world's leading companies across a number of industries.
www.msainteractive.com

Nestlé is the world's leading food company, with operations in almost every country, including many developing countries. The Nestlé culture is diverse, and focused on valuing people within the company and the people for whom it provides good food and a good life.
www.nestlé.com

Sunai offers individual coaching, counseling and psychotherapy, consultancy, and workshops including assertiveness workshops. Sunai seeks to "empower individuals in the way they need, so that they can achieve more of what they want in life."
www.sunai.co.uk

United Technologies Corporation (UTC) is a $42.7 billion company (2005) that provides high-technology products and services to the building systems and aerospace industries. UTC is made up of seven distinct business units: Carrier heating and cooling, Hamilton Sundstrand aerospace systems, Otis elevators and escalators, Pratt & Whitney aircraft engines, Sikorsky helicopters, UTC Fire & Security monitoring and protection, and UTC Power fuel cell and distributed generation. UTC's businesses are worldwide market leaders and carry the names of the industries' founders.
www.utc.com

Appendix 3

Website Resources

This appendix gives web addresses of organizations that provide consultancy, coaching, training and development, research, and materials related to assertiveness and diversity in organizations. The websites are listed in relation to the relevant part of the book, and are intended as a guide and resource for readers.

Part II: What is Assertiveness?

www.brieftherapy.org.uk	Providers of training and consultancy in brief therapy
www.hoffmaninstitute.co.uk	Personal development and change
www.bigtoptraining.co.uk	Training and development using NLP
www.career-change-coach.com	Career change coaching to help people reignite their working lives and to make changes; action-oriented coaching
www.vitalityforbusiness.com	Focus on the vitality, health, and well-being of people and organizations
www.spc.ac.uk	School of Psychotherapy and Counselling, Regents College, provides training in mediation and alternative dispute resolution
www.dovetail-partnerships.co.uk	Specialists in behavioral risk management solutions
www.cnvc.org	A global organization (for non-violent communication) whose vision is a world in which all people are getting their needs met and resolving their conflicts peacefully

www.banbullyingatwork.com	Online reflection questionnaire, commitment to dignity at work, and business case for eliminating bullying at work
www.bullyonline.org	Provides definitions of bullying and stress; publications and information
www.andreadamstrust.org	Research and publications, training and education, promoting good practice and campaigning for effective legislation
www.hse.gov.uk/stress	Research and information about benefits of overcoming work-related stress to business and individuals

Part III: Working with Personality Differences

www.opp.eu.com	Providers of psychometric materials including MBTI and FIRO-B, training and development
www.facetofaceleadership.com	Provider of coaching, learning, and development using MBTI and FIRO-B
www.belbin.com	Provides online Self-Perception Inventory, SPI, and Observer Assessment; and software package e-interplace® for organizations
www.peterhoney.com	Learning styles online materials and publications

Part IV: Multicultural Differences, Differences of Sexual Orientation, and Gender Difference

www.eve-olution.net	Training and development in gender awareness and focus on gender diversity
www.bitc.org.uk	Opportunity Now membership organization representing emp-loyers that want to ensure inclusivity for women. Opportunity Now runs the UK workplace award for gender equality, diversity and inclusion
www.stonewall.org.uk/workplace	Support for organizations in diversity and equality for all irrespective of sexual orientation
www.sunai.co.uk	Training and development courses for women from ethnic minority groups

www.womensaid.org.uk — A national (UK) voluntary organization that helps women and children who are being abused in their own homes. Campaigns for the right for everyone "to live in safety and to have a future without fear."

Part V: Assertiveness and Diversity in Organizations

www.schneider-ross.com — Leading consultancy in diversity, equality, and inclusion. Support for organizations and set up Global Diversity Network, GDN.

www.ombudsassociation.org — International organization provides training and networking for Ombuds

www.icasgroup.com — Provider of employee assistance programs worldwide

www.ppcworldwide.com — Provider of employee assistance programs worldwide

www.bacp.co.uk — Publications, advice, support, and best practice guidelines for counseling in the workplace

www.robertsoncooper.com — Specialists in leadership and well-being, offering organizations business benefits through developing the resilience and motivation of their people

www.ashridge.co.uk — Provider of training, development, and consultancy including 360 review feedback and the Ashridge Inventory of Management Skills (AIMS)

www.msainteractive.com — 360 performance reviews

www.mclanegroup.co.uk — Leadership training and development

www.ralphlewis.co.uk — Assertiveness training, leadership and team building, coaching of individuals and teams

www.thegarnettfoundation.com — Theatrical productions and workshops that address a range of organizational issues including diversity, communication, and bullying

www.humansynergistics.com — Providers of high-quality products and

	services, assessments and simulations for individuals, leaders, teams, and organizations
www.roffeypark.com	Research, conferences, consultancy, training, and development committed to diversity in organizations
www.workingfamilies.org.uk	Information, publications, resources, support, and advice to organizations and individuals on work–life balance and flexible working
www.managementfutures.co.uk	Consultancy in training and coaching
www.sustainabletactics.co.uk	Training and coaching for individuals and teams, includes using horses as part of learning about communication

References and Further Reading

Chapter 2 Philosophy of Assertiveness

Berne, E. (1975) *What Do You Say After You Say Hello?* Corgi.

Bowlby, John (2006a) *A Secure Base: Clinical applications of attachment theory*, reprint, Routledge.

Bowlby, John (2006b) *The Making and Breaking of Affectional Bonds*, reprint, Routledge.

Butler, Pamela E. (1981) *Self-Assertion For Women*, Harper and Row.

Cooperrider, David L. and Whitney, Diana (1999) *Appreciative Inquiry*, Berrett-Koehler.

Covey, Stephen R. (2004) *The 8th Habit: From effectiveness to greatness*, Simon and Schuster.

George, Evan, Iveson, Chris, and Ratner, Harvey (1990) *Problem to Solution: Brief therapy with individuals and families*, BT Press.

George, Evan, Iveson, Chris, and Ratner, Harvey (2002) *Solution Focused Brief Therapy, course notes*, Brief Therapy Practice.

Gerhardt, Sue (2005) *Why Love Matters*, Routledge.

Hallowell, Edward (2002) *The Childhood Roots of Adult Happiness*, Vermilion.

Hammond, Sue Annis (1996) *The Thin Book of Appreciative Inquiry*, Thin Books.

Harris, Thomas A. (1995) *I'm OK – You're OK*, Arrow.

Harris, A. and Harris, T. (1986) *Staying OK*, Pan.

Laurence, Tim (2003) *You Can Change Your Life: A future different from your past with the Hoffman Process*, Hodder and Stoughton.

Myss, Caroline (2005) *Invisible Acts of Power*, Simon & Schuster.

Orsillo, Susan M., Roemer, Lizabeth, Lerner, Jennifer Block, and Tull, Matthew T. (2004) "Acceptance, mindfulness and cognitive-behavioral therapy," in Steven C. Hayes, Victoria M. Follette, and Marsha M. Lineham (eds), *Mindfulness and Acceptance: Expanding the cognitive-behavioral tradition*, Guilford Press.

Seligman, Martin E. P. (2004) *Authentic Happiness*, Nicholas Brealey.

Spinelli, Ernesto (2000) *Tales of Un-knowing,* Duckworth.

Steiner, Claude (1990) *Scripts People Live*, 2nd edn, Grove Press.

Strasser, Freddie (1999) *Emotions,* Duckworth.

Strasser, Freddie and Strasser, Alison (1999) *Existential Time-Limited Therapy*, Wiley.

Watkins, Jane Magruder and Mohr, Bernard J. (2001) *Appreciative Inquiry,* Jossey-Bass/Pfeiffer.

Wilkinson, Margaret (2006) *Coming Into Mind, The Mind-Brain Relationship: A Jungian clinical perspective,* Routledge.

Chapter 3 Positive Self-Assertion

Hay, Louise (1998) *You Can Heal Your Life*, Eden Grove.

Klaus, Peggy (2003) *BRAG: The art of tooting your own horn without blowing it*, Warner Business Books.

Myss, Caroline (2005) *Invisible Acts of Power*, Simon & Schuster.

Ray, Sondra (1976) *I Deserve Love: How affirmations can guide you to personal fulfillment*, Les Femmes.

Chapter 4 Assertive Communication

Leeds, Dorothy (2005) *The 7 Powers of Questions: Secrets to successful communication in life and work*, Perigee, Penguin.

Luft, Joseph (1984) *Group Processes: An introduction to group dynamics*, 3rd edn, Mayfield.

Chapter 5 Assertive Relationships

Bandler, Richard and Grinder, John (1979) *Frogs into PRINCES*, Real People Press.

Bandler, Richard and Grinder, John (1981) *TRANCE-formations*, Real People Press.

Bandler, Richard and Grinder, John (1982) *Re-framing*, Real People Press.

Cameron-Bandler, Leslie (1985) *Solutions: Practical and effective antidotes for sexual and relationship problems*, Future Pace.

Cameron-Bandler, Leslie, Gordon, David, and Lebeau, Michael (1985a) *The Emprint Method: A guide to reproducing competence,* Future Pace.

Cameron-Bandler, Leslie, Gordon, David, and Lebeau, Michael (1985b) *Know How: Guided programs for inventing your own best future,* Future Pace.

Cameron-Bandler, Leslie and Lebeau, Michael (1986) *The Emotional Hostage: Rescuing your emotional life*, Future Pace.

Lankton, Steve (1980) *Practical Magic*, Meta Publications.

McDermott, Ian and Jago, Wendy (2001) *The NLP Coach: A comprehensive guide to personal well-being and professional success*, Piatkus.

Chapter 6 Managing Conflict

Benfari, Robert with Knox, Jean (1991) *Understanding Your Management Style: Beyond the Myers-Briggs Type Indicator*, Lexington Books.

Bush, Robert A. Baruch and Folger, Joseph P. (2005) *The Promise of Mediation: The transformative approach to conflict*, Jossey-Bass.

Fisher, Roger and Ury, William (1999) *Getting to Yes: Negotiating an agreement without giving in*, Random House Business Books.

Rosenberg, Marshall B. (1999) *Nonviolent Communication: A language of compassion*, PuddleDancer Press.

Thomas, K. W. and Kilmann, R. H. (1974) *Conflict Mode Instrument*, Xicom.

Chapter 7 Dealing with Bullying

Field, Tim (1996) *Bully in Sight: How to predict, resist, challenge and combat workplace bullying*, Success Unlimited.

Peyton, Pauline Rennie (2003) *Dignity at Work: Eliminate bullying and create a positive working environment,* Brunner-Routledge.

Chapter 8 Models for Working with Personality Differences

Belbin, R. Meredith (1985) *Management Teams: Why they succeed or fail,* Heinemann.

Belbin, R. Meredith (1993) *Team Roles at Work,* Butterworth-Heinemann.

Belbin, R. Meredith (2000) *Beyond the Team,* Butterworth-Heinemann.

Briggs Myers, Isabel with Myers, Peter B. (1980) *Gifts Differing*, Consulting Psychologists Press.

Fitzgerald, Catherine and Kirby, Linda K. (eds) (1997) *Developing Leaders: Research and applications in psychological type and leadership development*, Davies-Black.

Garden, Annamaria (2000) *Reading the Mind of the Organisation: Connecting the strategy with the psychology of the business*, Gower.

Honey, Peter (1994) *101 Ways to Develop Your People, Without Really Trying! A manager's guide to work based learning,* Peter Honey Publications.

Honey, Peter and Mumford, Alan (1992) *The Manual of Learning Styles,* 3rd edn, Peter Honey Publications.

Honey, Peter and Mumford, Alan (2006) *Learning Styles Questionnaire, 80-item,* July edn.

Lawrence, Gordon D. (1987) *People Types and Tiger Stripes,* CAPT.

Mumford, Alan (1993) *How Managers Can Develop Managers,* Gower.

Quenk, Naomi L. (1993) *Beside Ourselves: Our hidden personality in everyday life,* CPP Books.

Schnell, Eugene R. (2000) P*articipating in Teams: Using your FIRO-B results to improve interpersonal effectiveness,* CPP.

Schutz, Will (1966) *FIRO: A three-dimensional theory of interpersonal behaviour,* 3rd edn, Will Schutz Associates.

Schutz, Will (1984) *The Truth Option: A practical technology for human affairs,* 10 Speed Press.

Schutz, Will (1988) *Profound Simplicity: Foundations for a social philosophy,* Will Schutz Associates.

Waterman, Judith A. and Rogers, Jenny (2000) *Introduction to the FIRO-B,* OPP.

Chapter 9 Using the MBTI

Rogers, Jenny (1997a) *Sixteen Personality Types at Work In Organisations,* Management Futures.

Rogers, Jenny (1997b) *Influencing Others Using the Sixteen Personality Types,* Management Futures.

Tieger, Paul D. and Barron-Tieger, Barbara (1997) *Nurture by Nature: How to raise happy, healthy, responsible children through the insights of personality type,* Little, Brown.

Tieger, Paul D. and Barron-Tieger, Barbara (2000) *Just Your Type: Create the relationship you've always wanted using the secrets of personality type,* Little, Brown.

Chapter 10 Using FIRO-B

Tuckman, P. (1965) 'Developmental sequence in small groups,' *Psychological Bulletin,* 63 (6), pp. 384–99.

Chapter 11 Belbin Team Roles

Belbin, R. Meredith (1993) *Team Roles at Work*, Butterworth-Heinemann.

Chapter 12 The Learning Cycle and Learning Styles

Nicholson, William (2006) *The Creative Prostitute*, Speaking a Common Language, talk at Pelham House, Lewes.

Robinson, Ken (2006) TEDTalks Premieres, 27 June 2006 (online) www.ted.com/tedtalks/

Simmons, A, (2002) *The Story Factor: Secrets of influence from the art of storytelling*, Basic Books.

Chapter 13 Multicultural Differences

Berger, Mel (1996) *Cross-Cultural Team Building: Guidelines for more effective communication and negotiation*, McGraw-Hill.

Cornes, Alan (2004) *Culture from the Inside Out: Travel—and meet yourself*, Nicholas Brealey.

Gobodo-Madikizela, Pumla (2006) *A Human Being Died That Night: Forgiving Apartheid's chief killer*, Portobello Books.

Guirdham, Maureen (1999) *Communicating Across Cultures*, Macmillan.

Hofstede, G. (2003) *Cultures and Organisations: Software of the mind, intercultural cooperation and its importance for survival*, Profile Books.

Hughes, Robert (1994) *Culture of Complaint: The fraying of America*, Harvill.

Trompenaars, Fons and Hampden-Turner, Charles (2004) *Riding the Waves of Culture: Understanding cultural diversity in business*, Nicolas Brealey.

Chapter 14 Differences in Sexual Orientation

Steel, Ashley (2005) Article in *KPMG News*, 24 June (online) www.kpmg.co.uk

Chapter 15 Gender Difference

Babcock, Linda, Laschever, Sarah, Gelfand, Michele, and Small, Deborah (2003) "Nice girls don't ask: women negotiate less than men—and everyone pays the price," *Harvard Business Review*.

Baron-Cohen, Simon (2004) *The Essential Difference*, Penguin.

Fisher, Roger and Ury, William (1999) *Getting to Yes: Negotiating an agreement without giving in*, Random House Business Books.

Gilligan, Carol (1982) *In a Different Voice: Psychological theory and women's development*, Harvard University Press.

Gray, John (1993) *Men are from Mars, Women are from Venus*, Thorsons.

Senge, Peter (1995) *The Fifth Discipline Fieldbook: Strategies and tools for building a learning organization*, Nicholas Brealey.

Tannen, Deborah (2001a) *Talking from 9 to 5: Women and men at work, language, sex and power*, Virago.

Tannen, Deborah (2001b) *You Just Don't Understand: Women and men in conversation*, Quill.

Chapter 16 Working with Multicultural Differences

WorkChoice Survey (2005) *An Investigation into Employer of Choice Issues*, Summary results.

Chapter 17 Making the Business Case for Diversity

De Anca, Celia and Vazquez, Antonio (2007) *Managing Diversity in the Global Organization*, Palgrave Macmillan (for more on diversity at Ford, and particularly in Spain).

Chapter 18 Meeting the Work-Life Balance Needs of Employees

Swan, Jonathan and Cooper, Cary L. (2005) *Time, Health and the Family: What working families want,* Working Families.

Honoré, Carl (2004) *In Praise of Slow: How a worldwide movement is challenging the cult of speed*, Orion.

Litosseliti, Lia (2003) *Using Focus Groups in Research*, Continuum.

Chapter 19 Corporate Ombuds

Bensinger, Ann, Minor, Donald, and Semple, Grace (nd) *Ombuds Practitioners—HR Practitioners: Different paths—same objective*, Working paper archived with The Ombudsman Association, New Jersey.

Chapter 20 Workplace Counseling

Carroll, Michael (1996) *Workplace Counselling: A systematic approach to employee care*, Sage.

McLeod, J. (2001) *Counselling in the Workplace: The facts, a systematic study of the research evidence*, BACP.

PPC Worldwide (2005) *Milestone or millstone?* research report, PPC Worldwide.

Reddy, Michael (1994) "EAPs and their future in the UK: history repeating itself?" *Personnel Review*, 23 (7), pp 60–78.

Swan, Jonathan and Cooper, Cary L. (2005) *Time, Health and the Family: What working families want*, Working Families.

Chapter 22 360 Review Feedback

EMC (2003) *Global Training and Development*, March, EMC University.

Chapter 23 Assertive Leadership

Adair, John (1988) *Effective Leadership*, Pan.

Blanchard, Kenneth, Zigarmi, Patricia, and Zigarmi, Dream (1986) *Leadership and The One Minute Manager*, Willow.

De Pree, Max (2004) *Leadership Is an Art,* Currency.

Kotter, John P. (1990) *A Force for Change: How leadership differs from management,* Free Press.

LSI (1990) *Life Styles Inventory, LSI 2*, Human Synergistics International (online) (www.humansynergistics.com).

Chapter 24 Coaching

O'Neill, Mary Beth (2000) *Executive Coaching with Backbone and Heart,* Jossey-Bass.

Rogers, Jenny (2004) *Coaching Skills: A handbook*, Open University Press.

Whitmore, John (2001) *Coaching for Performance*, 2nd edn, Nicholas Brealey.

Chapter 25 Promoting Happiness at Work

Hallowell, Edward (2002) *The Childhood Roots of Adult Happiness*, Vermilion.

Harrison, Roger (1995a) "Leadership and strategy for a new age," in *The Collected Papers of Roger Harrison*, McGraw-Hill.

Harrison, Roger (1995b) "Organisation culture and the future of Planet Earth," in *The Collected Papers of Roger Harrison*, McGraw-Hill.

John Lewis Partnership (JLP) (1944), *Gazette,* Archives of the John Lewis Partnership.

JLP (1955) *Gazette*, Archives of the John Lewis Partnership, October.

JLP (2006) "The listeners," *Gazette*, 25 February, p. 17.

Law, Andy (1998) *Open Minds*, Orion.

Layard, Richard (2005) *Happiness: Lessons from a new science*, Allen Lane.

Martin, Paul (2006) *Making Happy People: The nature of happiness and its origins in childhood*, Harper Perennial.

Index